REAL WORLD
PDF WITH
ADOBE ACROBAT 5

ANITA DENNIS

PEACHPIT PRESS
BERKELEY, CALIFORNIA

REAL WORLD PDF WITH ADOBE ACROBAT 5
Anita Dennis

Copyright ©2002 by Anita Dennis

Peachpit Press
1249 Eighth Street
Berkeley, CA 94710
510/524-2178
Fax: 510/524-2221

Find us on the World Wide Web at: http://www.peachpit.com
To report errors, please send a note to errata@peachpit.com
Peachpit Press is a division of Pearson Education

Editor: Kelly Ryer
Production Coordinator: Kate Reber
Copyeditor: Jill Simonsen
Proofreader: Kate McKinley
Editorial Assistant: Suzie Lowey
Composition: Magnolia Studio
Indexer: Karin Arrigoni
Cover Design: Gee + Chung Design

ISBN 0-201-75894-6

9 8 7 6 5 4 3 2 1

Printed and bound in the United States of America

To Martin and Sarah

With gratitude I thank the many people at Adobe Systems who shared with me their knowledge and expertise about Acrobat, PDF, and other Adobe products and technologies: Rick Brown, Tricia Gellman, Macduff Hughes, Jim King, Carl Orthlieb, and Lydia Varmazis. Thanks in particular to Lonn Lorenz and Bob Schaffel for explaining to me how Acrobat and PDF workflows are used in the real world, to Mark Boodnick for the use of his PC, to Jill Merlin for providing me software and other resources; and to Brian Wiffin for a PDF-centric demo of InDesign 2.0 on the Seybold San Francisco show floor, when so many other customers awaited. And my deepest appreciation to Dov Isaacs, who kept setting me straight about what Acrobat and PDF do and don't do, and who debunked more PDF myths than I ever imagined existed.

Of no less importance in the research of this book are the many generous prepress experts, designers, and printers who shared with me their professional experiences with Acrobat. For your honest opinions, thank you to Margo Baker, Dave Bates, Gaby Brink, Paul Bunyar, Marco Cappuccio, Keli Davis, David DePaolo, Richard Dey, Gianna Tabuena-Frolli, Jennifer Gold, Diane Gould, Thomas Kuo, Charles Kurnow, Mark Martin, Mike McKee, Rowan McKinnon, Melinda Monti, Tom Mornini, Jerry O'Neal, Marvin Plummer, Larisa Sheckler, Paul Showalter, Sean Sullivan, Justine Trubey, Scott Tully, Warren Vegas, Jeff Wall, and Michael Weinglass.

Numerous vendors and other experts were also critical to the authoring of this book: Thank you to Martin Bailey, Dave deBronkart, Alan Darling, Stephen Herron, and Carl Young for sharing insights on your respective specialties. Thanks also to Mike Jahn for Agfa; Sandy Bozek at Apple; Olaf Drummer at Callas; Marc Mascara and Bob Kutsche at CreoScitex; Mark Atchley and Catherine McCarthy at Enfocus; Jon Maroney and Joseph Schorr at Extensis; Helmut Tschmernjak and

Bill Gram-Reefer for Helios; Bob Green at Lantana; Amy Leith, Andy Scott, and Hans Stoger at OneVision; Glen Turpin at Quark; and Jeff Peterson at Screen.

For keeping me motivated and on course, and for listening to me whine about my deadlines, thank you to my editor at Peachpit Press, Kelly Ryer. For wonderful line-editing, thank you to my copyeditor Jill Simonsen; and thank you, Kate Reber, my production manager, for your patience with this new author and for designing a beautiful book. Thank you also to Marjorie Baer and Nancy Ruenzel for having the confidence in me to assign this project.

Finally, thank you to John Farnsworth for the workflow diagrams on pages 7, 13, 14, 16, and 179; to Marty Beaudet for the screen shots; and, last but not least, to Jim Felici for pitching in even though my file crashed your computer.

—*Anita*

CONTENTS AT A GLANCE

Foreword xiii

Chapter 1: The World According to Acrobat 1

Chapter 2: How to Create PDF Files for Prepress 25

Chapter 3: The Lowdown on Distilling 83

Chapter 4: Collaborating, Repurposing, and Proofing 117

Chapter 5: PDF in Prepress 177

Chapter 6: Workflow Systems and Alphabet Soup 217

Chapter 7: Electronic Documents 241

Appendix One: Acrobat Assistants 289

Appendix Two: Online Resources . . . . : 301

Index 303

TABLE OF CONTENTS

Foreword . . . . **xiii**

Chapter 1: The World According to Acrobat 1

One, Two, Buckle Your Shoe 1

Three, Four, Open the Door 4

Five, Six... 6

PDF's Role in Prepress 10

   Out of the (Black) Box 10

   How RIPs Work 13

   PDF's Role 15

   Other Final File Format Options 17

   Benefits of PDF Production 20

   Making the Change 22

Chapter 2: How to Create PDF Files for Prepress **25**

Printing from an Application 26

Exporting from Applications 29

Distilling Files Manually 30

Before You Start 32

Illustrator 10 34

   Print 34

   Save As 36

Photoshop 6.0 39

   Print 39

   Save As 41

InDesign 2.0 43

   Print 43

   Export 45

PageMaker 7.0 52

   Print 52

   Export 53

FrameMaker 6.0 56

   Print 56

   Save As 58

FreeHand 10 59
   Print 59
   Export 61
QuarkXPress 4.11 and Later 62
   Print 62
   Export 66
CorelDraw 10 for Windows 68
   Print 68
   Export 72
Microsoft Office 2000 (Windows) and 2001 (Mac) 75
   Print 75
Create Adobe PDF Online 77
How to Use Transparency in PDF Workflows 79

Chapter 3: The Lowdown on Distilling **83**
Job Options 84
   General 85
   Compression 87
   Fonts 92
      How Distiller Accesses Fonts 94
      A Few Words About Double-Byte and Other Non-English Fonts 94
      Checking and Previewing Fonts 95
      Embedding and Licensing Fonts 96
   Color 98
   Advanced 104
Security 106
How Do You Prefer to Distill? 108
Get in Line 109
Watch Out 115

Chapter 4: Collaborating, Repurposing, and Proofing **117**
Collaborative Tools 117
   Making Comments 118
   Marking Up Pages 124
   Managing Comments and Annotations 128
   Digital Sign-off 138
   Comparing Documents 147

Editing Content 149
   Editing Text 149
   Editing Graphics 154
Extracting Content 157
   Managing Pages 159
   Plug-ins 162
Proofing Tools 163
   Color Management Preferences 163
   Proof Setup and Proof Colors 165
   Printing Managed Color 166
Preparing Final Pages 169
   Renumbering Pages 169
   Removing Comments and More 170
   Unsecuring Files 172
Batch Processing 172

Chapter 5: PDF in Prepress **177**
Homegrown PDF Workflows 178
Preflighting 180
   Features to Find 181
   Typical Tools 184
      Callas pdfInspektor 184
      Enfocus PitStop Professional 185
      Extensis Preflight Online and Preflight Pro 186
      Markzware FlightCheck and MarkzNet 186
      OneVision Asura 188
Trapping 189
   Application-Based Trapping 190
   In-RIP Trapping 191
   Dedicated Trapping 191
   The PDF Trap-22 192
   An Overprinting Primer 193
   Dedicated Trapping Tools 195
      ScenicSoft TrapWise 195
      Ultimate Technographics Trapeze Artist 195
      Heidelberg Supertrap 196

OPI 197
Imposition 200
    Imposition Lingo 201
    What to Look for 202
    Imposition Tools 204
        DK&A INposition 204
        Dynagram DynaStrip 205
        IPTech ImpozeIt 205
        OneVision Secare 205
        Quite Imposing 205
        ScenicSoft Preps 205
        Shira PDF Organizer 207
        Ultimate Technographics Impostrip and Impress 207
Separations 207
    The Magic of Screening 208
    FM Screening 211
    Color Separating Software 212
RIP 215

Chapter 6: Workflow Systems and Alphabet Soup **217**
What's Extreme? 217
    Process Players 218
    Process Management 219
Extreme Systems 219
    Make Room to RIP 219
    Agfa Apogee 221
    CreoScitex Prinergy 222
    Fujifilm CelebraNT 225
    Screen Trueflow 226
    CreoScitex Brisque 228
Alphabet Soup 229
    PJTF and JDF 229
    CIP3 and CIP4 231
    PDF/X and TIFF/IT 234
    PPML/VDX 237
Non-Extreme PDF RIPs 238

Chapter 7: Electronic Documents 241

PDF versus XML 242
  XMP 244
eBooks 246
  Structure and Tags 247
  Creating Tagged PDF Files 247
    Exporting Tagged PDF from PageMaker 248
    Exporting Tagged PDF from InDesign 251
  Reflowing Text 252
  Editing Tags 255
  Links and Bookmarks 256
    Creating Links 257
    Creating Bookmarks 258
    Creating Article Threads 260
  Finishing Touches 263
Electronic Forms 266
  How Acrobat Handles Forms 267
  Designing Forms 268
  Creating Form Fields 269
  Adding Interactivity and Intelligence 271
  Editing Form Fields 274
  Checking Spelling 277
  For Form Fanatics 278
Cataloging PDF Files 278
  Building an Index 279
  Searching a Catalog 285
  Staying Up to Date 287

Appendix One: Acrobat Assistants 289

Acrobat Plug-ins 289
  File Conversion/Compatibility 289
  Preflighting 290
  Output 291
  Content Manipulation 291
  Security 293
  Utilities 294
  Telecommunications 295

Stand-Alone Programs 295
Acrobat Distiller Clones 299
Browser Plug-ins 299
QuarkXPress Extensions 299

Appendix Two: Online Resources **301**
Information Sources 301
Online Services 302

Index **303**

FOREWORD

Real World PDF with Adobe Acrobat 5 should be considered an official Graphic Arts Desk Reference Manual for productive workflows in the 21st century. It will help you to realize the benefits of using Acrobat beyond PDF creation and at the same time cover more technical detail than you ever dreamed existed about how to create the best PDF files from your desktop applications.

I have to hand it to Anita for the great tenacity she has shown in completing this book. If you were to search within Adobe or in the graphic arts consulting world, it would be hard to find a single person that could share with you all the information contained in *Real World PDF.* The only way to compile this much useful knowledge is to call up lots of sources, read lots of documents and then synthesize this with an existing knowledge of the graphic arts industry. Anita Dennis has done it all for you. In *Real World PDF,* Anita draws on her expertise as a longtime writer in the graphic arts industry to help educate people on how—and why—to use PDF workflows.

As Acrobat has grown in popularity, so have its uses and audiences. In fact, Adobe Acrobat and PDF are used by more people in government and business than in the graphic arts/printing industries. Organizations like the IRS and the FDA have standardized entire document workflows on the usage of PDF. This popularity has introduced many non-graphic arts users to PDF workflows. Many of these workflows never even involve print. Today the use of Adobe Acrobat has extended beyond simply creating PDF files for business publishing in print on CD or on the Web. Users are actually implementing workflows that increase productivity through the value of having a single reliable document, the Adobe PDF file.

Tricia Gellman
Group Infrastructure Manager
Cross Media Publishing
Adobe Systems, Inc.

CHAPTER ONE

The World According to Acrobat

One of the best-named software applications on the market, Acrobat works on multiple levels: It not only performs acrobatics by offering flexible and independent viewing of content regardless of a file's source application, it has juggled more roles and demands in its ten-year life than any program should have been asked to manage in 20. Each of Acrobat's five full versions was designed for a market and purpose unique to that point in our technological and publishing history. Over the years, Acrobat has adapted beautifully, always living up to its goal of viewing and printing documents with integrity and consistency. To understand why Acrobat offers its particular blend of features, strengths, and limitations, it helps to know something about the program's evolution within the publishing industry.

ONE, TWO, BUCKLE YOUR SHOE

Despite Adobe's long leadership role as a graphic arts software developer, it created Acrobat (originally code-named Carousel) to solve a problem in the corporate world. Back in 1993, when Acrobat was first released, companies were creating documents using a wide variety of applications—primarily Microsoft Word, Excel, and PowerPoint, but also word processing, spreadsheet, and presentation applications from other companies. Many of these documents were text heavy; however, color graphics were quickly finding their way in, especially in presentations. The problem was that unless you printed and distributed hard copies to your colleagues, there was no way to ensure that your document's layout would remain intact—including the appearance of type and the position and appearance of graphics. Digital file exchange wasn't reliable because document creators had no way of knowing whether the receiving parties were on the same operating systems, much less whether they had the same applications and fonts on their hard drives or the appropriate color capabilities on their monitors.

Enter Adobe Acrobat. Well, enter Acrobat and No Hands Software's Common Ground and a couple other contenders for the portable document crown. You see, in the early 1990s the myth of the paperless office loomed large: Many believed that the rise of the Internet would lead to the demise of paper. Adobe's Portable Document Format (PDF) files were a giant step toward the realization of the paperless office.

Using its own PostScript page-description language, Adobe developed Acrobat to translate PostScript files into page-oriented, resolution-independent portable documents that could be viewed on any computer platform and output to any printing device, regardless of where, when, and how the original document was authored. All you needed to view the PDF file was Acrobat Reader, a viewing application for which Adobe initially charged $50. In addition to being costly, the Reader was a hefty file—more than a megabyte in Windows. The PDF files themselves, however, were compact. Files that once required a SyQuest disk or a portable hard disk to hold them could now fit on a floppy.

Files tended to be a little larger, however, if they were "written" with the Acrobat Writer plug-in rather than distilled to PDF; indeed, writing PDF files has been the more common practice for most corporate users throughout Acrobat's history. In contrast to distilling PostScript to create PDF files, the PDF Writer printer driver writes the PDF file based on screen-resolution data with a simple key command. This is fine for basic text documents but has always been a problem for complex layouts, especially those with EPS graphics, which typically display low-resolution proxies on screen.

Other companies used different technologies to create and view portable documents, resulting in different strengths and weaknesses. No Hands Software, for example, didn't require readers to pay for a viewing application; document authors could embed a mini-viewer in the portable file itself. In the end, Adobe's method of producing portable documents won out, largely because from the get-go PDF files did a superior job of maintaining the integrity of text (thanks to its ability to create substitutions) and complex layouts (because it was object-oriented)—even though the program wasn't perfect and it was significantly more expensive than the competition.

Multimedia was also a buzzword in the early and mid-1990s, and Adobe wasn't shy about quickly finding a niche for its PDF format among those content creators. With

Acrobat 2.0, Adobe added numerous features that made the files more interactive, and the company began touting PDF as a way to publish to CD-ROMs, kiosks, and the Web. Version 1.0 offered the bare-bones navigational features—internal hyperlinks and bookmarks—but version 2.0 added support for external links (to other PDF files), article threads, and the capability to display and play back embedded video and sound clips. PDF files could also now be indexed and searched with the Catalog feature; viewers could see a full-screen view of a document for slide-show presentations; and watched folders were introduced. Finally, PDF files got smaller, thanks to the addition of font subsetting.

	Acrobat 1.0 (PDF 1.0)	**Acrobat 2.0 (PDF 1.1)**	**Acrobat 3.0 (PDF 1.2)**	**Acrobat 4.0 (PDF 1.3)**	**Acrobat 5.0 (PDF 1.4)**
Released	1993	1994	1996	1999	2001
Navigational and structural features	Internal links and bookmarks	External links and article threads Can embed multimedia elements Searchable documents	Support for interactive forms	Larger page size allowed (up to 200 by 200 inches) Can embed portable job tickets	Tagged PDF allows export to RTF and makes text reflow onscreen XML metadata supported
Color	Device CMYK support	Spot color support via prologue.eps	Device-independent color Complete spot color support	ICC-based color management	Compression of DeviceN color Color management on par with other Adobe applications
Annotations	Sticky notes			Highlight, strike-through, and other new annotation tools	Online review and commenting

continued

Table 1-1 All good things in all good time. Truer lyrics could not be sung about using PDF files in prepress production. The first version of PDF was a bare-bones file format that offered few advantages for high-end printing. It wasn't until Acrobat 3.0 that PDF began to offer features of value to the prepress world. In the last five years, the PDF spec has grown to support improved color management, larger page sizes, and critical prepress data, such as screening and trapping information.

Table 1-1 *continued*

	Acrobat 1.0 (PDF 1.0)	Acrobat 2.0 (PDF 1.1)	Acrobat 3.0 (PDF 1.2)	Acrobat 4.0 (PDF 1.3)	Acrobat 5.0 (PDF 1.4)
Fonts	Embed Type 1 and TrueType fonts	Subset fonts	Support for double-byte fonts added		OpenType support added
Imaging			Halftone screens, transfer functions, black generation, UCR and over-print instructions Downsampling added		Transparency Separate controls for transfer functions, half-tones, and black generation JBIG 2 compression Export images to JPEG and other formats
PostScript	Level 2	Level 2	Level 2	Levels 2 & 3	Levels 2 & 3
Additional prepress features			OPI 1.3 Support for bleeds, trim, and art boxes	OPI 2.0	Overprint preview Tiling
Other features		Watched folders Plug-in architecture		Web capture Digital signatures Predefined job options	Encryption boosted to 128 bits Batch editing tasks

THREE, FOUR, OPEN THE DOOR

Along about version 3.0, Adobe began to take prepress users' needs more seriously, adding such features as support for screening and overprint instructions. However, this version came out in 1996, when the World Wide Web had risen to the midmorning sky and was shining down brilliantly on publishers, who were blinded by its glare. Thus, Acrobat 3.0 was promoted as a Web publishing tool.

It allowed links to URL addresses, which meant that someone reading a PDF file could click on a link and jump to a live Web page. An Adobe plug-in allowed PDF files to be displayed within Netscape Navigator, and an ActiveX control let them be displayed in Internet Explorer (Figure 1-1). Web surfers needed the Reader viewer to see PDF files online (and still do), but once it was free and available for download at Adobe's Web site, it began to propagate quickly. (The most recent count was 165 million and still growing strong.)

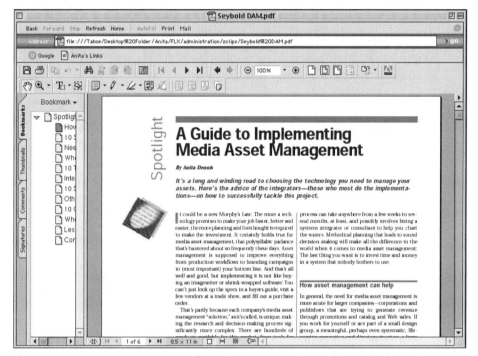

Figure 1-1 Since the introduction of Acrobat 3.0, you've been able to display and print PDF files from within Microsoft's Internet Explorer and Netscape Navigator. All you need is the free Acrobat Reader, which you can download from Adobe's Web site.

Acrobat 4.0, released in 1999, was all about workflow productivity—mostly for corporate users (who by then had become the product's primary market), but also for the creative community. Lots of annotation features were added, including highlighter and strike-through tools, and digital signatures were introduced. Now users could mark up and sign off on drafts and proofs using PDF (reminiscent of the way people work on hard copies), but with none of the mess of tracking and merging changes in authoring applications (and minus the associated version-control headaches). A plug-in allowed Windows users to click a button to distill a document from within Microsoft Office applications. And since the Web had become intrinsic to publishing workflows, Adobe offered a Web Capture feature in Acrobat for Windows (and a plug-in for the Mac), allowing HTML pages to be downloaded and translated into PDF. This was a boon to Web publishers, who could now use PDF files to circulate, proof, and mark up staged pages; they could even be used to test-drive navigational structures and links.

Distiller was also greatly enhanced: It now offered predefined job options that users could customize, save, and share for automating the creation of PDF files. In addition, the maximum page size was increased to 200 by 200 inches (making imposition more practical), and more downsampling provided users with greater control over the file-size versus file-quality trade-off.

FIVE, SIX...

With version 5.0, Acrobat and especially the PDF file format itself (in version 1.4) have evolved into essential tools for "network publishing." In this world—Adobe's vision of publishing's future—users will be able to publish content from any source (hard-copy scans; digital photos and graphics; page-layout files; sound, video, and animation clips) to any number of output formats and devices: not just print, the Web, and the occasional CD-ROM, but also handheld devices (such as Palm devices and cell phones), eBook readers, and DVDs (Figure 1-2). Before long the list will probably include tricorders and holodecks!

In this vision, Adobe sees its PDF file format as key. It is the "digital master" from which all other subservient (or device-specific) formats will be derived. Adobe views PDF as a "wrapper" around content: PDF files hold objects that are managed like a database, and these objects can be published where and how the content creator sees fit.

To this end, Acrobat 5.0 introduces structured and tagged PDF files—mechanisms that in essence divorce content from output medium so that it can be published anywhere, anytime, in any way. Both types of PDF files provide a logical structure "tree" that allows content to be repurposed for multiple types of output devices. XML-tagged PDF files go a step further by providing additional information about content, such as character spacing, recognition of soft and hard hyphens, and alternate text descriptions for images (Figure 1-3). Tagged PDF files—which you can export from PageMaker 7 and InDesign 2.0, create in Microsoft Office

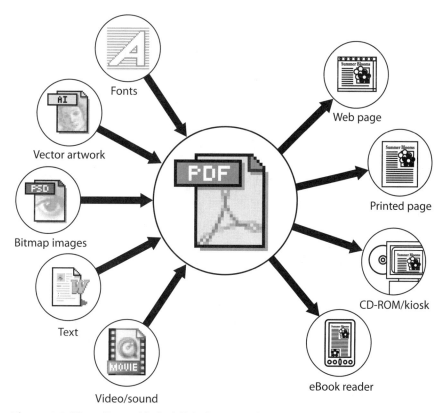

Figure 1-2 Virtually any kind of digital content, from fonts to video clips, can be embedded in a PDF file, which in turn can be published to any medium, including print, the Web, CD, kiosks, and handheld devices.

applications using the PDFMaker tool, or generate using Acrobat's Make Accessible plug-in—provide faithful repurposing of PDF files.

The most immediate application for structured, tagged PDF files is eBooks—a fact not lost on Adobe. The company now offers not only a dedicated Acrobat eBook Reader PDF viewer application but also versions of the good, old Acrobat Reader that run on the Palm OS and Pocket PC, which can also be used to read eBooks. Acrobat 5.0 (PDF 1.4) files can be structured with tags that allow text to be reflowed from a desktop PC (where an eBook can be downloaded) to a Palm device (where it might actually be read by a tired businessperson commuting home on the Metro North Hudson line).

Other major changes to Acrobat 5.0 continue version 4.0's trend of catering to the established corporate base. Forms features have been greatly enhanced, so that

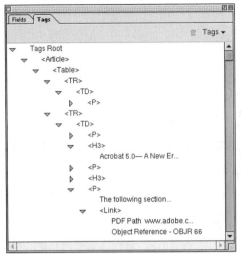

Figure 1-3 In the Tags palette of a tagged PDF file, you can see its HTML structure, including table (<Table>), row (<TR>), and cell data (<TD>) specifications; text tags such as paragraphs (<P>) and styles (<H3>); and image (<IMG>) and hypertext link markers (<Link>).

PDF files now include live fields that can be filled out online. Depending on what information is submitted, the form can update interactively to prompt for specific data. Then, using a CGI script (written outside of Acrobat, usually by a Web server administrator), the information can be collected and stored in a database. You can also edit PDF forms in Acrobat 5.0; you don't have to return to the source application to do so.

Adobe has also refined and streamlined Acrobat's annotation and comments features, adding the capability to export comments in their own file and place them on a server so that they can be accessed by anyone in a workgroup through a Web browser. Finally, Adobe has made it easier to export text and graphics from Acrobat so that they can be edited and reused in other applications, and the Acrobat interface is now more similar to that of Microsoft Office applications.

Despite the nod to Microsoft, Adobe has taken steps over the years to tightly integrate PDF with all of its own professional publishing applications. You can import and export PDF to and from most of them.

ADD IT UP

PDF 1.3, Acrobat 4.0, PDF 1.2, Acrobat 3.0—can't keep straight which version of Acrobat produces which version of PDF? Just do the math. The sum of the digits in the PDF spec equals the version of Acrobat to which it corresponds: PDF 1.2 = Acrobat 3.0; PDF 1.3 = Acrobat 4.0; and PDF 1.4 = Acrobat 5.0. No promises about Acrobat 6.0, of course!

Which Acrobat Do You Need?

Although modularity is what makes Acrobat so flexible, that very benefit has also been a barrier to many users. With each version of the software, Adobe has reconfigured the mix of what constitutes the application, causing confusion with every upgrade.

Acrobat 5.0 is the key ingredient to using PDF in design and production workflows. It includes everything you need under one roof:

- Acrobat, for viewing, editing, and printing PDF files
- Catalog, an indexing and search engine that's a plug-in to Acrobat
- Paper and Web Capture, also both plug-ins. The former is an OCR tool for scanning legacy print documents into PDF files; the latter allows HTML pages to be downloaded into PDF format
- Distiller, for creating PDF files, which can be run independently or launched from within Acrobat.

A handful of specialized Acrobat applications are also sold separately:

- Acrobat Capture, for high-volume conversion of paper documents to PDF
- Acrobat Messenger, a workgroup tool that uses a dedicated PC with an attached scanner or digital copier to convert hard-copy documents into PDF and distribute them by email or fax
- Acrobat Approval Business Tools, which adds a stand-alone PDF client tool for completing digital forms
- PDF Merchant, a server-based product for the production and secure electronic distribution of copyrighted PDF files (such as eBooks)
- Content Server and eBook Reader—the former allows distilled PDF files to be packaged, copyright-protected, and distributed as eBooks; the latter is a viewer for PDF-based eBooks
- Acrobat Distiller Server and Document Server—the former centralizes the creation of PDF files for high-volume production and accepts PostScript, not native application files; the latter allows PDF files to be viewed in Web browsers as GIF and JPEG, without a Reader

Free Readers—plain old Reader 5.0 for Mac, Windows, and Unix; the eBook Reader 2.2; and the Palm OS and Pocket PC Readers—can be downloaded from Adobe.com for those who just consume, and don't create, content.

Now that you understand all of the things you can do with Acrobat and PDF files, you can decide what you want or need to do with them. If you're a small independent publisher of self-help and business advice books, you might want to add PDF-based eBooks to your catalog. If you're producing an internal HR newsletter that typically goes through several rounds of approval, you might want to use PDF to circulate those drafts electronically. Finally, if you're constantly facing remakes because your application files crash your printers' RIPs, you might consider switching to PDF as a composite final file format. In all of these scenarios, Acrobat PDF can save you time and money.

PDF's Role in Prepress

Although Adobe didn't create its portable document format for streamlining prepress workflows, the graphics community quickly realized PDF was a natural for prepress because it's based on PostScript, the page-description language Adobe developed for putting pixels on paper back in the 1980s. While Adobe has always stressed other strengths and markets for Acrobat and PDF, the company has also (quietly and gradually) made the technologies more friendly to the graphic arts community (see Table 1-1). Today, users can employ Acrobat and PDF to manage PostScript data with aplomb, and take advantage of the supporting cast of tools to accomplish a wide variety of tasks.

If you plan to use PDF in your prepress workflow, it helps to know how the production process has evolved to the point where PDF is needed. I could go all the way back to Gutenberg, but let's fast-forward to the 1980s, when PostScript revolutionized the way desktop printers understand instructions for drawing marks on a page.

Out of the (Black) Box

At the time Adobe was developing PostScript, the printing world had moved from hot type (which involved systems like Linotype that automated composition using cast-metal slugs) to cold type, photographic typesetting that married computer screens for type entry with a back-end system that laser-imaged content onto photographic paper. Production assistants would take this paper, chemically developed, and lay out pages of text, art, and ads, all waxed down on the page. These flats would then be sent to a printer, who used a graphic arts camera to separate the pages into the film used to image the four CMYK printing plates, "stripped" into imposed signatures, and printed.

In the late 1970s and early 1980s, when these systems became capable of processing images and art as well as type characters, they became known as imagesetters. Entire high-end prepress systems developed around this technology, comprising optical scanners, color-correction software and imaging workstations, and networked storage devices. These systems came from many of the vendors whose prepress equipment we still use today, such as Scitex, Screen, and Linotype-Hell (which became just Linotype, and then got swallowed into the big belly of the German press manufacturer Heidelberg).

Initially, as you might imagine, these high-end prepress systems were closed and proprietary. Scitex, for example, used its CTLW (continuous-tone line work) format, which couldn't be read by Screen's systems. These systems also used dedicated processors to make the computationally intensive calculations required to rasterize output. These raster image processors, or RIPS, crunch the digital data that describes a page into a bitmap, which is an array of bits that can be used by a marking engine to image dots on film (or directly on plates or paper). With these early high-end prepress systems, RIPs were hardware-based, either built into the imaging device or into a "black box" tethered to the device. Although these early electronic prepress systems automated and streamlined the formerly complex and time-consuming tasks involved in preparing pages for print, they were cumbersome. For all their processing power, they were still slow, and a system that was busy rasterizing a page couldn't be used for other tasks. Finally, such systems were costly to upgrade—if they could be upgraded at all.

By the mid- to late-1980s, however, processing technology had begun to grow both more powerful and more affordable, and color displays and desktop publishing and imaging applications with graphical working environments were becoming available. Designers now had tools at their disposal to compose rich, graphical pages, and they wanted to output those pages as they appeared on screen. John Warnock and Chuck Geschke, the founders of Adobe, developed PostScript for just that purpose.

PostScript is both a page-description language—software that describes the contents of a digital page—and a programming language. Like C, VisualBasic, or Java, PostScript contains commands, or code, that tell an output device how to accurately render the described page. The difference between PostScript and other page-description languages is that it understands both text and objects as mathematical representations, which means it can render those objects to any output device: The words that describe this capability are *device independent*. Because Adobe allowed PostScript to be licensed to hardware manufacturers and made PostScript's specifications freely available to software developers, the language quickly began to take root, giving users tremendous flexibility in authoring tools and output devices, making both front- and back-end systems more compatible, and ensuring high-quality final printed output.

A breakthrough, yes, but like other software applications, the first version of PostScript, called Level 1, left something to be desired. Like the systems it was beginning to replace, it was slow and required a lot of processing power. More importantly, it couldn't handle four-color separated files. However, PostScript Level 2, which came along in 1994, changed that. In addition to supporting color separations, Level 2 offered improved performance and reliability, better font handling, and more reliable drivers (Table 1-2).

	PostScript Level 1	**PostScript Level 2**	**PostScript Level 3**
Released	1985	1994	1998
Color capabilities	Device-dependent output parameters, including RGB color and resolution	CMYK, RGB, and other color models, including device-independent color	DeviceN color space added, allowing non-CMYK images, such as duotones and spot-color blends, to be separated
Font features	Type 1 Roman, Cyrillic, Greek, Hebrew, and Arabic fonts	Support for composite fonts, such as Chinese and Japanese	Type 42 fonts for native TrueType support under PostScript Extended font set: 136 Type 1 fonts typically built in
Imaging features	256 levels of gray	Filters for JPEG and other compression algorithms	Up to 4,096 levels of gray, which reduces banding in high-resolution output devices Smooth shading also reduces banding in gradients produced by high-resolution output devices
Prepress features		Improved halftone screening algorithms, including Adobe's Accurate Screening Support for in-RIP separation of composite files	Support for in-RIP trapping

Table 1-2 High-resolution printed pages require PostScript Level 2 at minimum. PostScript 3 offers more gray levels and smooth shading for reduced banding in gradients—features that can be carried into PDF files distilled from PostScript 3 data. PDF files created in Acrobat 4 or higher should be made with PostScript 3 to produce the highest-quality page data.

Combine this with other industry advances—the development and release of color PostScript printers; support for PostScript in graphical desktop applications such as PageMaker, Illustrator, and QuarkXPress; and improved processing power in desktop CPUs—and the stage was set. Not only was there critical mass for the generation of PostScript pages, but the crunching of that data by RIPs could now be handled much more efficiently in software (turning those pixels of color into dots of toner or ink). By the mid-1990s, those proprietary black boxes and closed, hardware-bound imaging systems were becoming ancient history.

How RIPs Work

Rasterizing PostScript data is a multistep process. First the PostScript data stream must be interpreted, meaning all the objects and their locations on the page are read and saved to something called a *display list.* The resulting description of a word of text, for example, includes the typeface, point size, spacing, position, color, and all of the other characteristics that describe it on the page. Using this display list, the RIP rasterizes, or renders, the objects into the precise bitmapped data that will appear on the page; this includes a screening process that defines the shape and placement of the dots, which are finally imaged on paper (proofing device or digital press), film (imagesetter), or plate (platesetter) by a marking engine (Figure 1-4).

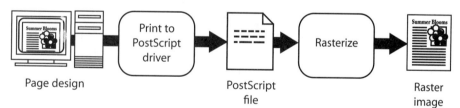

Page design → Print to PostScript driver → PostScript file → Rasterize → Raster image

Figure 1-4 In a PostScript workflow, pages are laid out in a desktop publishing software application, printed to a PostScript file via a printer driver, and then rasterized to an output device.

Despite PostScript's advantages, there are several drawbacks to the rasterization process. First, the PostScript data has to be interpreted in page order. PostScript RIPs process pages sequentially, one at a time. When you're talking about an 8-up signature or larger, this can entail some huge digital files that take a l-o-o-o-o-n-g time to process, even with the fastest of CPUs.

Second, every object on the page must be interpreted, including any data that's hidden under an overlapping object on another layer. Even if such obscured data isn't intended to be imaged on the page, the RIP must calculate it (see Figure 1-5).

Figure 1-5 PostScript interprets all the data in a file, even extraneous information, on layers or under objects that won't be printed. This is called "flattening" a file.

Third, it's difficult to edit PostScript files late in the production process. Because of the way PostScript is constructed, the language works best when it contains irrevocable, final data. Otherwise, PostScript has to be reinterpreted by each application that edits it—a tedious process. PostScript's cousin, encapsulated PostScript (EPS), however, can be used to exchange graphics files. EPS includes a low-resolution preview of the PostScript that can be displayed and edited onscreen.

Finally, PostScript workflows are extremely error prone: Among other things, the fonts and images associated with a PostScript file are often only linked to it, and those links are easily broken, which can cause all kinds of prepress bottlenecks. Also, each application writes PostScript code with its own unique quirks, and when PostScript files are imported and exported into and out of numerous applications, the final interpretation may end up having to parse redundant or conflicting code, which increases the risk of errors and makes the final output unpredictable. Various prepress packages attempt to "preprocess" PostScript, which is ineffective unless you have a complete PostScript interpreter. Many also attempt to pattern-match against Document Structuring Convention (DSC) comments in PostScript to guess intent of the PostScript page. Such packages tend to break every time applications and drivers change. Furthermore, each output device may rasterize the PostScript slightly differently, which means the page may not look the same on different devices.

Now think about the ways technological advances are changing the way we work. The historic model for publishing is to create a page, print it, and then distribute it. Increasingly, however, we're creating pages, distributing them, and then printing them. In part, this is because telecommunications have opened up, and T1, T3, and other high-bandwidth channels (even DSL and cable modems for us small fish) are now used by virtually every corporation, agency, prepress house, and printer. It's become commonplace to send files across the country (or even the world) for production rather than calling a bike messenger to carry flats across town or shelling out a few bucks to have FedEx deliver SyQuest disks overnight.

With the Internet reinforcing the need for customized, targeted, and timely delivery of printed information, we've had to adapt our publishing strategies. By distributing pages quickly over high-bandwidth channels to multiple destinations before they're printed, we're able to achieve more flexible, customized printed pages: Magazines can publish ads localized to a particular geographical region; direct mail and catalogs can be targeted to gender or other demographics; newspaper inserts can advertise goods and prices for local markets. These days, a printer with multiple manufacturing plants might take your job and queue it to an available press in any number of states from one central dispatch site, keeping presses humming and customers happy with timely turnarounds.

PDF's Role

Although all of this sounds great, you may be wondering how PDF fits into these and other scenarios. Because PDF is based on PostScript, it offers all of the benefits we've come to associate with that type of high-quality, high-resolution output. However, it also addresses some of the drawbacks that can plague PostScript-based prepress production.

First and most obvious, PDF is object-oriented, which is really just a fancy way of saying that it displays the contents of the PostScript file onscreen with pages and page elements visually intact; the file is not just a string of impenetrable code that you have to view in a word processor (although you *can* edit it if you need to). Better yet, PDF files are device- and resolution-independent, which means that pages appear identical onscreen and in print, regardless of the application or platform being used.

PDF files are also smaller and more reliable than PostScript files (which are notoriously huge and prone to error messages). The reason for this is that the Distiller application that generates PDF files is itself a RIP. It "normalizes" a string of PostScript code—that is, it flattens the file, strips out hidden data that won't be imaged for print, compresses images and text, and then writes the file to PDF instead of to a display list. The result is a self-contained file, with font and image data embedded rather than referenced externally, eliminating the broken links that result in PostScript errors. The judicious application of image compression also results in smaller files that can be transferred and processed more quickly. Indeed, it's accepted practice among prepress operators to debug or simply clean up PostScript files by running them through Distiller. Distilled PDF files print and image more reliably, giving prepress operators greater confidence in the data they're managing.

In addition to having the device- and resolution-independent characteristics of PostScript files, PDF files are page independent. Pages, like their contents, are simply data objects in PDF. This means that a multipage PDF file can be sliced up and individual pages rasterized on one or several systems, then rendered to one or more output devices simultaneously (Figure 1-6). This is a huge change from monolithic PostScript files, which have to be processed one at a time and in page order—an improvement that can speed production exponentially. It also adds a degree of flexibility and control previously unavailable: Output devices can be at different locations, employ different resolutions, and be of different types (an imagesetter at one location and a platesetter at another). In addition, pages can be swapped in and out of imposed signatures, allowing the final piece to be customized in a way that PostScript files never could.

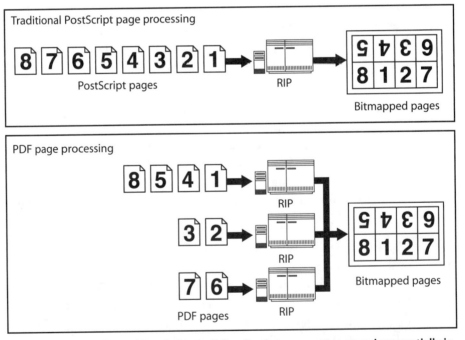

Figure 1-6 In a traditional PostScript workflow (top), pages are processed sequentially in a RIP. PDF workflows (bottom), however, allow you to process pages individually, speeding and streamlining rasterization.

Finally, a key advantage of PDF over plain old PostScript in prepress is editability: Because the PDF file format is so visual, it's natural for users to want to make corrections on pages. Acrobat itself includes some basic editing tools to accommodate review processes and late-stage touch-ups, and there are a wide variety of third-party plug-ins that you can use for more complex editing, preflighting, and prepress tasks. You have to be careful, however, when editing text within PDF files: You can only edit line by line (because text doesn't reflow or repaginate). However, the upside to this is that edits made to single pages can be re-rasterized individually, without having to re-RIP entire signatures. Similarly you can make significant changes to an individual page in, for example, a page-layout application, redistill that page, and then insert it into the larger document without having to redistill the entire file.

Other Final File Format Options

The use of PDF in prepress production is often described as a composite workflow. This is because PDF files contain all of the color channel data in one flat, composite document. Usually, it's not until after the PDF files reach the prepress shop that the digital grayscale separations are created and used to image film or plates. The alternative is a preseparated workflow, in which the document creator produces separations, usually by employing the DCS file format. The DCS, or desktop color separations, format is an enhanced version of EPS that was developed by Quark but is supported in other applications as well. You can, for example, export images from Photoshop as DCS and then import them into a page-layout application such as InDesign, where they can be cropped and resized before being output.

DCS 2.0 files contain multiple channels: cyan, magenta, yellow, and black, as well as up to one alpha channel and multiple spot channels and a composite preview (Figure 1-7). When you provide DCS files to your prepress house, you must separate the channels yourself and also specify all of the screening options for the various inks in your page layout application. The benefit here is that you save your prepress provider the work of creating separations and you can create them with as much precision as you desire; the drawback is that if your prepress provider has to make changes, they will probably need to be made on a composite file. The preseparated workflow also requires that you know in advance how the file will be imaged and printed so that you can make all of the appropriate decisions regarding halftone screen angles, frequency, dot gain, and so on—something that may not always be possible. What's more, your prepress partner may prefer to create the separations to ensure the task is performed to its standards. After all, most of us don't think in terms of grayscale CMYK channels and would have a difficult time, for example, determining from a quick visual assessment of a preseparated file whether a cyan channel was going to print too dark.

```
%!PS-Adobe-2.0 EPSF-1.2
%%Creator: QuarkXPress(R) 4.11
%%Title: sad sarah (Page 1)
%%CreationDate: 7/24/01 11:19 AM
%%DocumentProcSets: QuarkXPress_EPS_4.11 1.0 0
%%DocumentSuppliedProcSets: QuarkXPress_EPS_4.11 1.0 0
%%DocumentProcessColors: Cyan Magenta Yellow Black
%%DocumentData: Binary
%%LanguageLevel: 1
%%BoundingBox: 0 0 612 792
%%PlateFile: (Cyan) EPS #1278228 338850
%%PlateFile: (Magenta) EPS #1617078 338850
%%PlateFile: (Yellow) EPS #1955928 338850
%%PlateFile: (Black) EPS #2294778 338850
%%EndComments
%%BeginProcSet: QuarkXPress_EPS_4.11 1.0 0
```

Figure 1-7 The header in a DCS file (top) points to the four individual cyan, magenta, yellow, and black plates (bottom), each of which contains grayscale image data.

You can also hand off final files in their native application format—a common practice. There are, however, numerous drawbacks to this method. To start, because all the graphics are linked to the page-layout file, you must manually include all images with the document, as well as all of the fonts you used. This can be cumbersome, and even if you do remember to include everything, the links can be tenuous. If the links are stable *and* your service provider has the same application on the same platform *and* doesn't accidentally swap in a different version of Times, the service provider *should* be able to view the file as you intended. It may even be able to proof and separate the file! But that's a lot of *ifs*. How many times has your prepress shop called to say that the document has reflowed and doesn't match the hard-copy proof?

SLEEP AT NIGHT

We used to send application files to our printers, and I'd worry that someone would move something or that a font would default to Courier. I hated always being unsure when I sent a book out what we were going to get back. It was a terrible feeling. Now when I send a book to prepress as PDF, I'm sure it's going to work out. I know when I send them the PDF that we'll get what we expect.

—Keli Davis, director of production, Evan-Moor Educational Publishers

There's one other file format option for prepress that I'll mention for good measure; however, I won't dwell on it because it really serves a niche audience. Called TIFF/IT, the format is used exclusively in magazine advertising production. A raster format derived from the Aldus-developed tagged image file format (TIFF), TIFF/IT (the *IT* stands for *image technology)* was developed in the 1990s and advocated by the DDAP, an association of graphic arts professionals who wanted to integrate digital advertising into publication production processes. Although TIFF/IT is a reliable and predictable format used by many magazines and supported by a number of prepress vendors, it's not a mainstream format. You can't save or export TIFF/IT files from your desktop applications. Instead, your prepress provider must convert PostScript files to TIFF/IT and then integrate them with the rest of the magazine pages.

Prepress managers like TIFF/IT because it's basically uneditable—meaning you can't accidentally introduce errors into high-end (read: expensive) color advertising. But this lack of editability also has its downsides, as I mentioned earlier, and TIFF/IT files are known for their heft. This is at least part of the reason that the same group of graphics pros who came up with the format has also embraced a version of PDF, called PDF/X, as a complementary digital format for vector-based magazine advertising. (For more on PDF/X, see Chapter 6. For a features comparison of the various types of final output file formats, see Table 1-3.)

File Type	Application	DCS 2.0	PostScript	PDF
Structure	Composite but layered, proprietary	Separated with composite preview	Program code and binary data	Composite, object oriented, includes binary data
Fonts	Linked	Embedded	Embedded	Embedded
Images	Linked	Linked	Linked	Embedded
Size	Medium	Large	Very large	Small
Average reliability	Moderate	Moderate	Moderate	High
Security	None	None	None	Optional, flexible, robust

Table 1-3 PDF files are self-contained and composite, providing designers with greater assurance that their production partners will be viewing and printing exactly what they intended.

Benefits of PDF Production

The flexibility and consistency of PDF files make them an attractive proposition to prepress shops and printers that desire a more reliable alternative to PostScript, DCS, or application files. A well-distilled composite PDF file translates into smoother and more efficient workflows that save prepress and print shops time and money: Files can be processed faster; fewer consumables are used; and financial resources aren't tied up in expensive, proprietary equipment that's costly to upgrade. A stable, normalized file will behave predictably when output, and provide enough editability (with the help of plug-ins) for service providers to perform such mandatory prepress tasks as trapping, screening, and imposition.

PDF workflows also offer significant benefits for designers and print content producers. Once you get the hang of distilling them (preferably using predefined job options provided by your prepress partner or printer), you'll find they're much easier to hand off—no more collecting files for output; zipping pages, images, and fonts together; no more checking and printing the contents of folders. You simply prepare one file containing all of the page elements, which you can check at a glance. And because the composite format is familiar, you don't have to wonder whether you separated the channels correctly. PDF files are especially useful in environments where lots of contractors (and thus many different tools) are used: Just give your freelancers a job options file, and you can be confident they'll provide you with a usable final file. You may even find that PDF saves you money because your prepress partners aren't spending as many billable hours getting your files to print.

In addition to being ideal for final output, PDF files have myriad other uses in the design and prepress world: Because they can be viewed on any platform, you can use them to circulate proofs. And the intrepid among you might even use Acrobat's ICC color management features to print remote proofs or to soft-proof pages, confident that the color your client or prepress partner sees is what you saw and is what will appear when the ink hits the page. Annotation features and support for digital signatures facilitate the collaborative creative process: You can mark up proofs with comments and requests for changes, and sign off on final versions. Finally, because they're compact and self-contained, PDF files are also great for archiving: When you go back and reopen the file, you don't need to worry about being able to access the application the file was designed in, or about lost fonts or broken links from outdated paths and directories.

TURN AROUND ON A DIME

We used to print hard-copy galleys and send them via courier to our authors. Since our head office is in Melbourne, Australia, and our authors live as far away as Nepal, turning around these proofs could take a month—a month of down time! Now we distill PDFs, use FTP as an electronic-exchange mechanism, and we can turn around author proofs with text, maps, color, and cover art in 24 hours. The authors love it and the production crew loves it, and we've had massive savings on printers, print supplies, and the cost of international shipping.

—Rowan McKinnon, Lonely Planet Publications

Despite their many benefits, PDF files are not a panacea for all production woes. If the files are poorly prepared (RGB images not converted to CMYK, fonts not embedded), your prepress partner will still go crazy trying to fix them. In fact, the biggest problem with PDF workflows may well be that properly distilled PDF files are difficult to create. All the functionality that Adobe has added over the years has, in many ways, only made the process more confusing. You have to dot your *i*'s and cross your *t*'s in more dialog boxes than even the most competent computer wizard cares to navigate to ensure that your final PDF file is in order.

Also keep in mind that PDF files can't compensate for poorly designed pages. For example, hairline rules and tiny, process-color type will still be a challenge to print sharply and without press registration mishaps. Thus, as the designer, it remains incumbent on you to prepare pages wisely, using sound document-construction techniques.

Making the Change

When your bottom line depends on sending pages out the door, you can't necessarily adopt a PDF-based workflow overnight. You need to properly plan the transition, determining how this type of workflow can best serve both you and your prepress and printing partners. Here are a few ideas to get the ball rolling:

- **Talk to your partners.** This is the first step in the planning process. Find out what systems and processes your partners use now, and ask whether and how PDF might help. You may find out that they redo a lot of your work (such as specifying halftones) and that they'd be happy to receive the format. On the other hand, you may find out that they want you to ease into a PDF workflow. If this is the case, you could allow your partners to generate proofs from PDF files before committing to producing film or plates from them. Make sure that your prepress service provider has Acrobat, supporting and up-to-date prepress tools, the proper RIPs, and, most importantly, the training and experience to accept and process PDF files. If it doesn't, you should go elsewhere. Attempting to teach a service provider that doesn't know or embrace PDF workflows can be an expensive and frustrating lesson in futility.

- **Provide your partners with final composite PDF files *along with* your final application or PostScript files for a couple of jobs.** Your partners may or may not have time to look at them right away, but at least you'll get some practice distilling PDF files while giving your partners an opportunity to get used to them.

 KEEP UP WITH THE TIMES

People resist change, like years ago when we first installed a multiline phone in the shop, my mother refused to use it. Don't fear PDF; it's a good working tool. It can be user-friendly for all aspects of the printing environment.

—Margo Baker, graphics specialist, ProPrint, Inc.

- **Visit your partners' shops.** The more you know about what your partners do, the more effectively you'll be able to use PDF—and the smoother the transition will be for all involved. You may find out that your partners are ready to go on their end, or you may learn that a PDF workflow is simply incompatible with the larger systems and processes they employ. Once again, if you're committed to making the transition, it's essential to work with partners who are open to PDF and fit with the way you want to work.

- **Talk with your clients.** Find out whether they have Acrobat and to what degree they're open to receiving digital PDF comps for print or onscreen review, as well as whether they can use Acrobat's collaboration tools for design reviews. Keep in mind that everyone involved in the PDF workflow should have the full, licensed version of Acrobat. If your clients only have the free Reader, they can't digitally mark up pages or sign off their approval. Plus they can't control the way color files are displayed and printed.

FIRST SMALL WINS, THEN BIG

We've been concentrating on using PDF for some small wins. We use it in our review cycle so that product development, merchandising, and quality assurance can see an electronic color proof instead of a hard-copy black and white. This has resulted in a significant cost and time savings for us. We also use it to produce an "FYI mechanical": Again, we used to print and circulate bound black-and-white copies when the catalog was finished, but now we put a composite PDF on our intranet. That way, the call center can see it and anticipate questions; planners can reforecast if they need to; and everyone enjoys it being in color because they get the true impact of how the book looks. I think we'll ultimately use PDF for some big wins, such as sending out final files to our separator, as we continue to try to improve collaboration across departments and build catalogs more efficiently.

—*Larisa Sheckler, creative services director of operations, Eddie Bauer, Inc.*

- **Determine a timeline for the transition.** Finally, you need to decide whether you want to phase in PDF use over time or jump in feet first without looking back. Not surprisingly, the former is the more rational approach. This way, you can continue to be productive as you work out kinks in the new workflow, learn what happens to your files in prepress, and get the hang of producing good, clean PDF files. Still, if you're only using PDF like stucco—to patch holes in your workflow—then you're not realizing its full potential. Since the name of the game is consistency, PDF can provide the greatest efficiency boosts when it serves as the standard for whatever processes you apply it to. In any case, give yourself more time than you think you'll need to make the transition because you'll likely have to continue producing live jobs as you phase in new processes.

CHAPTER TWO

How to Create PDF Files for Prepress

Few things in life are easy, so why should creating PDF files for prepress be any different? The good news is, there's a multitude of ways to go about the task; the bad news is, it can be difficult to sort through all the options. Should you choose PDF from Illustrator's Save As dialog box, or should you use the Create Adobe PDF option in the Print dialog box (new in Acrobat 5.0)? And if you're a Windows-based designer, what about that Convert to Adobe PDF button that appears in your Microsoft applications now that you've upgraded to Acrobat 5.0? You'll find the answers to all of these excellent questions and more in this chapter.

You can produce PDF files for prepress in three basic ways: Print them from an authoring application, export them from an authoring application, or distill them manually. Because each alternative has advantages and disadvantages, this chapter will first describe how the various procedures work and then tell you how to execute them in some of the most common authoring applications. By the time we're finished, you should be able to produce a PDF file that your prepress partner won't kick right back to you. (There are other ways to create PDF files, but you'll want to avoid them when your files are destined for four-color or offset printing. See "How NOT to Create PDF Files for Prepress," page 31.) Speaking of prepress partners, talk to your service providers before you start sending them PDF files. Really. They may not want you to provide composite PDF files; instead, they may want the raw PostScript or an application file so that *they* can distill the files. (They may not even use a PDF or PostScript workflow, but if that's the case, you may want to work with them to develop one.) The best-case scenario would be for them to provide you with the Distiller job settings optimized for their imaging hardware and RIPs—this could save you tons of guesswork, aggravation, and time.

SHOOTING FOR 100 PERCENT

Our goal is to teach customers to create PDF files for us, but we make them, too. Up to 80 to 85 percent of the files we receive are PDF. We've worked out the job options settings with Distiller and provide them to customers. We work closely with our customers to help them set up PDF servers and get them trained on using watched folders and distilling files correctly.

—Melinda Monti, manager of electronic prepress training and development, Vertis, Inc.

PRINTING FROM AN APPLICATION

With Acrobat 5.0, Adobe has greatly streamlined the process of creating PDF files. In the past you had little choice but to print a PostScript file to disk from your page-layout (or word processing or drawing or whatever) application and then run the PostScript file through Distiller to convert PostScript to PDF, but Adobe now lets you distill PDF files from within the Print dialog box of virtually all major design or publishing applications.

On the Mac, this method uses the AdobePS 8.7 printer driver, which Acrobat 5.0 installs automatically. On PCs, Acrobat installs the AdobePS 4.5 PostScript printer driver in Windows 95/98 systems, AdobePS 5.2 on Windows NT systems, and the system PostScript driver on Windows 2000 systems. On both platforms, Acrobat takes the PostScript data stream from the driver, launches and runs Distiller in the background, and produces the PDF.

Just as when you send a file to a printer, many applications display a progress bar onscreen that indicates they're spooling and printing the file—in this case to the Adobe PostScript driver. Then, if you want, you can "see" the file being distilled from your desktop. On the Mac, double-click the Create Adobe PDF desktop printer icon to view progress in the Printer Monitor dialog box (Figure 2-1). In Windows, open your Printers Control Panel and double-click the Acrobat Distiller printer icon (Figure 2-2).

If you set up your driver properly, when you create PDF files by "printing" them from an authoring application on the Mac, in most cases you invoke the same familiar PostScript Print dialog box that indicates Create Adobe PDF is your printer and lets you choose a Distiller settings file from the Job Options pop-up menu. You can also opt to launch Acrobat right after the PDF is created. Click OK, and you're off. The trick, of course, is to define your job options in Distiller before you start. Job options (which are described in detail in Chapter 3) tell Distiller what to do with the PostScript file as it converts it to PDF: for example, whether and how to embed fonts, how to compress data, and how to manage

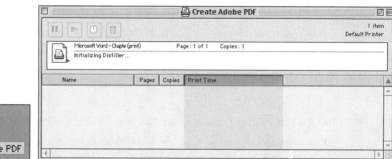

Figures 2-1 When you create a PDF file through the Print dialog box of an authoring application on the Mac, you can watch your file being distilled by double-clicking the desktop printer icon (left) and looking at the Print Monitor (right).

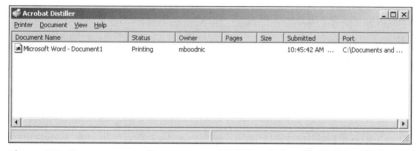

Figure 2-2 You can watch the progress of PDF files being distilled in Windows by looking at your Printers Control Panel and double-clicking the Acrobat Distiller icon.

color, security, and other parameters. In some applications' Print dialog boxes, you'll find that you can specify choices that are also available in Distiller—and which may ultimately conflict. Luckily, you can tell Distiller through job options whether or not to defer to the instructions in the application. Acrobat ships with four predefined job options settings files—eBook, Print, Press, and Screen (all of which are based on PDF 1.3 or 1.2)—but you can create your own or use one provided by your prepress partner if you'd rather.

On Windows PCs, you can also set up Distiller as your default printer and specify a default conversion settings file (which is the same as job options on the Mac), greatly simplifying the process of printing PDF files through Distiller. However, each authoring application's Print dialog box varies slightly, so you may have to search a bit to find the Acrobat Distiller Document Properties dialog box, where you can select your conversion setting as well as a few other options from the

Adobe PDF Settings tab. The nice thing about this dialog box is that you can click the Edit Conversion Settings button to access job options directly. You can create new ones or edit existing ones right in the dialog box that opens; however, the Mac doesn't afford this convenience.

The Role of Printer Drivers and PPDs in Producing PDF Files

When creating Adobe PDF files, you rely on two other types of files—printer drivers and PPDs—which can be confusing unless you understand what they do and how they relate to each other.

A printer driver is a program that takes data out of an application and feeds it to a printer (or filmsetter or platesetter). Adobe makes printer drivers that stream data from documents in the PostScript page-description language. PostScript files contain a slew of commands that describe the content of a given page or document. A RIP in a PostScript output device interprets those commands and produces the hard copy. However, output devices rely on another file to tell them how and where to image that content's dots: That file is known as a PPD.

PPD (PostScript Printer Description) files describe the fonts, paper sizes, resolution, and other device-specific capabilities of PostScript output devices. Typically produced by the printer manufacturer and distributed with your printer, they reside in the Printer Descriptions folder in the System Extensions folder on the Mac. In Windows, you'll usually find them in the Windows System subdirectory or a deeper directory.

When you produce PDF files, Acrobat Distiller acts as a device-independent PPD. After you click Print, Acrobat essentially simulates a printer and becomes your PPD. The authoring application actually uses a PostScript printer driver, but Adobe has put a nice wrapper on it—called Create Adobe PDF on the Mac and Acrobat Distiller in Windows. By selecting that printer driver, you tell your application to print your document to a PostScript file, and then use the Acrobat Distiller PPD to convert the PostScript into PDF using Distiller job options.

Don't be like me, though, and allow yourself to be confused by PPDs versus job options. PPDs describe a range of characteristics of specific output devices. Job options, in contrast, describe how the content of a file should be handled when output. The job options settings that you specify (which include compression, font embedding, and so on) are applied to the PostScript file by the Distiller PPD when it converts it to PDF.

Finally, on the Mac you may notice that after you install Acrobat 5.0 and begin using its included PostScript drivers, "virtual printers" appear on your desktop when you print PDF files. Virtual Printer is a plug-in that installs automatically with AdobePS 8.6 or later, and it's there in case there's no PostScript output device attached to the system running Acrobat: The PostScript driver needs a printer to which it can send data—even if it's virtual and the data is ultimately channeled into an electronic PDF file. Virtual printers are most commonly used to create PostScript files from QuarkXPress.

Exporting from Applications

Even though Adobe has made it much easier to produce distilled PDF files with Acrobat 5.0, most of the leading design and authoring tools give you an alternative: exporting as PDF. In Photoshop, Illustrator, and FrameMaker, for example, you can use the Save As command in the File menu to save documents as PDF. In InDesign, FreeHand, and QuarkXPress, meanwhile, you can use an Export command. These applications use varying methods to export PDF files: Some go through Distiller, while others bypass PostScript and use their own engines or Acrobat's PDF libraries to produce the PDF file directly.

Exported PDF files differ from distilled PostScript PDF files in one significant way: They're the size of the actual document as defined in the authoring application. Distilled PDF files, in contrast, are the size of the page that's specified by your PPD. If your document and page size are both 8½ by 11, for example, you may not notice. This means that if you want to include off-page marks, you should distill the PDF file and make sure that your page size is larger than your document size to accommodate them. If you want the PDF file to reflect the actual document size, sans off-page marks, go ahead and export (Figure 2-3).

Because applications export to PDF in a variety of ways, it's safer to distill PDF files for prepress than to export them: You usually have more control over the process and you know you're getting reliable, clean PostScript. The times to export PDF files are when you want to take advantage of PDF 1.4's features, such as transparency, or to create structured and tagged PDF files for electronic documents, such as from PageMaker or InDesign.

PostScript itself doesn't support transparency; digital files that contain transparent objects must be flattened before they can go through a PostScript RIP. Since creating a PDF file from an application's Print dialog box sends the file through a PostScript stream, any transparency in the file is flattened in the process. If you want the transparency to remain live so that you can reopen the PDF and edit the transparency in Photoshop, Illustrator, or InDesign 2.0, you must export from those applications and specifically instruct the software to maintain transparency. (This doesn't hold true for CorelDraw or FreeHand because they cannot import PDF 1.4 files.) Transparency gets confusing because applications support it differently; for more on this topic, see "How to use Transparency in PDF Workflows," page 79.

When you save as or export to PDF, each application prompts you with its own series of PDF options dialog boxes that generally reflect the type of content that the

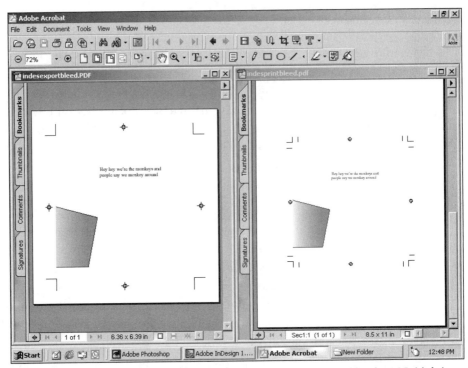

Figure 2-3 Distilled documents are the size of the page as specified by the PPD (right); exported documents are the size of the document as defined in the application (left).

application produces. In Photoshop, for example, you select compression methods, but you can't subset fonts because Photoshop images don't usually contain enough type for subsetting to save much space. InDesign's export options, on the other hand, are almost as robust as Distiller's job options—not surprising since this page-layout application was developed with PDF workflows in mind. Although these dialog boxes can be confusing, just think of them as being analogous to job options, and you should be OK.

DISTILLING FILES MANUALLY

The third and final way to produce PDF files for prepress is to distill your files manually—which in essence was what you did in previous Acrobat versions when you performed the two-step process of printing a PostScript file to disk and then distilling it. Acrobat 5.0 automates this process by letting you print distilled PDF files directly from authoring applications. Thus, if you want to distill a file manually, you have to take the process apart: You simply revert to the old method of printing a PostScript file or saving as EPS and then launching Distiller, where you create the PDF file.

But why would you manually distill a file when Acrobat can do it automatically? Well, for one, your prepress provider may want to produce the PDF file instead of letting you do it. Or you might not have Distiller on your system (say you're working remotely and won't be able to distill the file until you're back in the office). You may also want to distill PDF files manually if you're using watched folders to automate the routine conversion of multiple PostScript files to PDF, or when you want to combine multiple PostScript files into one PDF file. The next chapter explains how to do this, as well as everything else you need to know about Distiller settings, options, and processes.

How *Not* to Create PDF Files for Prepress

Although Acrobat 5.0 streamlines the process of creating PDF files, there are a number of other ways of creating PDF files that aren't suitable for prepress because none of them comprise distilled PostScript. These include the following:

1. **Capturing PDF.** Acrobat 5.0 lets you "capture" PDF files from the Web by choosing Open Web Page from the File menu or Tools > Web Capture > Open Web Page. Both commands create 72-dpi RGB PDF files, which are fine for viewing Web page comps (complete with links) but not for sending through a raster image processor.

2. **Import Scan.** Acrobat 5.0's File > Import > Scan command lets you scan paper documents that contain text or images directly into PDF. This results in files whose content is "image only," meaning the page elements can be edited only as bitmapped images; text cannot be searched or edited. If you want to make the text searchable, Adobe offers the Paper Capture online service, accessible from the Tools menu. Note that Paper Capture is *not* a way to create PDF files, nor is it a way to convert scanned documents into distilled PostScript. Rather, it's a way to substitute characters and words for bitmapped text in a PDF file so that it can be searched. It's used for editing scanned business documents and for making scanned PDF files accessible to visually impaired and motion-challenged readers, not for pages destined for a four-color press.

3. **Open as Adobe PDF.** This command in Acrobat 5.0's File menu lets you convert a number of file types to PDF on opening. It works with text and HTML files as well as many common image file formats—including GIF, JPEG, and TIFF—but it's mostly for putting a PDF wrapper around Word for Windows files.

continued

How *Not* to Create PDFs for Prepress *continued*

4. **PDFWriter.** Although Adobe eliminated the PDFWriter utility on the Mac with Acrobat 5.0, some Windows users who are too smart for their own good may still find it as a Custom Install option. If it's on your system, either from a previous or current installation of Acrobat, don't use it! PDFWriter, which you can invoke in the Print dialog box of an authoring application, captures a PDF 1.2 file! While this is an acceptable way to create and circulate PDF files of simple text-based business documents, these PDF files are the bane of the prepress workflow because they don't support PostScript commands and can't handle embedded EPS graphics. Show some mercy on prepress providers and never send written PDF files!

5. **OS X.** Although it's true that OS X lets carbonized applications create PDF files, they're based on PDF 1.2 and 1.3—which means they can be viewed in Acrobat 5.0 (as well as Apple's own PDF Viewer), but they don't print transparency or support some other PDF 1.4 features. Based on screen data, Apple's PDF files support only a subset of the PDF document model (for example, no bookmarks, links, or compression or downsampling). Like PDF files created using the Open As command or PDFWriter utility, Apple's PDF tool is suitable for exchanging and viewing business documents that aren't going to be sent to a PostScript RIP.

BEFORE YOU START

One could fill a book with instructions about how to print or export PDF files from every iteration of every design, publishing, and business application (not to mention various flavors of operating systems), but I don't want to write that book and I doubt you want to read it. Instead, this book will show you how to produce PDF files from the current versions of some popular applications on Mac OS 9.1 or later and Windows 2000 Professional (or its equivalent) using the PostScript drivers that ship with Acrobat. If your setup varies, I apologize. Hopefully the explanations provided here will be clear enough that you can extrapolate from these generic setups and make informed choices that yield high-quality PDF files.

Also keep in mind that these techniques are not intended as tutorials on the printing and output capabilities of the various applications. This book presumes that you know not only when you want to tile a document on a larger page size but also how to find the proper command in whatever application you're using. This chapter is intended to show you how to produce composite, device-independent PDF files so that you can leave device-dependent considerations up to your prepress provider. As you'll soon see, however, there will be times when you have to dip into separation setup dialog boxes to invoke bleeds or page marks. If you want to produce actual separations, use your software manuals and get some guidance from your prepress partner so that you can choose the appropriate screening and other options.

To produce PDF files efficiently, you must set up your printer driver properly before you start distilling files. On the Mac, that means clicking the Create Adobe PDF desktop printer icon and pressing Command-L to set it as your default printer. Then go into one of your regular publishing applications and press Command-P. In the dialog box that appears (Figure 2-4), don't worry about job options for now; just click the PDF Settings pop-up menu and go to the PostScript Settings panel (Figure 2-5). Choose PostScript Job as your format, Level 3 as your PostScript level, and Binary as your data format, but don't include fonts. Your destination should be File. Now click Save Settings, then Cancel, and you're ready to roll.

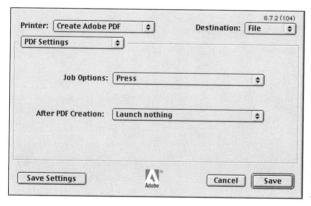

Figure 2-4 The Print dialog box in most Mac authoring applications.

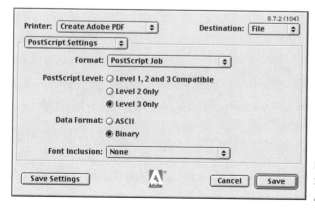

Figure 2-5 The PostScript Settings panel of the Create Adobe PDF Print dialog box.

In Windows, click Acrobat Distiller in the Printers Control Panel to choose it. Then choose Printing Preferences from the File menu. In the Adobe PDF Settings tab of the Acrobat Distiller Printing Preferences dialog box (Figure 2-6), make choices about your default distillation setup: Choose a conversion method such as Adobe's high-end Press option or click Edit Conversion Settings to tweak an existing setting and create a new one. Check "Do not send fonts to Distiller." It's a counter-intuitive click, but Distiller has an efficient way to find the fonts it needs to embed in the PDF file, and sending the fonts is less efficient. When you're finished with this panel (and any other choices you make in the others), click OK. Then choose File > Set As Default Printer, and make Acrobat Distiller your default printer. The preferences you specified will now be the defaults for the applications we're about to cover.

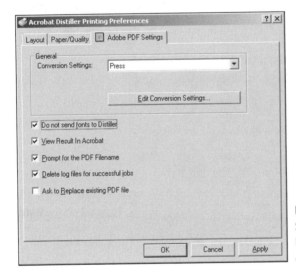

Figure 2-6 The Adobe PDF Settings tab of the Acrobat Distiller Printing Preferences dialog box.

ILLUSTRATOR 10

Print

Before actually distilling, make sure the file is ready. If you want to include page marks and bleeds in your PDF file, choose Separation Setup from the File menu. In the Separations dialog box (Figure 2-7), you can define Distiller PPD settings (page size, orientation, and so on) as well as document settings. Check the Use Printer's Marks box and specify a bleed if you want them to carry over to the PDF file you're about to distill. Make sure the page size is large enough to accommodate those definitions. Click OK.

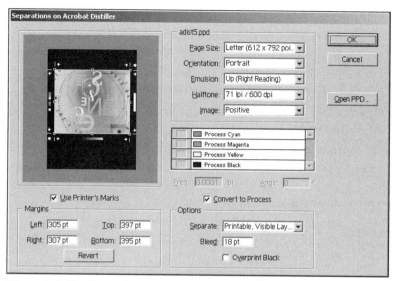

Figure 2-7 The Separations setup dialog box in Illustrator 9.0.

Now select Print from the File menu or press Command/Control-P. Depending on your platform, Create Adobe PDF or Acrobat Distiller should appear as your chosen printer. If another printer driver appears, choose Create Adobe PDF (Mac) or Acrobat Distiller (Windows) from the pop-up list. Be aware, however, that if you've chosen a non-PostScript driver (for example, a LaserWriter driver) on the Mac, you won't be able to choose the PDF driver. Go back to your desktop, select the Create Adobe PDF driver, and try again.

If you're on a Mac, you should now be able to choose from a pop-up list of available Distiller job options (Figure 2-4): As I mentioned earlier, Acrobat ships with four default options; they should be available to you here. If you or your prepress provider create others and save them in the Settings folder inside the Distiller application folder, they'll be available from this list, too. (Again, see Chapter 3 for more on job options.) For all of my examples, I've chosen the default Press option, which is geared for high-quality printing in that it preserves the maximum amount of information possible from the original document without concern for final file size. You can also specify whether you want to launch Acrobat, Acrobat Reader, or Adobe Circulate after the PDF file is created to view it right away. (Circulate, if you aren't familiar with it, comes with PressReady and displays PDF document thumbnails.) After you've made your choices, click Save, and in the dialog box that appears next, name your PDF file and select where you want it saved. Click Save again, and you're finished.

If you're in Windows, click the Properties button in the Print dialog box (Figure 2-8). In the Adobe PDF Settings tab of the Acrobat Distiller Document Properties dialog box (Figure 2-9), specify your conversion setting from the pop-up list (notice that this is the same dialog box as Distiller's Printing Preferences, in Figure 2-6.) If you want to edit the settings or create a new one, click the Edit Conversion Settings button here. Make sure the "Do not send fonts to Distiller" box is checked; check the other options as you see fit. Click OK when you're finished, and when you're back in the Print dialog box, click OK. In the Save PDF File As window that appears, name your file, choose a destination, click Save, and let Acrobat do its thing.

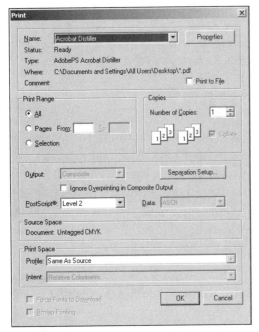

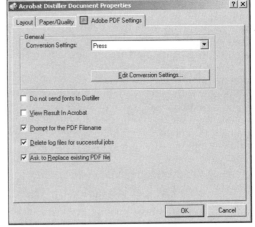

Figure 2-8 The Print dialog box in Illustrator for Windows.

Figure 2-9 The Acrobat PDF Settings tab of the Acrobat Distiller Document Properties dialog box.

Save As

To export an illustration as a PDF file so that you can bypass PostScript and maintain editable transparency, choose File > Save As. In the Save As dialog box that appears (Figure 2-10), choose Adobe PDF as your format on the Mac or your Save as type in Windows, and specify where you want the file saved. Make sure your file name has a .pdf extension (so as not to confuse it with another version of the file), then click Save.

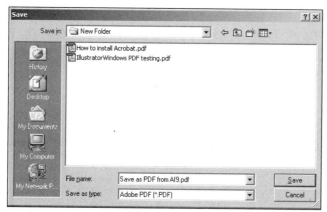

Figure 2-10 The Save As dialog box in Illustrator.

Illustrator now presents you with the Adobe PDF Format Options dialog box, which is the same on both Mac and Windows. You can choose from three Options Sets: Default, Custom, or Screen Optimized. For each of these sets, you must toggle through two pop-up panels of settings: General and Compression. Choose either the Default or Custom Options Set and view its General panel (Figure 2-11). Notice that it specifies Acrobat 5.0 as the default File Compatibility option, but you can also choose Acrobat 4.0. If you choose the former, Illustrator creates a PDF 1.4 file; if you choose the latter, it writes a PDF 1.3 file. Check the Preserve Illustrator Editing Capabilities box if you plan to later open the file in Illustrator (which you probably will, since that's why you've chosen to export it). This keeps fonts, color characteristics, patterns, vertical type blocks, and other objects intact.

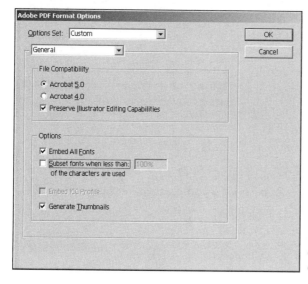

Figure 2-11 The General panel of the Adobe PDF Format Options dialog box in Illustrator.

The rest of the options are similar to those you specify in Distiller. Thus, if you want a fuller explanation of them, see Chapter 3, where they're discussed in detail. Check the Embed All Fonts box so that the resulting PDF file will display and print fonts without having to approximate them. When the embed fonts box is checked, Illustrator automatically checks the Subset Fonts box, specifying a 100 percent threshold. Since Illustrator files are often single-page documents without an abundance of fonts, it's fine to either uncheck the Subset box or leave the setting at 100 percent. You won't save much in file size by reducing the threshold.

The Embed ICC Profile box will be available if you've specified a profile for the file in the Color Settings dialog box (which I haven't). Check this box if you want the profile to be attached to the PDF file you're creating so that the color is consistent when you view it in Acrobat 5.0 or reopen it later in Illustrator.

When you're finished with these options, click and hold the General menu to access the Compression panel (Figure 2-12). I've accepted the default settings, which produce fairly high-quality PDF files: They invoke 8-bit ZIP compression, a lossless method that's good for images with large areas of single colors or repeating patterns. You probably don't need to downsample images since you won't save much on file size unless you dramatically resample (for example, repurposing a high-resolution print illustration for the Web). Do check Compress Text And Line Art: It's lossless and efficient.

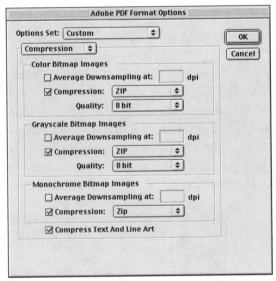

Figure 2-12 The Compression panel of the PDF options dialog box in Illustrator.

If you opt to export a screen-optimized PDF file because your file is destined for the Web, Illustrator applies automatic compression (either JPEG or ZIP, depending on the content of the page). It also downsamples images to 72 dpi and does not preserve the file's editing capabilities.

When you're finished, click OK to save the PDF file.

PHOTOSHOP 6.0

Print

In Photoshop you can specify bleed and printers' marks among other things in the Print Options dialog box, accessible from the File menu. To view them, check the Show More Options box (Figure 2-13). In Windows, you can also find and select printers' marks in the Page Setup dialog box (what you check in one dialog box is reflected when you open the other).

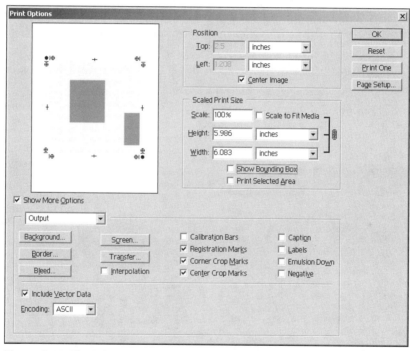

Figure 2-13 The Print Options dialog box in Photoshop 6.0.

Now select Print from Photoshop's File menu or press Command/Control-P. The Print dialog box should reflect your printer driver. If Create Adobe PDF isn't in the Printer pop-up list on the Mac, choose it in the Chooser or go back to the desktop to select a PostScript or PDF driver if you don't have any options in that menu.

With the Create Adobe PDF driver selected, the Mac Photoshop Print dialog box (Figure 2-4) lets you choose from a pop-up list of Distiller job options: the four default Acrobat job options as well as any you've created. I've chosen my favorite default Press option, which is geared for high-quality printing, and opted not to launch Acrobat after the PDF file is created. Click Save, and in the dialog box that appears next, name your PDF file and select where you want it saved. Click Save again, and you're finished.

In the Print dialog box in Windows (Figure 2-14), you must now jump through some hoops: Click the Setup button to access the Page Setup dialog box, where you can choose Acrobat Distiller from the Name list (if you need to) as well as any printers' marks you'd like (Figure 2-15). Then click the Properties button to access the Acrobat Distiller Document Properties dialog box. In the Adobe PDF Settings tab (Figure 2-9), specify your Conversion Setting from the pop-up list. I've chosen Press in my example. When you've finished, click OK to go back to Page Setup, then click OK again to go back to the Print dialog box. (If you're certain the proper conversion settings are selected, you don't have to go through this rigamarole.) Back in the Print dialog box, select Binary as your encoding method and any color management settings you'd like to apply. Then click OK. In the Save PDF File As window that appears, name your file, choose a destination, click Save, and you're finished.

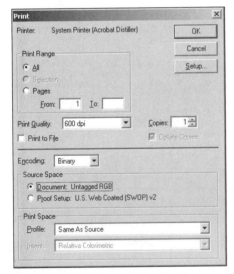

Figure 2-14 The Print dialog box in Photoshop 6.0 for Windows.

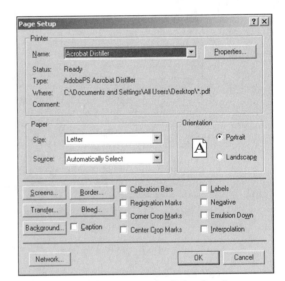

Figure 2-15 The Page Setup dialog box in Photoshop 6.0 for Windows.

Save As

As with Illustrator, exporting PDF files from Photoshop is the same on both Mac and Windows. Choose Save As from the File menu. In the Save As dialog box, specify where you want to save the image, and choose Photoshop PDF from the Format list. This automatically appends a .pdf extension to your filename (Figure 2-16). Depending on the structure and contents of your file, you can choose to preserve alpha channels, layers, spot colors, and annotations. You'll want to retain whatever makes sense for your file and your workflow: For example, if you plan to open and edit the file again, you'll probably want to preserve layers and alpha channels (at a minimum). If you're working with a color-managed file, you'll also be able to check Use Proof Setup. If you want to create a color-managed file, you can check Embed Color Profile (on the Mac) or ICC Profile (in Windows) as long as that's OK with your prepress partner. When you've made your choices, click Save.

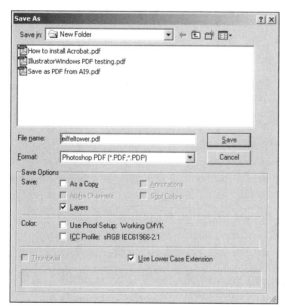

Figure 2-16 The Save As dialog box in Photoshop.

In the PDF Options dialog box that appears next (Figure 2-17), you can select either ZIP or JPEG as the encoding method. ZIP is better suited for graphics with large areas of flat color, such as screen shots, while JPEG is more appropriate for photographic images. If your Photoshop artwork combines continuous-tone imagery and flat areas of color, you'll have to decide which area's integrity is more important to preserve. When you choose JPEG, as in my example, you must decide how much compression to apply: The greater the compression, the more image quality is compromised, because JPEG is a lossy technique. For PDF files destined for prepress and printing, choose Maximum as your quality level.

If your file includes transparency, you should now check the Save Transparency box so that you can edit it again when you reopen the PDF file in Photoshop. Don't bother to check the Image Interpolation box: You only need to select that if you want to

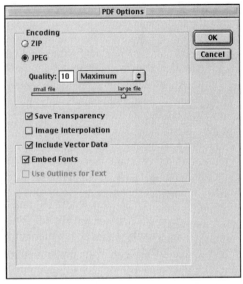

Figure 2-17 The PDF Options dialog box in Photoshop.

antialias low-resolution images when they're printed. Since you're dealing with high-resolution images for print, it doesn't apply.

If your image contains vector data, preserve those resolution-independent objects in the PDF file by checking Include Vector Data. This will ensure smoother edges for type and paths when printed. Then you can choose either Embed Fonts or Use Outlines for Text. The former is preferred, even though it produces larger files. If I haven't made it clear yet, let me be explicit now: Don't be too worried about file size when it comes to producing PDF files for prepress. Content integrity should be your primary concern—which is why we're conservative about using compression and choose to embed fonts rather than converting text to paths.

Finally, click OK, and Photoshop will write the PDF file. On the Mac you'll notice that the resulting file icon is a little different from the usual Acrobat PDF document icon. This is because the PDF file was created in Photoshop.

InDesign 2.0

Print

When you press Command-P on the Mac, you'll immediately notice that InDesign's Print dialog box isn't the familiar dialog box you've encountered in Photoshop and Illustrator. On both Mac and Windows systems, InDesign's Print dialog box offers a list of panels—the first is the General panel (Figure 2-18)—that you can tab through to choose print options. On the Mac, Create Adobe PDF will be selected in the Printer pop-up list, and Acrobat Distiller will be selected in the PPD pop-up list. In Windows, Acrobat Distiller should appear in the Printer Name field. To check or change your job options or conversion settings, on the Mac click the Printer button at the bottom of the box and in Windows click the Properties button, then make your selections. Click Save or OK to return to the InDesign Print dialog box, and then click through the seven other panels: Setup, Marks & Bleeds, Output, Graphics, Color Management, Advanced, and Summary. Make the choices appropriate to your document, such as Composite CMYK in Output (Figure 2-19). The Graphics panel is where you specify PostScript options, such as generating PostScript Level 3 and

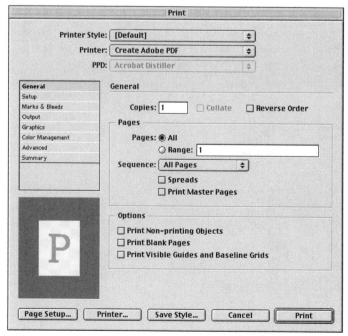

Figure 2-18 The General panel of InDesign's Print dialog box for Mac.

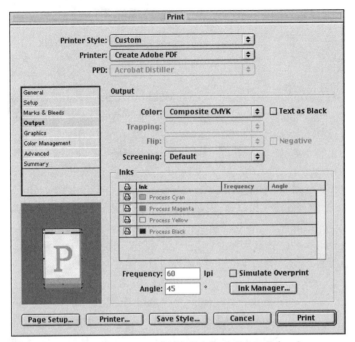

Figure 2-19 The Output panel of InDesign's Print dialog box.

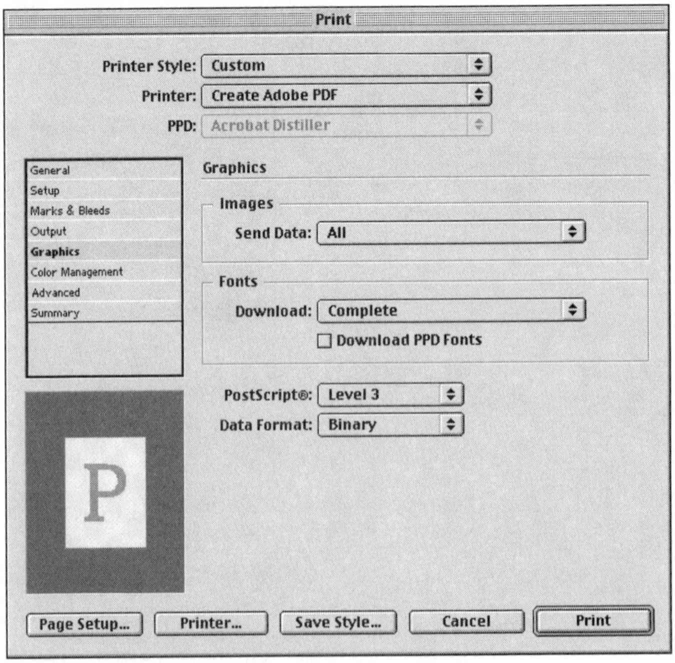

Figure 2-20 The Graphics panel of InDesign's Print dialog box.

choosing Binary as your data format (Figure 2-20). Notice that the preview in the lower-left corner of the dialog box updates to reflect your choices, and the printer style changes to Custom.

When you've made your choices, click Print: InDesign willl begin generating PostScript, and Acrobat will distill the PDF file.

Export

Many of InDesign's Export PDF options bear an uncanny resemblance to Distiller's job options (the Compression panel in particular). When you export, however, you have access to a few unique controls that aren't available through Distiller, such as the ability to include tags and hyperlinks for electronic documents or to flatten transparency. For print publishing, though, there's little reason to export to PDF unless you want to circumvent the PostScript stream and generate PDF files directly from libraries so that your files are document size rather than page size. Hold onto your hats while we hike through that process—which, happily, is the same for both the Mac and Windows.

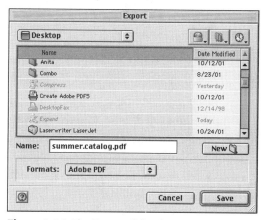

Choose Export from the File menu. In the Export dialog box that appears (Figure 2-21), choose Adobe PDF as your format on the Mac or as your Save As Type in Windows, and give your filename a .pdf extension. Click Save.

Figure 2-21 The Export dialog box in InDesign 2.0.

A PURPOSE FOR THUMBNAILS

We recommend including thumbnails because they are useful during preflight: it may add a tiny amount to the file size, but we can see at a glance if page orientation is off, if bleeds are there, and so on.

Justine Trubey, prepress product manager, R.R. Donnelley Print Solutions

The Export PDF dialog box that next appears onscreen looks a great deal like the Print dialog box, with its set of tabbed panels. You start out in the General panel (Figure 2-22), where you can select which pages you want to distill. In that same panel, from the Compatibility pop-up menu, you can choose which version of

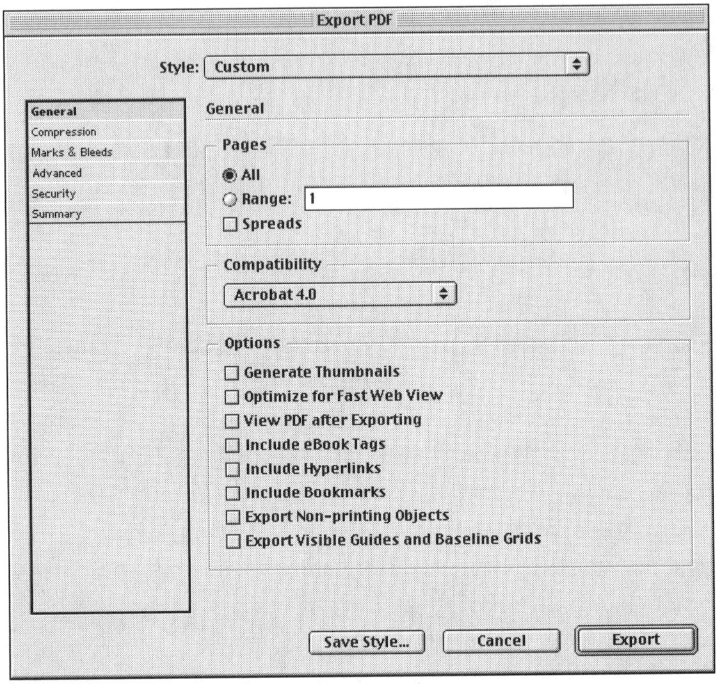

Figure 2-22 The General panel of InDesign's Export PDF dialog box.

PDF file—Acrobat 4.0 (PDF 1.3) or Acrobat 5.0 (PDF 1.4)—you wish to generate. You can also decide whether you want to create thumbnails and preserve links (see Chapter 7 for more on these options). Unless you want to export nonprinting items (say, to preserve their editability in PDF once they've been imported into Illustrator or back into InDesign), you can leave all of these boxes unchecked. Checking Optimize for Fast Web View saves on file size by removing repeated background elements and replacing duplicates with pointers to the originals. It's safe to check this box even if your PDF file is destined for prepress since it results in a slightly cleaner file and also speeds viewing of the PDF file from a network. Checking Spreads exports pages as they would appear in bound reader spreads.

In the Compression panel (Figure 2-23), you can specify parameters for down-sampling and compressing color, grayscale, and monochrome images, as well as text and line art. As mentioned earlier, these options are comparable to those in Distiller's Job Options dialog box. You can leave the Compression setting on Automatic for color and grayscale bitmap images because InDesign can automatically detect where those types of images are in the document and apply suitable compression. Alternatively, you could use the guidelines described in the section

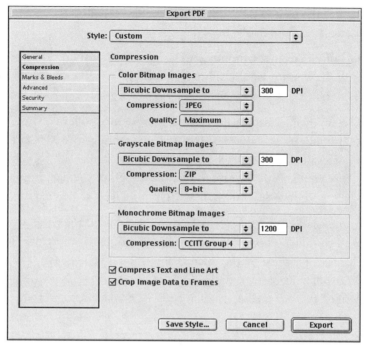

Figure 2-23 The Compression panel of InDesign's Export PDF dialog.

on compression in Chapter 3 (page 87). When you choose JPEG compression, leave the Quality setting at Maximum.

Monochrome images should be compressed with CCITT Group 4 technology, and do check the Compress Text and Line Art box: InDesign applies lossless ZIP compression to these page elements. One choice offered in this panel that doesn't exist in Distiller is the option to crop image data to their frames. Check Crop Image Data to Frames to rid the PDF file of image data hidden behind frames and not intended to print, or leave the box unchecked if your service provider needs this image data for repositioning or bleeds.

If you know what output device your PDF will be sent to as well as the resolution and line screen it supports, you can safely resample images so that you don't bog down the RIP with extraneous pixel data. Keep in mind, however, that if you haven't used the PDF file to generate intermediate or final proofs yet, those proofing devices may support different resolutions and line screens. Thus, you don't want to strip the PDF file of image data it needs for the highest-resolution device. The safest settings are those optimized for high-resolution devices: Resample color or grayscale bitmap images to 300 dpi and monochrome images to 1,200 dpi. If you do this, the resulting PDF file will include enough pixel data to be imaged on just about any output hardware.

To prevent over-resampling, InDesign has a sampling threshold of 1.5—which means it won't resample an image unless its resolution is more than 1.5 times the resolution value you enter in the DPI text box.

The following chapter provides a thorough overview of how compression and resampling work; however, the important thing to understand now is that you don't want to guess at what settings to use here. Talk to your prepress partner before you compress or resample images: Once the data is gone, it's gone. You'll have to produce an entirely new PDF file if you've deleted too much.

In the Marks & Bleeds panel (Figure 2-24), as in the panel of the same name in the Print dialog box, you can expand the boundaries of the PDF file to include bleeds or printers' marks. Bleed value should be between 0 and 1 inch (in whatever unit you prefer), indicating the area that needs to be imaged beyond the defined page size. Check which types of marks you want to include on the pages.

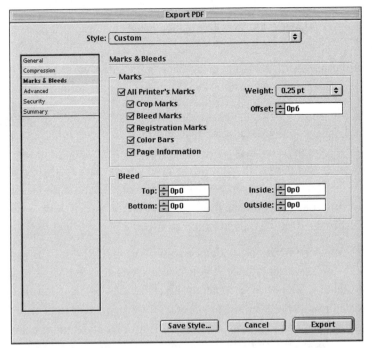

Figure 2-24 The Marks & Bleeds panel of InDesign's Export PDF dialog box.

The value you enter in the Offset box specifies how far from the edge of the page the marks are drawn (6 points by default).

Now for the Advanced panel (Figure 2-25): If your file is destined for a printing press, choose CMYK to make InDesign convert any RGB images to process colors, so that the PDF file can be separated later. If your document is being color-managed, check the Include ICC Profiles box so that attached profiles travel with the PDF file to its next destination; then choose a destination profile. Check the Simulate Overprint box if you want to preview overprints in Acrobat.

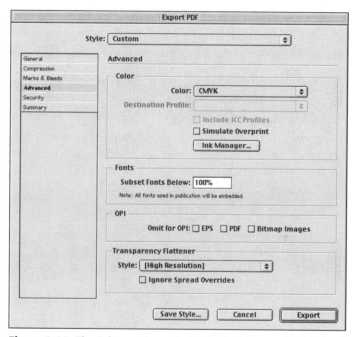

Figure 2-25 The Advanced panel of InDesign's Export PDF dialog box.

In the Fonts area, set the threshold for subsetting embedded fonts at 100 percent. Although InDesign automatically embeds fonts (as long as there are no licensing restrictions), subsetting at 100 percent saves a little space. The benefit of reducing the threshold further is that it makes the final PDF file smaller; however, if you're using multiple fonts in a document, it may not be worth the effort to calculate an accurate percentage. The reason for this is that InDesign applies the one threshold to all of a document's fonts. Thus, if you undersubset, you don't get the benefit of the smaller PDF file, and if you oversubset, InDesign protects you by not subsetting at all. Leaving the threshold at 100 percent is your safest option.

If you're working in an OPI environment, you can choose to omit EPS or bitmapped images or PDF pages. Checking any of these boxes leaves only the OPI links in the file, which means that although your service provider will be able to view the low-res proxy in the InDesign document itself, the exported PDF file will contain gray boxes for those omitted images. If you choose any of these options, remember that your service provider will need to have the high-resolution versions of the images when it's time to output the file.

Finally, choose the degree of flatness you want to apply to any transparency in the file. The Style pop-up menu lets you trade off quality for processing time: Choose High Resolution if you want a high-quality interpretation of the transparency effects and don't mind waiting for your computer to crunch the file. Choose Medium or Low Resolution to speed processing for lower quality results.

Lastly, we arrive at the Security panel (Figure 2-26), where you can apply password protection and permissions to the file. For example, you can assign one password to open the document and another to change security settings. You can also restrict users' ability to print the PDF file, change anything in the file, select and copy text and graphics, or add or change notes or form fields. Regardless of which type of

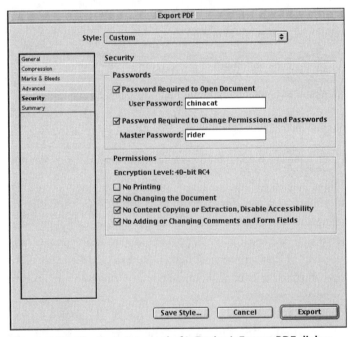

Figure 2-26 The Security panel of InDesign's Export PDF dialog.

PDF file (Acrobat 4.0 or 5.0) you're creating, you can only apply 40-bit security. In Acrobat and Distiller, however, you can apply 128-bit security to Acrobat 5.0 files, giving you more control over the types of restrictions you can assign.

We won't visit the Summary panel; it just shows you what you've selected. However, it does contain a handy button that lets you save the summary—which you can print out and give to your service providers in case they have questions about your file. When you're ready, click Export.

If you feel like you've just trekked up Mount Everest and are gasping for oxygen, you'll be glad to hear about two convenient InDesign features: PDF Styles and Printer Styles. You've probably already noticed the Style pop-up menu and the Save Style button in the Export PDF dialog box, as well as the Print Styles pop-up menu in the Print dialog box. Styles streamline the process of creating these PDF files by letting you save print or export settings for easy reuse: Say, for example, you want to produce low-resolution RGB files that simulate a CMYK press for soft-proofing, or you want to create a slightly customized press style for a client whose design is templated and printing is routine. In such cases you can customize styles available in the Print or Export dialog box rather than manually slog through panels, text boxes, and radio buttons.

To create PDF export styles, select File > PDF Style. In the PDF Styles dialog box (Figure 2-27), you'll see a list of available styles based on Distiller's default job options, with their characteristics described in the Style Settings scrolling list. Select one of the job options and click New to create a PDF style based on that style. This opens the New PDF Style dialog box (Figure 2-28), where you can rename the selected style and modify its settings as desired. You'll notice

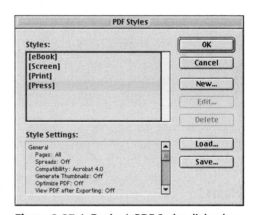

Figure 2-27 InDesign's PDF Styles dialog box.

right away many familiar panels that you can click through: General, Compression, Marks & Bleeds, Advanced, and Summary.

Click OK when you've finished creating or editing a style, and from then on it will be available from the Style pop-up menu in the Export PDF dialog box. You can create Printer styles by going through a similar process after selecting File > Printer

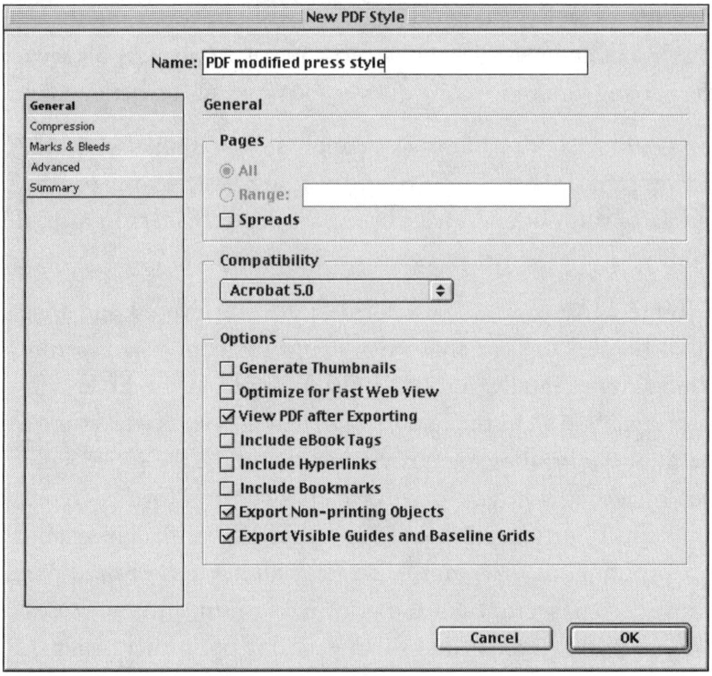

Figure 2-28 InDesign's New PDF Style dialog box.

Styles > Define. I like to use styles so that I don't forget to check certain essential boxes, like Convert to CMYK. Your prepress partner can give you styles, too, which will save you from manually sifting through the entire Export dialog box and accidentally subsetting 10 percent rather than 100 percent of embedded fonts.

PAGEMAKER 7.0

Print

As with InDesign, PageMaker's Print dialog box is all its own (Figure 2-29). Not to worry: Although PageMaker's Print dialog box looks different from any we've seen so far, it contains all of the required options and is identical on Macintosh and Windows systems. Create Adobe PDF or Acrobat Distiller should be your Printer; select it from the pop-up list if it's not. Acrobat Distiller should be your PPD; if it's not, select it from that pop-up list. Then click the Paper, Options, Color, and Features buttons to make choices about paper size (Figure 2-30), printers' marks, downloading fonts, sending binary image data, printing composite color, and other options.

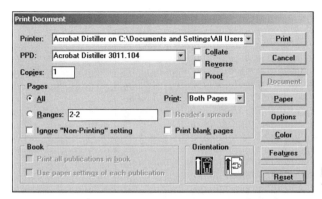

Figure 2-29 PageMaker 7.0's Print dialog box.

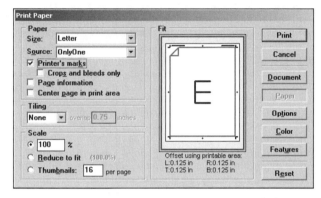

Figure 2-30 The Paper options panel of Page-Maker's Print dialog box.

Export

When you export documents from PageMaker, the application invokes Distiller to produce the PDF file; unlike with Photoshop, Illustrator, and InDesign, it doesn't use libraries, so except for page size, you produce essentially the same PDF file as you would if you printed the file using the Create Adobe PDF or Acrobat Distiller printer driver and PPD. It's nice, however, because you can apply PDF styles, à la InDesign, to speed file creation and also include links, article threads, and book-marks for files destined to become electronic documents.

Choose File > Export > Adobe PDF, and PageMaker presents a PDF Options dialog box, where on Windows you can select from tabs and on the Mac you can select from a pop-up menu of equivalent choices. In General (Figure 2-31), choose your job option or invoke a style (if you've already created one from these panels). In Doc. Info (Figure 2-32), enter author and keywords for the PDF file. In Hyperlinks and Articles/Bookmarks (Figures 2-33 and 2-34, respectively), you

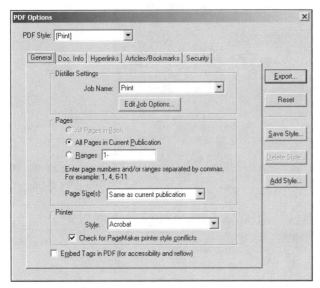

Figure 2-31 The General panel of PageMaker's PDF Options dialog box.

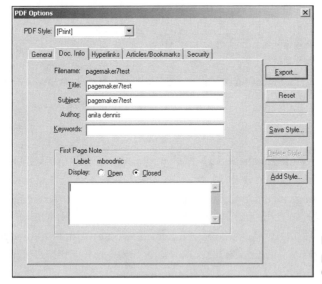

Figure 2-32 The Doc. Info panel of PageMaker's PDF Options dialog box.

can specify navigational aids for the document if it's going to become, for example, an eBook. And, finally, in Security (Figure 2-35), you can control access to the document, which is also helpful for documents you plan to publish or circulate electronically.

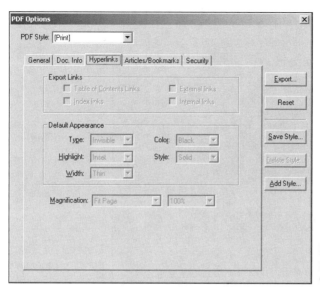

Figure 2-33 The Hyperlinks panel of PageMaker's PDF Options dialog box.

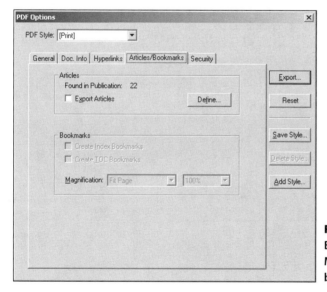

Figure 2-34 The Articles/ Bookmarks panel of Page-Maker's PDF Options dialog box.

After making your choices, click Export, and the Export PDF As dialog box will appear (Figure 2-36). Choose PDF from the Save as type or Format pop-up list if it's not already chosen, name your file, and choose the folder you want it to be saved in. Then click Save. PageMaker now sends the file to Distiller to create the PDF file.

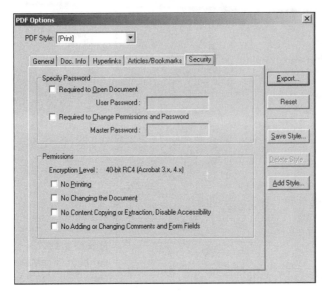

Figure 2-35 The Security panel of PageMaker's PDF Options dialog box.

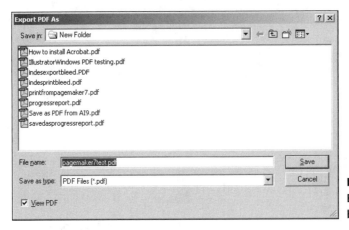

Figure 2-36 The Export PDF As dialog box in PageMaker 7.0.

FRAMEMAKER 6.0

Print

On the Mac, the familiar PostScript Print dialog box (Figure 2-4) lets you choose a Distiller job options setting: Press, Print, eBook, Screen, or any other setting you have created. Click and hold the PDF Settings pop-up menu to access other print options panels such as PostScript and Background Printing. Choose FrameMaker 6.0. Here, in the printing options panel (Figure 2-37), you can choose which pages to distill and whether to include registration marks. If you click the PDF Setup button, you'll see a dialog box where you can click through panels and indicate how you want to generate bookmarks, structure, document info, and links (Figure 2-38). Since you won't need any of this stuff for prepress, click Cancel to back out of this dialog box, and uncheck Generate Acrobat Data. (We'll revisit the PDF Setup dialog box and learn more about it in the Save As section.)

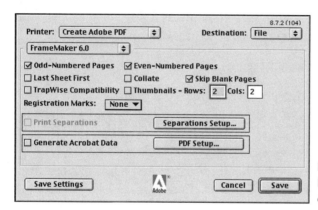

Figure 2-37 The Macintosh FrameMaker 6.0 printing options panel.

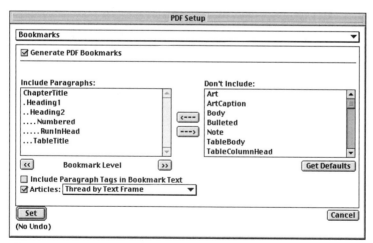

Figure 2-38 The PDF Setup dialog box, accessible from FrameMaker's Print and Save As PDF commands.

After you've finished specifying your print options, click Save, and in the dialog box that appears next, name your PDF file and select where you want it saved. Click Save again, and Acrobat will distill your PDF file.

In Windows, these same options—printing selected pages and accessing PDF Setup for bookmarks and links—are at your fingertips in the Print dialog box (Figure 2-39). If you want to check or change your conversion settings, click Setup at the bottom of the dialog box, and in the Print Setup dialog box that appears (Figure 2-40), click Properties. You should now see your friendly Acrobat Distiller Document Properties dialog box (Figure 2-9), where you can specify your conversion settings. Click OK twice to back out to the Print dialog box, and click Print to distill the PDF file. In the Save PDF File As dialog box that appears, name the file, choose where you want it saved, and click Save.

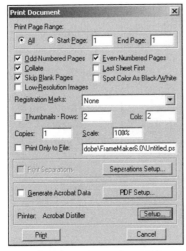

Figure 2-39 FrameMaker's Print dialog box for Windows.

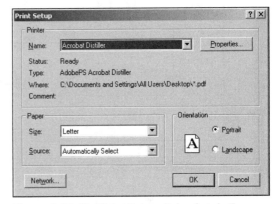

Figure 2-40 The Print Setup dialog box in Frame-Maker for Windows.

Save As

If InDesign offers little reason to export PDF files for prepress, FrameMaker offers even less. The latter program, like PageMaker, exports to PDF via Distiller, which means it doesn't make much of a difference whether you print a FrameMaker file to Distiller or perform a Save As. Both operations also provide access to settings that facilitate the production of electronic documents and books. However, if you watch the progress bar as FrameMaker spools your document to a .tps file and Distiller 5.0 launches in the background, converting the temporary PostScript file to PDF (using currently specified job options), you'll see that the implementation isn't very smooth. On the Mac, you're likely to get an error message—along with the distilled file (go figure)! Because this process isn't very reliable, Adobe doesn't recommend exporting PDF files from FrameMaker 6.0.

Just in case you're the curious type, though, if you *did* choose File > Save As, this is what would happen: First you would get a Save As dialog box. Choose PDF from the Format (Mac) or Save as type (Windows) pop-up menu. Then select a destination, name the file, and give it a .pdf extension. Click Save.

You will now be prompted with the PDF Setup dialog box (Figure 2-38), where you can specify (using a context-sensitive pull-down menu on the Mac or tabs in Windows) how you want to manage the document's bookmarks, structure, document info, and links—just as you could from the Print dialog box. Make your choices and click Set. Then confirm the name and location of the PDF file and click Save.

FreeHand 10

Print

Printing a PDF file from FreeHand for Macintosh to Distiller is exactly the same as doing so in Illustrator and Photoshop. After your printer driver is set to Create Adobe PDF and your PostScript options are configured, open your illustration in FreeHand and press Command-P.

In the dialog box that appears (Figure 2-4), Create Adobe PDF should be your printer. Select or change your job and launch options if desired or required, and then click and hold the PDF Settings menu to access FreeHand's print options (Figure 2-41). Check the Use PPD box and click on the ellipsis button to choose Distiller if the wrong PPD is selected.

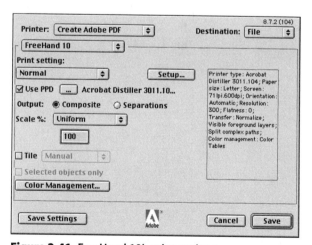

Figure 2-41 FreeHand 10's print options.

Check the Composite radio button and make other choices as desired, such as scaling and tiling, and then click the Setup button to check your print setup. In the Separations tab of the Print Setup dialog box (Figure 2-42), the Composite radio button should be checked; check "Print spot colors as process" if you want any spot colors in the file to be printed with process inks. In the Imaging tab (Figure 2-43), indicate what labels and marks you want on the page; set Images to Binary; and make sure "Convert RGB to process" is checked. Finally, in the Paper Setup tab (Figure 2-44), change the paper size and orientation if desired. Click OK when you're done and then click Save to distill the file, naming it when prompted.

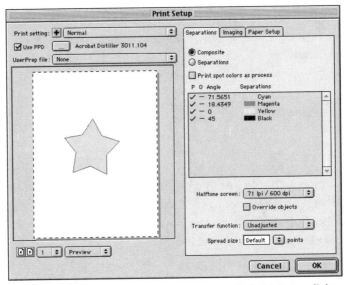

Figure 2-42 The Separations tab of FreeHand's Print Setup dialog.

Figure 2-43 The Imaging tab of FreeHand's Print Setup dialog.

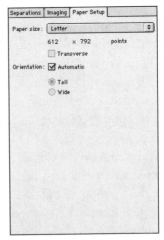

Figure 2-44 The Paper Setup tab of FreeHand's Print Setup dialog.

In Windows, the process is almost identical. With Distiller chosen as your printer driver, open your illustration in FreeHand and press Ctrl-P. In the Print dialog box that appears, Acrobat Distiller should be your Printer; if not, select it from the pop-up menu. Click Properties to access the Acrobat Distiller Document Properties dialog box (Figure 2-9), where you can select or change your conversion settings. Click OK to return to the Print dialog box, where you should check the Print to File box and choose Level 2 as your PostScript print setting.

Now click Setup, and you'll see the same Print Setup dialog box as on the Mac, with tabs for Separations, Imaging, and Paper Setup (Figures 2-42, 2-43, and 2-44). Choose Distiller as your PPD and make all the other appropriate choices for your document, including specifying composite output and making images binary (cross-platform). Return to the Print dialog box by clicking OK and finish making your selections here (tiling, color management, and so on). When you're finished, Click OK to distill the file, naming it when prompted.

Export

FreeHand 10 lets you export (and import) Acrobat 4.0 (PDF 1.3) or earlier files using the software's own PDF filters. This means that although the process circumvents PostScript, you still don't gain the benefit of transparency or structured and tagged PDF; what you do gain are speed and a PDF the size of the FreeHand document itself.

To export an illustration as PDF from FreeHand on either Mac or Windows, choose File > Export. In the Export dialog box that appears (Figure 2-45), choose PDF as your format, then name your file and specify where you want it saved. Now click the Setup button. In the PDF Export dialog box (Figure 2-46), choose the PDF version you want to produce and make other appropriate choices. Generally, you should embed fonts, convert colors to CMYK, and compress text and graphics, but limit image compression. By selecting Editable text format, you keep text blocks intact for later editing in FreeHand or Illustrator; however, you also end up with a larger PDF file. When you're finished, click OK. Back in the Export dialog box, click Export (Mac) or OK (Windows) to save the file as PDF.

Figure 2-45 FreeHand's Export dialog box.

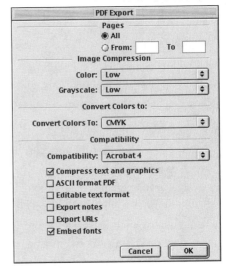

Figure 2-46 FreeHand's PDF Export options dialog box.

QUARKXPRESS 4.11 AND LATER

Print

Perhaps it won't surprise you to learn that it's not as easy to distill a PDF file from QuarkXPress' Print dialog box as it is from an Adobe application's Print dialog box. It's not that tricky once you get the hang of it, but to do it right, you must click through numerous dialog boxes to make sure everything is properly set up. Let's tackle the Mac first: As always, make sure Create Adobe PDF is chosen as your printer, and then make sure QuarkXPress recognizes it. Choose PPD Manager from the Utilities menu, and see whether Distiller is on the list and checked off (Figure 2-47). If it's not, make sure the correct System PPD Folder is selected, and update it if necessary.

Now you can jump from the frying pan into the fire of the QuarkXPress Print dialog box: Press Command-P and select the Setup tab in the Print dialog box or choose Page Setup from the File menu to go directly there (Figure 2-48). Check to make sure that Acrobat Distiller is your specified Printer Description; if not, select it now. Make any other appropriate changes (for example, customizing page size) and then click through the other tabs to make other choices for your PDF file: in Document (Figure 2-49), for example, decide whether you want to print

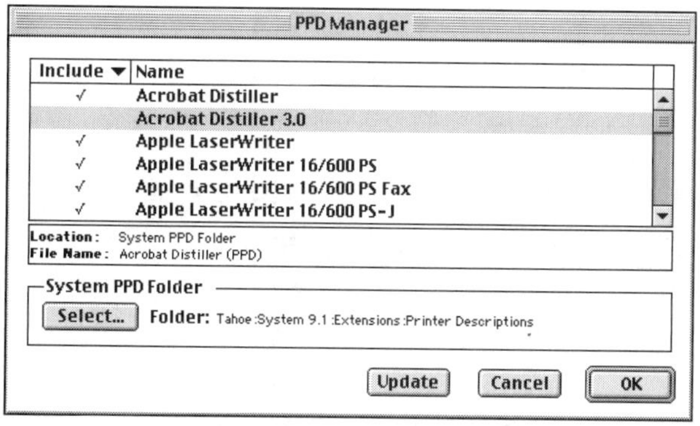

Figure 2-47 QuarkXpress' PPD Manager utility.

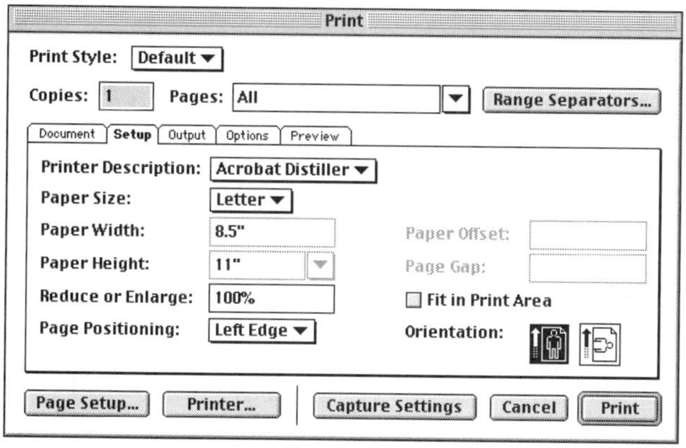

Figure 2-48 The Setup tab of QuarkXPress' Print dialog box on the Mac.

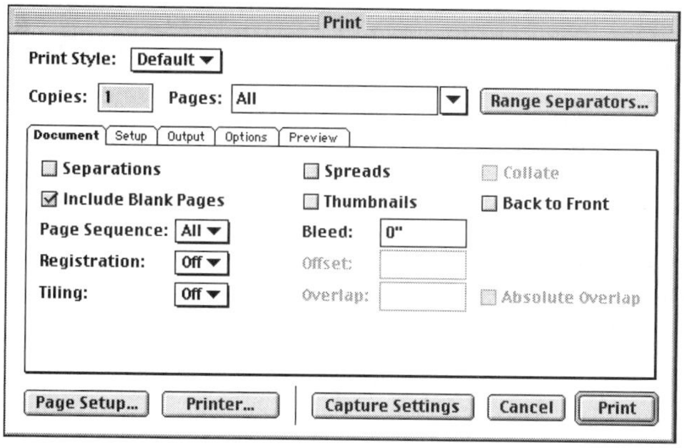

Figure 2-49 The Document tab of QuarkXPress' Print dialog box.

separations, tiles, and registration marks. In Output (Figure 2-50), specify a resolution. In Options (Figure 2-51), choose Normal as your picture output; Binary is the type of data you send, and specify how you want QuarkXPress to manage OPI images. Click Preview anytime to see how your document is fitting onto the page.

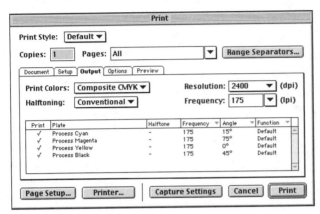

Figure 2-50 The Output tab of QuarkXPress' Print dialog box.

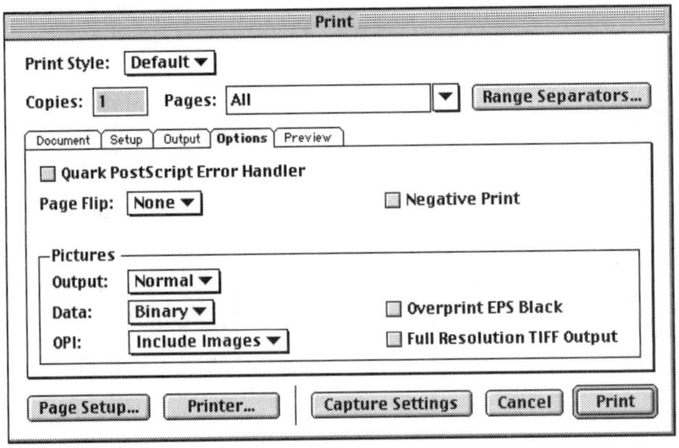

Figure 2-51 The Options tab of QuarkXPress' Print dialog box.

In QuarkXPress 5.0, use the Bleed and OPI panels to specify those options: the type and size of your bleed, and whether and how to include OPI comments for TIFF and EPS images.

But wait: It's not time to print just yet! First, you must click the Page Setup button to verify that Create Adobe PDF is selected as your printer and that all of the listed attributes are correct. If everything is correct (Figure 5-52), click OK to go back to the Print dialog box. *Now* click the Printer button: At last, a dialog box you recognize (Figure 2-4)!

Specify your preferred Distiller job option and whether or not you want to immediately launch Acrobat. Then click through the other panels: Most importantly, go to PostScript Settings and make sure that PostScript Job is your format, 3 is your level, Binary is your data format, and that you've included all fonts. Then click Save.

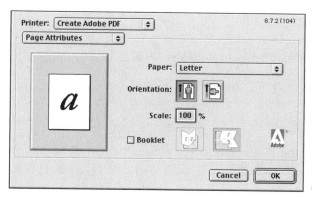

Figure 2-52 The Page Setup dialog box in QuarkXPress.

Choose where you want to save the file and what you want to name it, then click OK. You'll now be returned to the Print dialog box, where you can finally click Print.

In Windows, choose Acrobat Distiller as your printer and make sure you have a PostScript printer configured to print to file. (If you don't, use the Add a Printer wizard to choose a local PostScript printer: On the panel that shows available ports, choose File.) Then, with your document open in QuarkXPress, make sure Acrobat Distiller is available and selected in the PPD Manager. Press Ctrl-P and select the Setup tab in the Print dialog box or choose Page Setup from the File menu to go directly there (Figure 2-53). Acrobat Distiller should be your specified printer and your printer description; if it's not, select it now. Make other changes for your document here and in other tabs (for example, customizing page size in Setup; deciding whether you want to print separations, tiles, and registration marks in Document; and so on). In QuarkXPress 5.0, you can also visit the OPI and Bleed panels.

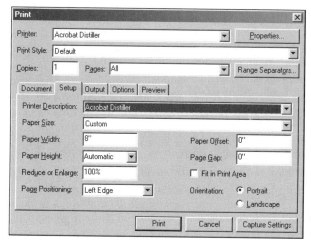

Figure 2-53 The Setup tab of QuarkXPress' Print dialog box for Windows.

Now click the Properties button to access the Acrobat Distiller Document Properties dialog box (Figure 2-9), where you can choose a conversion setting. When everything's set, click OK to return to the Print dialog box, and click Print to distill the PDF file.

Export

In addition to using the PostScript driver (in the Print dialog box) to distill your QuarkXPress files, you can also use a Quark-developed PDF export filter to distill PDF files. (The filter is built into XPress 5.0 and available for download from the company's Web site for XPress 4.x.) There are a few differences between printing and exporting PDF files, however: First, as with other applications, when you export a PDF file from QuarkXPress, the resulting file has the dimensions of your Quark document. Printing PDF files via Distiller, on the other hand, results in files with page sizes that match the selected PPD. In addition, the export filter runs Distiller in the foreground, while the print operation runs Distiller in the background. Most importantly, when you print a PDF file from QuarkXPress, you can choose which job option or conversion settings file you want to invoke. In contrast, when you export the PDF file, you must rely on the currently chosen Distiller settings—which means you might wind up with some other surprises in your file if you're not sure what those settings are.

Once you set up the PDF export filter, however, it provides a convenient means of generating PDF files from QuarkXPress—and there are a lot fewer dialog boxes to navigate! To set it up on either platform, first make sure Acrobat Distiller is your chosen PPD in the PPD Manager.

Once you've done this, choose Edit > Preferences > PDF Export in 4.0; in 5.0, choose Edit > Preferences > Preferences, and then choose PDF from the list in the left-side dialog box. Also in 5.0, choose Options from the Default Settings area of the box. In both versions you should now see a tabbed dialog box where you can make selections that correspond to the job options or conversion settings that Distiller will apply. For example, you can enter document information (author, title, and so on), and instruct lists and indexes to be converted to hyperlinks and bookmarks. In the Job Options tab (Figure 2-54), you can override Distiller's font embedding and compression options and manually set your own. Generally speaking, though, choose your job options or conversion settings properly in Distiller so that you don't have to override them. In fact, Quark warns that overriding the font options on the Mac may result in extremely large PostScript files.

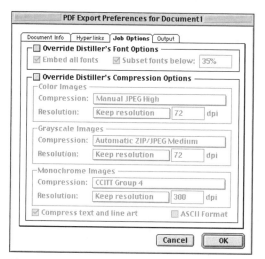

Figure 2-54 The Job Options tab of XPress' PDF Export dialog box.

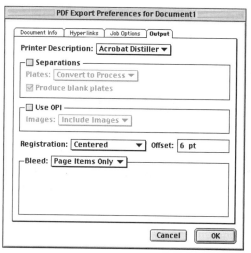

Figure 2-55 The Output tab of XPress' PDF Export dialog box.

In the Output tab (Figure 2-55), make sure Acrobat Distiller is your printer description and indicate whether and how you want to produce separations, use OPI links, and print registration marks and bleeds. When you're finished, click OK.

In 5.0, you can now define your workflow; in 4.x, you must first open your Application Preferences, then jump to the PDF tab (Figure 2-56). Browse to select the Distiller 5.0 application file (if it's not already initialized), and then choose to either distill your files immediately or create a Post Script file to be distilled later, perhaps using a watched folder. Click OK.

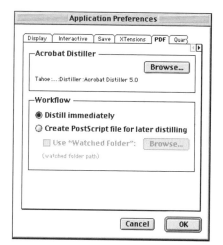

Figure 2-56 The PDF tab of XPress' Application Preferences.

Now you can export the PDF. In XPress 4.x, choose Export as PDF from the Utilities menu; in XPress 5.0, choose File > Export > Document As PDF. In the dialog box that appears (Figure 2-57), name your PDF file and select a destination for it. Clicking Preferences (in XPress 4.11) or Options (in 5.0) takes you to the PDF Export Preferences/Options dialog box we just visited; however, you can confirm or change settings for individual export operations. Click Save to export the file. Assuming you've set up Distiller to produce the PDF file right away, QuarkXPress will launch it—and you can go get a cup of chai.

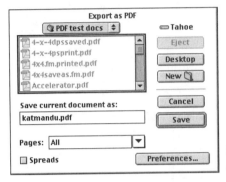

Figure 2-57 The Export As PDF dialog box in QuarkXPress.

CORELDRAW 10 FOR WINDOWS

Print

To distill a PDF file from a CorelDraw 10 illustration, set up Distiller as your default printer (as discussed in "Before You Start," page 32). Then, with your file open in CorelDraw, choose File > Print (Ctrl-P). The Print dialog box (Figure 2-58) offers several tabs where you can specify your print options. First, however, click the Properties button to access Acrobat Distiller Document Properties to change or edit your conversion settings (Figure 2-9).

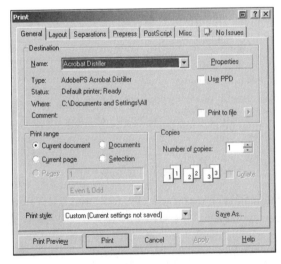

Figure 2-58 The General tab of CorelDraw 10 for Windows' Print dialog box.

Click OK when you're finished, and back in the Print dialog box click the following tabs to set your options:

- **Layout** (Figure 2-59). Here you control where and how your image appears on the page, as well as specifying bleeds.

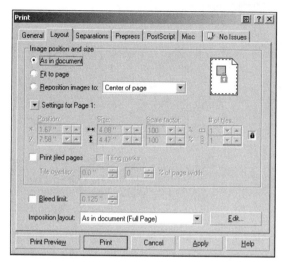

Figure 2-59 The Layout tab of CorelDraw 10 for Windows' Print dialog box.

- **Separations** (Figure 2-60). This panel is where you set options for printing separations and specify screening and trapping information. As I recommend throughout this book, you usually want to distill composite PDF files for prepress and leave trapping and screening options to your prepress partners.

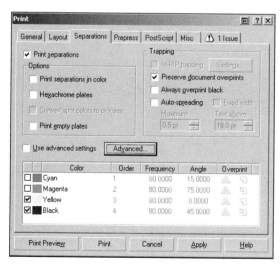

Figure 2-60 The Separations tab of CorelDraw 10 for Windows' Print dialog box.

- **Prepress** (Figure 2-61). This panel offers options for printing off-page marks.

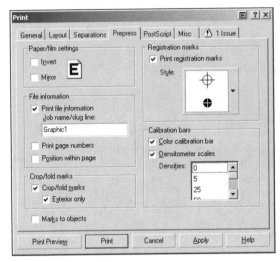

Figure 2-61 The Prepress tab of CorelDraw 10 for Windows' Print dialog box.

- **PostScript** (Figure 2-62). This is where you specify Level 2 or 3 output, high-quality JPEG compression for bitmap content, and whether you want to embed fonts and convert TrueType to Type 1.

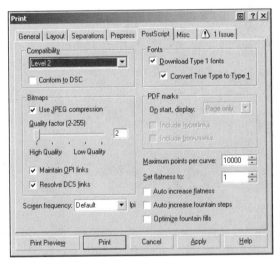

Figure 2-62 The PostScript tab of CorelDraw 10 for Windows' Print dialog box.

- **Misc** (Figure 2-63). This panel lets you include ICC profiles and specify image resampling (if you've already told Distiller to do it, don't select it here). You can even print a job information sheet: Click the Info Settings button to specify what type of information you want to include (Figure 2-64).

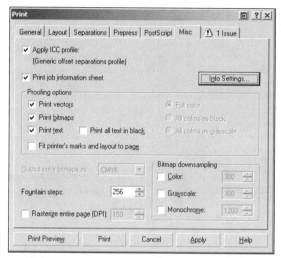

Figure 2-63 The Misc tab of CorelDraw 10 for Windows' Print dialog box.

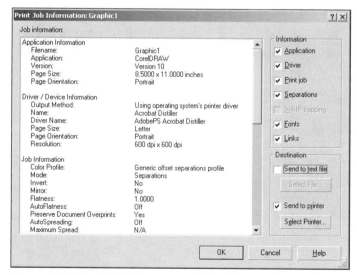

Figure 2-64 The Info Settings area of CorelDraw 10 for Windows' Print dialog box.

- **Issues** (Figure 2-65). This handy panel warns you of potential problems, such as printers' marks not fitting on the page.

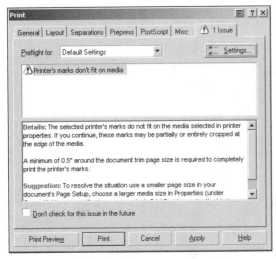

Figure 2-65 The Issues tab of CorelDraw 10 for Windows' Print dialog box.

When you're finished, go back to the General tab (Figure 2-58). You can save your custom settings as a print style by clicking the Save As button. Or you can go ahead and click Print. You'll be prompted to name the file; do so and then click Save to distill the PDF file. You can also check or change Distiller preferences at any time in the Print Setup dialog box (Figure 2-66), accessible from the File menu.

Figure 2-66 CorelDraw's Print Setup dialog box.

Export

Corel calls its Publish to PDF capability an engine, not an export filter. In essence, the PDF engine is a Corel-built PDF writer that converts files from the company's native format to PDF. Although the process circumvents PostScript (and is therefore faster than Distiller), it's based on PDF 1.3, which means it doesn't pre-serve editable transparency or generate structured PDF. CorelDraw 10 for Macintosh, however, does publish PDF 1.4 files.

To use Corel's PDF engine, open your illustration and choose File > Publish To PDF. Corel will display the Save As PDF dialog box (Figure 2-67), which differs subtly from Acrobat's Save As PDF box. The Save as type is automatically set to PDF; choose a location for your file and name it. Then chose a PDF style. You can choose from among Corel's five defaults—PDF for the Web, for document distri-bution, for editing, for prepress, or PDF/X-1—or create a custom style.

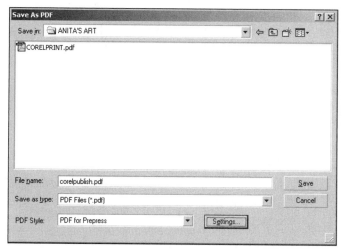

Figure 2-67
CorelDraw's Save As
PDF dialog box.

Choose Prepress or click the Settings button to access the Publish To PDF tabbed dialog box where you can create a custom style from one of the following panels:

- **General** (Figure 2-68). In this panel, you can select the pages or documents you want to export, and whether you want to produce an Acrobat 4.0 (PDF 1.3), Acrobat 3.0 (PDF 1.2), or PDF/X-1 file.

- **Objects** (Figure 2-69). This where you choose compression (ZIP or JPEG), downsampling, and whether to embed fonts.

- **Document** (Figure 2-70). This is where you specify bookmarks and hyperlinks, which are unnecessary for prepress but desirable for electronic documents.

- **Prepress** (Figure 2-71). This is where you opt to print bleeds and printers' marks. It's also where you opt to generate job tickets.

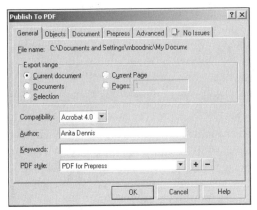

Figure 2-68 The General tab of CorelDraw's Publish To PDF dialog box.

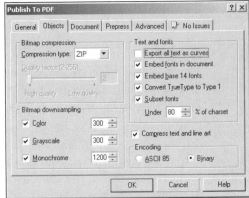

Figure 2-69 The Objects tab of CorelDraw's Publish To PDF dialog box.

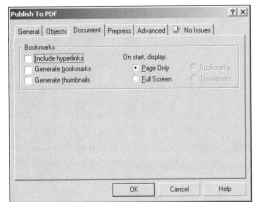

Figure 2-70 The Document tab of CorelDraw's Publish To PDF dialog box.

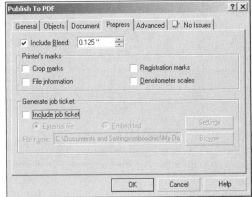

Figure 2-71 The Prepress tab of CorelDraw's Publish To PDF dialog box.

- **Advanced** (Figure 2-72). In this panel, you can preserve a variety of options, such as overprints and OPI links and whether to apply ICC profiles.

- **Issues** (Figure 2-73). Like its counterpart in the Print dialog box, this panel warns of potential problems.

When you're finished customizing your style, click OK. Back in the Save As PDF dialog box, click Save to write the PDF file.

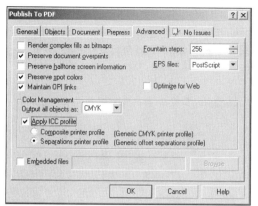

Figure 2-72 The Advanced tab of CorelDraw's Publish To PDF dialog box.

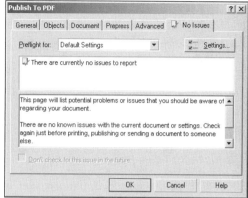

Figure 2-73 The Issues tab of CorelDraw's Publish To PDF dialog box.

MICROSOFT OFFICE 2000 (WINDOWS) AND 2001 (MAC)

Print

I'm going to tell you how to print PDF files from Microsoft Word (indeed all Office apps) because, well, they're Microsoft Office apps. Professional publishing applications such as InDesign have more and fancier layout and graphics capabilities, but you can still generate good PDF files for print from Office applications. And indeed, many designers do—for circulating and exchanging proposals, style guides, contracts, and the like that will be viewed onscreen or printed from an office printer, if not sent out for offset reproduction. Because Adobe makes it so easy to produce PDF files from Office applications, and because we all use them in everyday business, it's worth knowing how to do it right, whether for text-based documents used in business or for four-color offset printing.

When you create PDF files from Word, it's especially important that you choose the proper printer driver in advance. If you change to Create Adobe PDF or Acrobat Distiller in the Print dialog box, your document may reformat in PDF. If you're on a Mac, choose Create Adobe PDF as your printer. Then, with your document open in Word (or any Office application), press Command-P. In the dialog box that appears—again—the Printer pop-up menu will reflect your PDF printer (Figure 2-4). Choose a Distiller job option and choose whether you want to launch Acrobat after the PDF file is created. Then click Save, name your PDF file in the next dialog box, and click Save again.

PROOFREAD YOUR PAGES

The most important thing is for designers to know that their files are ready to print when they leave their shops. That is, they won't have type changes; they will include bleeds; and so on. The biggest thing is, read it! Make sure it's right: Don't wait for your prepress partner to send you a proof and tell you it's wrong.

—Jerry O'Neal, prepress supervisor, Scholin Brothers Printing Company

In Windows, choose Acrobat Distiller in the Printers Control Panel. Then go to your open document in Word and press Ctrl-P. In the Print dialog box (Figure 2-74), Acrobat Distiller should appear in the Printer Name box. Click the Properties button and select the Adobe PDF Settings tab of the Distiller Document Properties dialog box (Figure 2-9), where you can choose eBook as your conversion setting. Click OK to get back to the Print dialog, and click OK again to distill your document. Name your document in the next dialog box that appears, then choose a destination and click Save.

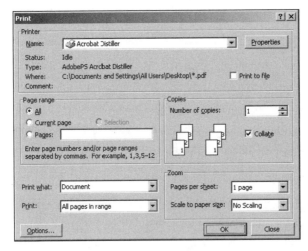

Figure 2-74 The Word 2000 Print dialog box.

As if that weren't easy enough, Acrobat 5.0 for Windows and Acrobat 5.05 for Mac install a macro called Adobe PDFMaker onto systems that manifests as both a button and a menu item in Office applications. Simply click the Convert to Adobe PDF button (Figure 2-75) or choose Convert to Adobe PDF from the Acrobat menu (Figure 2-76).

Figure 2-75 The Convert to Adobe PDF button appears in Microsoft Office applications in Windows.

Figure 2-76 An Acrobat menu also appears in Office applications in Windows.

Whichever you do, Office apps will zip you right to the Save As PDF File dialog box. When you name and save the file here, Distiller will produce a PDF based on the currently selected conversion setting. Choose Change Conversion Settings from the Acrobat menu to see or change selected conversion settings, as well as to access the Security, Office, Bookmarks, and Display Options tabs (Figure 2-77).

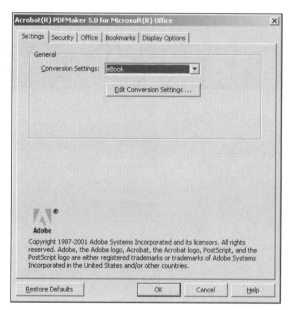

Figure 2-77 The Acrobat PDFMaker 5.0 dialog box lets you choose a conversion setting and other options for PDF files prepared in Office apps on Windows.

CREATE ADOBE PDF ONLINE

If the options presented here for creating PDF files for prepress have raised the hair on the back of your neck, try this more mellow alternative: Create Adobe PDF Online, a subscription service from Adobe at https://createpdf.adobe.com (also accessible from the Tools menu in Acrobat). This service, available only in North America, costs $10 a month or $100 a year and will create an unlimited number of PDF files for you automatically. You can try it for free for up to five files.

You can submit almost any file format, including Microsoft Office application files, native formats of every professional Adobe print application, Corel, EPS, TIFF (and other image file formats), and HTML. (The notable exception is QuarkXPress: You must convert XPress documents to PostScript and submit the PostScript file.) You upload the file from your hard drive, and it is distilled for you within a few minutes according to one of Distiller's five preset conversion settings—Web, Screen, eBook, Print, or Press. Files must be 10 MB or less (which can be limiting), and must be able to be processed in 15 minutes or less. You can opt to have the final PDF file display in a browser or emailed to you. Adobe also converts Web pages to PDF if you submit a URL, and it offers Paper Capture and Search PDF online services. See the company's Web site for more information (Figures 2-78 and 2-79).

Figure 2-78 When you log in to the Create Adobe PDF Online service, you can choose to convert a file (for example, a page-layout document), convert a Web page, or create a searchable scanned document.

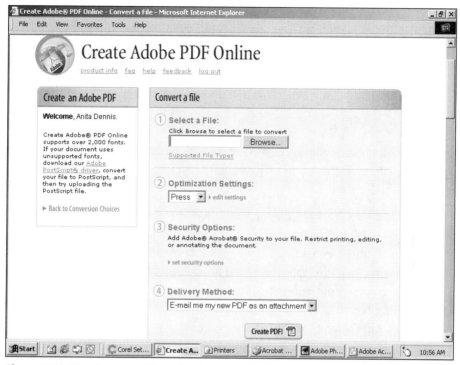

Figure 2-79 The Convert a File option lets you specify a file on your hard drive, then choose optimization, security, and delivery options.

HOW TO USE TRANSPARENCY IN PDF WORKFLOWS

We all love transparency and transparent effects: the digital panache that comes from gradient meshes and blending modes, or any effect in which the color of an object on a page is composed of all of the pixels in the stack (rather than just the color of the single opaque pixel on top). However, in PostScript workflows, transparency can be hell on RIPs. Thus, documents that contain transparency must be flattened at some point in the workflow—that is, all transparency effects must be irreversibly calculated and the final object rendered opaquely—before the PostScript file can be rasterized.

Most of us routinely flatten files we've created in Photoshop or Illustrator and then save them as EPS before we import them into page-layout apps. And running files through Distiller to create PDF files will flatten them, too. Thus, if you want to preserve transparent effects created in Photoshop or Illustrator so that you can go back and edit them after you've saved the file as PDF, you must use the application's Save As command to produce a PDF 1.4 file. Whether you distill or export to 1.3 or 1.4, you'll be able to see the effect in Acrobat, but you must export to PDF 1.4 to be able to go back and edit the effect in one of those applications.

PDF 1.4 files exported from Photoshop and Illustrator can also be placed in InDesign 2.0 documents, where transparent effects can be see onscreen, printed, and even created. When the final page is designed you can distill the composite PDF file to flatten it, or you can export the final PDF file and choose the degree of flattening you desire in the Advanced panel of InDesign's Export PDF dialog box (see page 49).

Non-Adobe design applications, however, don't support transparency in PDF 1.4 files. QuarkXPress 4.11, for example, doesn't even let you import a PDF 1.4 file; XPress 5.0 can import PDF 1.4 files, but it doesn't display or print "live" (unflattened) transparent effects. As a result, transparent effects that are exported to PDF 1.4 from say, Illustrator, and then placed in a XPress 5.0 picture box will appear as opaque, overlaid areas of color. If, however, you flatten the transparency by distilling the PDF (either to 1.3 or 1.4), you can see the effect in XPress—but you lose the ability to edit it back in Photoshop or Illustrator.

Illustrations created in FreeHand and CorelDraw for Windows, meanwhile, can be distilled to PDF 1.4 or exported to PDF 1.3 or earlier, but both methods flatten transparency. In addition, neither program can import a PDF 1.4 file, much less edit any transparent effects therein.

What all of this boils down to is that PDF 1.4's transparency features can only be fully leveraged within three Adobe applications: Photoshop, Illustrator, and InDesign 2.0. If you work in any other programs, you'll still need to place flattened EPS, TIFF, or PDF graphics files in them. And ultimately, transparency still needs to be flattened before it can be rasterized on a PostScript imaging device. Figure 2-80 illustrates how a PDF 1.4 file with transparency appears in several of the applications I've covered here.

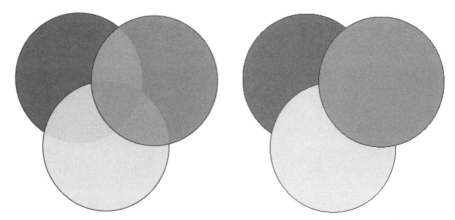

Figure 2-80 The Illustrator document above consists of overlapping red, blue, and yellow circles with a Luminosity blending mode applied. When exported as a PDF 1.4 file with editable transparency, the effect is maintained exactly in Acrobat 5.0 and InDesign 2.0. In QuarkXPress 5.0, however, the effect is lost, as shown at right. To see the effect in Quark-XPress, you need to distill (flatten) the PDF in Illustrator before placing it in a picture box.

PDF File Preparation Checklist

Most prepress shops like you to do the following before you hand off your jobs:

- Prepare one PDF document for each print job
- Give each document a unique and intuitive .pdf filename
- Create document pages in a logical, sequential order
- Delete unnecessary pages
- Convert RGB images to CMYK
- Embed and subset fonts at 100 percent
- Don't apply device-specific parameters, such as traps and screens, to composite PDF files
- Build document pages that are the final trim size
- Extend bleeds onto the pasteboard at least one-eighth inch
- Label any disks or other media that you submit with your company's name and phone number
- Provide a printout of the contents of the disk or other media's directory structure
- Provide a hard-copy laser composite and separated proofs; include file names and printers' marks on printouts; and print at 100 percent.

CHAPTER THREE

The Lowdown on Distilling

If you're still with me, take a bow! Successfully navigating the maze of application Print, Export, and Save As dialog boxes is an achievement worthy of an advanced degree.

With that behind you, you're now ready to learn about Distiller—an application that emulates a printer but creates a different kind of output. Instead of sending PostScript files (usually generated from another graphics application) to printers, this program outputs them as PDF files.

As should be clear by now, the decisions you make when creating offset- or digital-press-bound PDF files can make or break them. Poorly created PDF files are just as detrimental to the production process as improperly saved application files, often requiring cumbersome last-minute editing or color conversions as well as acrobatics on the part of the prepress operator who must generate film or plates for your job. Poorly prepared PDF files add up to remakes, held presses, and bottlenecks—all of which will hit you where you feel it most: your pocket.

Always keep in mind the old adage: Garbage in, garbage out—or GIGO—when producing composite PDF files for prepress. If, for example, you fail to convert RGB or spot colors to CMYK when your content is distilled, your prepress provider will have to fix the problem before the PDF file can be separated. And if you provide your prepress partner with a screen-optimized PDF file downsampled to 72 dpi, it's going to look really lousy in print. Likewise, if you've been saving your images repeatedly as JPEG—and thus losing image data with every Save operation—it won't matter what compression setting you use when distilling the file: Your image integrity will already have been compromised.

This is why it's so important that you implement Distiller settings wisely. In this chapter, we'll expand on many of the settings described in the previous chapter, explaining the reasoning behind various decisions as well as why some choices are more important than others. We'll then go on to describe ways you can use Distiller to streamline your production process. Ready? Let's go.

JOB OPTIONS

Distiller's four default job options provide a starting point from which to create PDF files for a wide gamut of publishing needs. If you're producing PDF files to post on a Web site, for example, use Screen: This keeps your PDF files small by using RGB color, downsampling images to 72 dpi, optimizing files for page-at-a-time viewing, and saving in Acrobat 3.0 (PDF 1.2) format for the millions of old Readers currently installed. One step up in quality is the eBook job option. This conversion setting is also optimized for onscreen PDF viewing; however, it provides slightly higher image resolution and Acrobat 4.0 (PDF 1.3) compatibility. (I'll go over eBook job options in more depth in Chapter 7. Here, I want to focus on optimizing settings for prepress.)

In addition to these settings, two higher-quality job options exist: Print and Press, both of which are intended primarily for serious print designers and publishers. For exchanging comps or generating proofs, you can use Print. Intended for output to desktop printers and copiers as well as for CD-ROM publishing, this setting downsamples images to 300 dpi and provides high-quality JPEG compression. It also embeds all fonts and subsets at 100 percent, and it tags images for color management.

The Press job option produces the best-quality (and largest) PDF files. Suitable for most prepress needs, this setting also downsamples images to 300 dpi but provides maximum-quality JPEG compression. Like Print, Press embeds and subsets fonts at 100 percent; however, it leaves color unchanged.

With the help of your service provider, you may also want to create custom conversion settings for certain jobs or output devices. To customize Distiller's job options, choose Job Options from the Settings menu. The multipanel dialog box that appears displays the currently selected options; you can customize these in a new file by clicking Save As. (Don't worry, though: You can't overwrite the defaults.) Even if you don't plan to change Distiller settings, read on to understand their functions.

General

Although the settings in the General panel (Figure 3-1) are fairly straightforward, the choice you make in the Compatibility pop-up menu is important. Select either Acrobat 4.0 (PDF 1.3) or Acrobat 5.0, which generates a PDF 1.4 file. You're always better off using the highest possible level of PDF (and PostScript), but you may want to find out if your prepress partner has a RIP that can handle PDF 1.4 files. Your prepress partner won't want to choke production with a file that contains live transparency that it cannot handle. In addition, depending on its content, your PDF 1.4 file may or may not be compatible with earlier versions of Acrobat. For example, masked images and documents larger than 45 inches in either direction might not display or print correctly. Of course, by the time you read this, things may have changed, so be sure to check with your prepress provider.

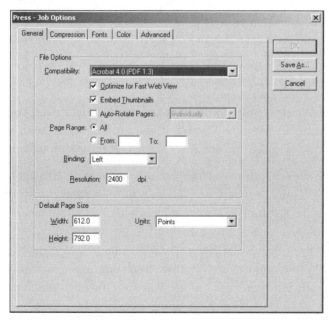

Figure 3-1 In the General panel of Distiller's Job Options dialog box, you can specify which PDF version you want to use, as well as other basic settings. Acrobat 4.0 (PDF 1.3) or higher is best for prepress.

Because the Acrobat 3.0 format (PDF 1.2) isn't as robust as that of Acrobat 4.0 (PDF 1.3), it's not recommended for prepress. Among other things, it doesn't support ICC color management, patterns and masked images display incorrectly, page size is limited, and double-byte (Kanji) fonts can't be embedded.

Optimize for Fast Web View. If this option is checked, Acrobat structures multi-page PDF files so that pages can be downloaded individually and thus displayed more quickly in viewers' browsers—a process called *byte serving*. This option also reduces file size by compressing text and line art, even if you haven't checked that option in the Compression panel (we'll get there in a minute). Although this option doesn't offer significant benefits for prepress PDF files, it certainly doesn't hurt to optimize them this way. It's always a good idea to compress text and line art.

Embed Thumbnails. If you choose this useful but nonessential setting, Distiller 5.0 creates thumbnail previews of each page of a PDF document, which you can then view when the file is open in Acrobat. If you uncheck this option but invoke the Thumbnails palette in Acrobat, that program will generate them on the fly for display purposes (you have to manually save them to keep them). Although thumbnails increase final file size, your prepress partner can strip them out later, so there's no harm in including them. Doing so, in fact, can call attention to obvious problems, such as incorrectly oriented pages.

Auto-Rotate Pages. By checking this option, you can individually or collectively rotate pages in a file based on either the orientation of the text or the document structuring conventions (see the Advanced panel).

Page Range. This option allows you to specify the range of pages you want to distill. Usually, however, you'll want to specify All.

Binding. This option determines how pages and thumbnails are displayed in the Facing Page-Continuous view in Acrobat; it has nothing to do with postpress binding. For Western-language documents, choose Left for traditional orientation.

Resolution. PDF files do not have an inherent resolution, so this option might be misleading: The value entered here doesn't have anything to do with the inherent quality of the resulting PDF file, or for when downsampling occurs. The value in the Resolution text box is a backup: If no resolution is provided by the PostScript file itself, PostScript can query this value, which must be between 72 and 4,000 dpi. PostScript jobs rarely perform such queries, so it is fairly rare for this value to have any effect on your output. You can either ask which value your prepress provider prefers, or accept 2,400 dpi as a reasonable default.

Default Page Size. As with Resolution, this setting only kicks in when the PostScript or EPS file that Distiller attempts to process doesn't explicitly specify a page size. This often occurs when PostScript is exported from InDesign or QuarkXPress. Remember that Acrobat 3.0 (PDF 1.2) or earlier files must be 45 by 45 inches or smaller; Acrobat 4.0 (PDF 1.3) or later files can be as large as 200 by 200 inches. (To find out how to generate good PostScript for use by Distiller, see "How to Create PostScript Files," page 110.

SURF AND YE SHALL FIND

Visit the Web site of your prepress provider or printer: Many of us have guidelines for producing PDF files, file-preparation checklists, downloadable PostScript drivers and PPDs, and more. All of these can help you submit files that we won't have to kick back at you.

—Marco Cappuccio, digital technology manager, SS Studios

Compression

Compression is one of those make-or-break settings: Executed well, it can reduce file sizes with little or no impact on quality; executed poorly, it can wreak havoc with your PDF content. Although maintaining small file sizes isn't as critical as it once was (say, back in the days when we had to use 44 MB SyQuest disks or 14.4 Kbps modems and 10BaseT Ethernet to exchange files), effective compression can still save on file size and eliminate unnecessary pixel data (Figure 3-2).

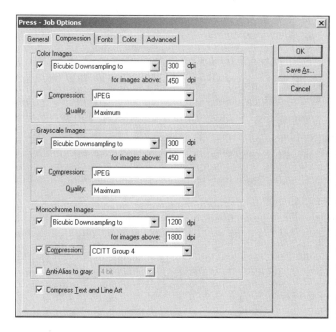

Figure 3-2 The Compression panel in Distiller's Job Options is where you define JPEG or ZIP compression for color and grayscale images and for continuous-tone or graphic images, respectively, as well as where you define CCITT or RLE compression for black-and-white art.

Distiller applies compression to four types of content: color images, grayscale images, monochrome images (1-bit, or black-and-white, images), and text and line art. Go ahead and check Compress Text and Line Art at the bottom of the Compression panel to apply lossless ZIP compression to those page elements. By doing this, you'll preserve the quality of those elements and end up with a smaller PDF file.

After you've made this selection, things get a bit more complicated. For color and grayscale images, you can choose between JPEG, ZIP, and Auto compression options. In general, you should use JPEG compression for color or grayscale photographic images with smooth, gradual transitions, and you should apply ZIP compression to graphic content composed largely of single, flat areas of color and/or detailed or repeating patterns.

The JPEG compression algorithm analyzes image content in small, 8- by 8-pixel blocks, eliminating any redundant data that it finds at those intersections. The result is what's called *lossy compression:* JPEG actually removes pixel data from the image that cannot be retrieved. The more you compress, the smaller the file, but the worse the image looks and the more detail is lost. With excessive JPEG compression, images look blocky and blurry. The nice thing about JPEG, however, is that you can control this trade-off between final image quality and file size: If you instruct JPEG to maintain Maximum image quality, it compresses less but keeps more pixel data intact; if you specify Minimum image quality, it compresses the image dramatically but quality suffers.

Maximum-quality JPEG compression is fine for images in PDF files that are destined for prepress, with one important caveat: Never apply JPEG compression to an image that's already been saved as JPEG. You will be compressing an already-compressed image, potentially compromising the quality and integrity of your final image. Whenever possible, work with TIFF or other non-compressed image file formats through the creative process and only apply JPEG at the final-output stage.

ZIP compression, a lossless alternative to JPEG, sometimes reduces file size more effectively but always preserves image integrity when applied correctly. It is typically the best compression option for screen shots. In a nutshell, ZIP compression works by finding repeating patterns in an image and storing them more efficiently. When you use ZIP compression on color or grayscale images via Distiller, your Quality choices are 4-bit or 8-bit. Use the type that is equal to or greater than the bit depth of your image, otherwise you lose colors.

Bit depth refers to the number of bits per pixel in your image: 1-bit images are black and white; 4-bit images have 16 shades of gray or 16 colors; and 8-bit images have 256 grays or colors. Artwork with more than 256 colors is usually considered continuous tone—that is, it has subtle, rather than sharp, color transitions and is more suitable for JPEG compression.

If your art contains 16 or fewer colors, use 4-bit ZIP compression; if it contains 17 to 256 colors, use 4-bit or 8-bit ZIP compression to achieve smaller file sizes without losing data. Using 4-bit compression on 8-bit art, however, will result in data loss that can compromise image quality.

If you're poking around in Distiller as you read this, you've probably noticed that Acrobat offers an Automatic option for compressing color or grayscale images. When you choose this option, Distiller examines the color changes that occur in images in the PostScript file and applies ZIP or JPEG compression based on the contents, in much the same way that InDesign's PDF export engine does (see Chapter 2). Generally speaking, if it determines that color transitions are smooth, it applies JPEG compression (you specify the quality); if it finds sharp color changes or indexed color, it applies ZIP compression. Also, if Distiller encounters RGB color in the file, it swaps luminance color data for chrominance data.

Distiller doesn't include an Automatic option for monochrome bitmap images. Instead, you have to tell it to compress black-and-white artwork using a ZIP, CCITT (3 or 4), or RLE algorithm. The CCITT (Consultive Committee on International Telephony and Telegraphy) compression methods were developed for fax transmission, while RLE (Run-Length Encoding) is another lossless compression method for images with large, discrete areas of black or white. Any one of these is acceptable. One final checkbox for monochrome images is Anti-Alias to Gray: If you check this, Distiller will smooth jagged edges; however, this can make small type or thin lines look fuzzy. If you invoke this option, specify how many levels of gray you want Distiller to generate: 4 (2-bit), 16 (4-bit), or 256 (8-bit). In case you were wondering, anti-aliasing does add to file size, but not enough to warrant concern.

For all types of bitmap images—color, grayscale, and monochrome—Distiller also lets you reduce resolution through a process called *resampling*. More accurately described as subsampling or downsampling, resampling uses a mathematical algorithm to combine multiple pixels into fewer but larger pixels. Downsampling provides a powerful means of reducing file size; however, you need to resample dramatically to see any benefit. And since pages destined for an offset press ultimately will be sent through high-resolution imaging devices, you don't need to be aggressive about it. In addition, because the process removes image data, you have to be careful when you apply it. You're better off scanning images at the proper resolution to begin with, and then resampling (if necessary) in Photoshop. If you create images that contain more pixels than needed by the final output device, it's not a big deal since today's software RIPs are very effective at processing page data. Thus, you won't be slowing down imaging devices by leaving high-resolution images intact, and the RIP will downsample extraneous pixel data if necessary.

How Compression Affects Image Size and Quality

To illustrate the effects of the various JPEG compression qualities on a continuous-tone image, I scanned a 4- by 6-inch photo at 300 dpi and then distilled the resulting CMYK Photoshop file with three different JPEG and downsampling settings (Figure 3-3). You'll have to take my word for it, but the changes are much more dramatic in color.

The original image, at left, weighed in at 8.01 MB. As you can see from both the bird's-eye view and the close-up, the image is sharp and well-defined.

When distilled using Adobe's default Press conversion setting, the image is compressed as a maximum-quality JPEG; no downsampling occurred because the original was only 300 dpi. The resulting PDF file is 1.44 MB. Despite the significantly smaller file size, the image remains well-defined and detailed.

Here, the image was distilled with Adobe's eBook job option, which applied medium-quality JPEG compression and bicubic downsampling to 150 dpi. The resulting file is 150 KB—very compact— but quality is slightly worse than in the PDF file produced with the Press job option. Notice in the close-up of the girl's eye that definition begins to soften just slightly.

The PDF file of the image distilled with low-quality JPEG compression (slightly worse than Adobe's Screen job option) and downsampling to 72 dpi is quite poor. In the close-up especially, you can see large blocky artifacts and fuzzy detail. This file, however, is a miniscule 30 KB.

Figure 3-3

If you decide to apply resampling, you can choose one of three types:

- **Average Downsampling.** Averages pixel values in a given area and replaces them with one average pixel color value at the new resolution.

- **Bicubic Downsampling.** Uses a weighted average to calculate the new pixel value at the new resolution.

- **Subsampling.** Replaces several pixels in a given area with the value of the pixel at the center of that region at the new resolution.

Bicubic downsampling is the best option for high-end imaging. This method takes longer to calculate, but it results in the smoothest tonal gradations. Whichever you choose, you must specify a resolution threshold for resampling: A rule of thumb is that final image resolution should be twice the line-screen ruling at which the file will be printed (see Table 3-1). If image resolution falls below this threshold, quality may be compromised, particularly where the image contains straight lines and geometric patterns. When you downsample, always ask your prepress provider the resolution at which your pages will be imaged (generally the threshold should be 240 or 300 ppi). For best results, the resampled image should be an even divisor of the original image. If the original is 1,200 ppi, for example, the resampled image should be 600, 300, or 150 ppi.

Output device resolution* (dots per inch)	Output device line screen (lines per inch)	Image resolution (pixels per inch)
300 dpi	60 lpi	120 ppi
600 dpi	85 lpi	170 ppi
1,200 dpi	120 lpi	240 ppi
2,400 dpi	150 lpi	300 ppi

* Devices with resolutions from 300 dpi to 600 dpi include laser, dye-sub, inkjet, and other printers used for generating comp or final proofs; 1,200- and 2,400-dpi devices include imagesetters, platesetters, and direct-imaging presses.

Table 3-1 When calculating how to resample a PDF file, keep in mind that the final image resolution should be twice the line screen ruling of the printed image.

Distiller applies compression and resampling to all images in a PDF file; if you want alternative compression settings for different images, or if you want to resample them at different resolutions, adjust them in Photoshop and then uncheck all of the options in the Color and Grayscale areas of the Compression panel. Alternatively, if the images requiring different treatment are on disparate pages, distill the pages as discrete PDF files and merge them in Acrobat (or save pages as individual PostScript files and follow the steps in "Get in Line" later in this chapter).

Fonts

The Fonts panel (Figure 3-4) contains two essential options that must be checked: Embed All Fonts and Subset Embedded Fonts. Nothing can grind prepress operations to a halt faster than a PDF file without embedded fonts, and there's nothing uglier than a PDF file printing Courier because it couldn't find and substitute a proper replacement. Acrobat makes Multiple Master substitutions either from the metrics of the font itself when it's available, or using the SuperATM database that installs with the program, when the font metrics are not available. Not all substitutions are obvious, but none are desirable (Figure 3-5).

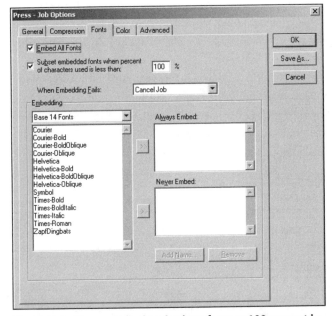

Figure 3-4 Always embed and subset fonts at 100 percent in the Fonts panel of Distiller's Job Options dialog box. This ensures that your PDF file displays and prints the exact fonts used in your document.

Embedding ensures that the fonts you used in your document travel with the PDF file, so when someone who doesn't have that font opens your PDF file it will still display and print properly. Acrobat actually creates a unique name for embedded fonts, which do increase PDF file sizes but also preserve the integrity of your document's text. (Caution: Embedded fonts must be properly licensed. See "Embedding and Licensing Fonts," page 96, for more information on this topic.)

The prepress world almost universally agrees that embedded fonts should be subset with a threshold of 100 percent. Subsetting embedded fonts results in slightly smaller file sizes, and satisfies some type foundries that require subsetting as part of their licensing agreements. If you only use a handful of letters of a display face in a headline, you could certainly significantly reduce the size of your file by subsetting at 50 percent or more, but subsetting is applied universally to all typefaces that are used in a document. That means if you try to subset at 50 percent but you use more than 50 percent of the character set in your Garamond body type, the entire font is embedded but the subsetting fails altogether. For that reason, it's safest to set a 100 percent threshold, which saves a little file size but doesn't compromise your embedded fonts (Figure 3-5).

The quick brown fox jumped over the lazy dog. (18-point Frutiger Roman)	The quick brown fox jumped over the lazy dog. (24-point Khaki Two)
The quick brown fox jumped over the lazy dog. (18-point Frutiger Roman)	The quick brown fox jumped over the lazy dog. (24-point Khaki Two)

Figure 3-5 If you fail to embed fonts, Acrobat will make the best possible substitution it can using a Multiple Master typeface. If your font is a straightforward serif or sans serif, such as Frutiger at upper left, it can do a fairly good job—but notice in the substituted version (lower left) how the *c* in the word *quick* is narrower than in the original. Also, when your typefaces are scripts or elaborate display faces, such as Khaki Two (upper right), Acrobat's substitution (lower right) doesn't come close to approximating the original.

If you check Embed All Fonts, you don't have to worry about the area at the bottom of the Fonts panel. This is where you can specify individual fonts that you want to always or never subset by moving them to the corresponding box on the right. Base 14 Fonts are the 14 Type 1 fonts that Acrobat installs into its Resources folder. By clicking and holding on that menu, you can locate and select fonts in various other folders on your system or network: within the Fonts folder in the System folder on the Mac, for example, or within Windows' psfonts folder. Fonts with license restrictions on embedding, by the way, should have a symbol indicating that in the display list.

FRIENDS AND ENEMIES

Fonts are one of our biggest enemies. We have 2,000 fonts loaded on our RIPs and we still miss them occasionally. If you don't have Distiller pointed in the right place, you can instruct it to embed fonts but it won't be able to find them. We restrict our creative departments to using fewer than 90 typefaces, and everyone has a license so that minimizes problems.

—*Mike McKee, prepress manager,* Contra Costa Times

How Distiller Accesses Fonts

By now you may be wondering how the heck Distiller finds the fonts it embeds in your PDF files. If you embed fonts into the PostScript file (described later in this chapter), no problem. If not, you have to give Distiller a clue about where to find them.

From Distiller's Settings menu, choose Font Locations. The Font Locations dialog box (Figure 3-6) lists the folders that Distiller recognizes as containing TrueType, Type 1, Type 3, or OpenType fonts, including those within its own directory structure and associated with Adobe Type Manager. Every time Distiller launches, it checks these folders and updates its internal font list. To customize the list of folders, add to it by clicking Add, and browse to identify the ones you want to add; or highlight a folder and click Remove.

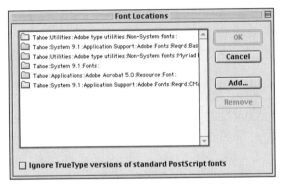

Figure 3-6 Instruct Distiller where to find fonts on your system using the Font Locations dialog box, which you access from the Settings menu. The application checks the folders you specify every time it launches.

Distiller monitors the contents of the folders in this list for actual fonts as well as for the Adobe Type Manager font database, whose font shape information it uses to generate substitutions.

Don't check the "Ignore TrueType versions of standard PostScript fonts" box. Leaving it unchecked allows whatever font the original document contains to be displayed, which ensures greater integrity and prevents substitutions.

A Few Words About Double-Byte and Other Non-English Fonts

Acrobat gets a bad rap when it comes to displaying and printing non-Western fonts, but it's a bit unjustified. As long as you embed them, you can safely and accurately display and print not only Roman, but Cyrillic, Eastern European, and Middle Eastern as well as Kanji, Chinese, and Korean double-byte fonts in Western versions of Acrobat 5.0. This is because Acrobat 5.0, on both platforms, complies with the Unicode standard, which is a system of encoding fonts in all of these as well as many other international languages.

Things do get a little dicey, however, when you try to view a PDF file in the English version of Acrobat that was created by, for example, the Japanese version of Word and the Japanese version of Acrobat. If the Japanese fonts are not embedded in the PDF file, the document won't display properly in the English version of Acrobat. In any such case when the Asian-language font is not embedded, you need to have installed the Asian Language Support options through a custom install in Windows, or the Asian Langauge Kit and Distiller Extensions on the Mac.

These double-byte support options provide Acrobat with "width only" versions of many common Japanese, Korean, and Traditional and Simplified Chinese typefaces so that you can embed them in PDF documents, and so that Acrobat and Acrobat Reader can display and print them. (Width-only fonts are special Distiller-only fonts that don't contain outlines.) There are, however, several limitations you need to keep in mind when viewing Kanji fonts in Western (Roman) versions of Acrobat:

- Kanji text cannot be cataloged or searched.

- The digital signature features in Western Acrobat viewers don't work with double-byte fonts.

- Western versions of Acrobat don't let you select or edit Kanji text.

Checking and Previewing Fonts

To make sure that you've properly embedded and subset fonts in your PDF file, open it in Acrobat and use the View > Use Local Fonts command. With this menu item toggled off, Acrobat displays the PDF using substitute fonts for those that haven't been embedded. Bullets appear for fonts that Acrobat can't substitute. If all fonts have been embedded and subset at 100 percent, they should appear intact because no substitutions will occur.

Since not all substitutions will be immediately obvious this way, you can also choose the Fonts submenu under File > Document Properties. Acrobat will tell you which fonts were in the original document, whether they were Type 1 or TrueType, how they were encoded (for example, as MacRoman, Windows, or CID), whether they were embedded and/or subset (an empty column under Actual Font means that the font wasn't embedded or subset or that it's not used on the page that's currently displayed), and whether the resulting font is Type 1 or TrueType (Figure 3-7).

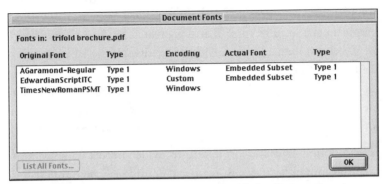

Figure 3-7 You can see what fonts are embedded, substituted, and encoded in your PDF file by choosing File > Document Properties > Fonts in Acrobat.

Embedding and Licensing Fonts

There's a big catch to embedding fonts that producers of creative content, graphic designers, and publishers need to be aware of: Many type foundries don't allow their fonts to be embedded willy-nilly—*willy-nilly*, of course, being a technical term. The colloquial term is *illegally*.

Fonts are intellectual property that you pay a license fee to use in your documents. When fonts are licensed for individual use, this usually means that the licensed typeface can be installed on your hard drive or networked storage device and used with just one output device. You cannot transfer the typeface to other systems or users, or permanently download the font to more than one device. These days, we rarely download fonts permanently to any device. However, site licenses usually let you install the one font on multiple computers at one company and at one physical location; global or worldwide licensing usually allows unlimited access to the font for an entire company at multiple physical locations. In all cases, you're not necessarily allowed to share the fonts with service providers without extending the license to them or making sure your partners have their own license. This has always been the case, even pre-PDF, but some foundries have specific rules or restrictions that pertain to embedding fonts in PDF files.

Adobe, for example, lets you embed its fonts without restriction for viewing and printing. Agfa/Monotype, on the other hand, lets you embed its fonts "for the sole purpose of printing or viewing such document, and not for editing or altering such document," according to its licensing policy. If the PDF file will be edited or altered, you must pay for a multi-user license agreement. Emigre requires that fonts embedded in PDF files and shared with unlicensed partners be subset at a threshold of 99 percent, and that the person who is embedding the fonts apply security settings that prohibit the file recipient from selecting or editing text.

Font licenses vary widely—which means it's vital that you research the rules. When you want to embed a font, check with the foundry to make sure that you have (or can acquire) the proper license. Also check with your service bureau or printer to see which fonts it has licensed. Some such companies have standing licenses for foundries' entire or partial libraries of fonts, which means you can embed without worry.

There are several ways to determine a font's foundry—and to see whether you've actually licensed the font. On the Mac the easiest way is to use the Get Info command. In the Finder, select the font's screen suitcase or the printer font file and choose Get Info from the File menu (Command-I). Non-System fonts will display the name of the foundry, and any available copyright infomation will appear in the Comments field. System fonts will display Mac OS under the font name; fonts installed by Microsoft will be identified as Microsoft Typography or Microsoft Internet Explorer (Figure 3-8).

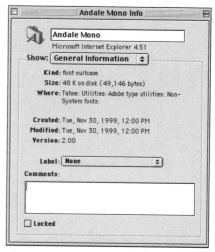

Figure 3-8 On a Mac you can determine a font's foundry by clicking it in the Finder and then choosing File > Get Info. In Windows, right-click the font and access its properties.

In Windows you can use Microsoft's Font Properties Extension 2.1 to right-click any font and view its properties: The tabbed Properties dialog box provides extensive information about the font, including the name of the foundry (in the Name tab), the foundry's URL (in Links), and details about embedding and licensing policies (in Embedding and Licensing, respectively). You can also double-click a font name to display a sample sheet that identifes the foundry. (If your version of Windows is earlier than Windows 2000, this only works for TrueType fonts.)

On both platforms you can also use a font management utility such as Adobe Type Manager Deluxe or Extensis Suitcase to identify a font's foundry. In Suitcase, for example, select a font and choose Get Info from the File menu; in ATM, choose Tools > Report. In the case of Microsoft-installed TrueType fonts, you'll get the name of the actual foundry, such as Monotype, this way (Figure 3-9).

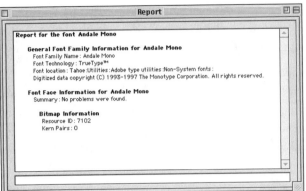

Figure 3-9 Another way to determine a font's foundry is by using a font management utility such as Suitcase or ATM Deluxe. Here is the same info about Andale in an ATM report. Note that it shows the foundry that designed the typeface (Monotype), not the company that installed it on your computer (Microsoft).

Color

Even if you're not using ICC color management (the standard system for producing consistent, predictable color on a wide range of devices), you can't avoid the Color panel of the Distiller Job Options dialog box. Color management is one of those hairy technologies that designers are constantly confronted with but rarely understand completely. To make matters worse, technology vendors—with the laudable goal of "simplifying" and "streamlining" their implementations of ICC color management—are constantly tweaking and updating their color management settings and systems, forcing us to relearn or avoid them so as not to damage our files.

Ranting aside, understanding how Distiller handles color is critical to producing printed pages using PDF that will yield the color you expect. Prepress folks tend to put designers between a rock and a hard place when it comes to color: They want you to supply a color proof indicating the output you expect them to produce; however, they also want you to understand that CMYK dots on paper will never match the oversaturated color of laser-printer toner comps. This is one more reason you need to understand how your software applications manage color.

The good news is that Adobe is standardizing how it handles color and color management. Its professional publishing applications (including current versions of Photoshop, Illustrator, InDesign, and Acrobat) all employ virtually the same Color Settings dialog box (Figure 3-10), with the same options and default settings for using color management, applying conversions and rendering intents, and choosing from available working spaces (Adobe's term for profiles).

Color Management 101

Color management is a topic that could fill volumes, but I'll try to succinctly synthesize here what you need to know about its theory and implementation. The first thing to know is that your computer displays color in RGB—adding red, green, and blue light—to produce a wide gamut of colors on your monitor. Printing presses, in contrast, produce color subtractively, using cyan, magenta, yellow, and black (CMYK) inks. RGB yields fewer colors than our eyes can see; CMYK yields an even smaller, yet different, range. The job of color management is to resolve these discrepancies so that the color we want and see is uniform across all devices—monitor, proof printers, and press—and predictable as we move documents through our workflow.

ICC color management, developed by the International Color Consortium, tackles this challenge with a two-pronged system. First every device in the workflow, including scanners, monitors, printers, and presses, gets tagged with a profile. A profile is a small file that tells a software application, such as Photoshop, what colors the device can produce: that is, whether the device displays in RGB or CMYK, the range of color it can produce, whether certain blues gravitate to a green hue, and any other pertinent color idiosyncrasies. Software applications crunch this data through a color engine: They back the color out to a huge color space called CIE, named after the Commission Internationale de l'Eclairage, or International Committee on Illumination. Within this larger, device-independent color space, the color engine maps color values across devices, displaying or printing consistent and predictable color regardless of each device's capabilities. The color engine also uses a translation algorithm called a rendering intent to preserve colors faithfully based on the content of the image.

Color management gives you tremendous flexibility: You can have your monitor simulate a four-color press for soft proofing, or you can have your service bureau produce an Iris proof that simulates a press, giving you greater confidence that the colors you used early in the design process are what you'll get off the press.

If you're interested in learning more about color management, there are many resources to choose from. Two places to start are Adobe's Web site, which includes an area devoted to the topic (www.adobe.com/print/prodzone/colormgt.html), and Apple's Web site, which includes extensive information about ColorSync, its system-level implementation of ICC color management (www.apple.com/colorsync/).

Because Distiller accepts files from applications where you may have already specified some form of color management, it defers to the PostScript file's color management information unless you tell it otherwise in the Color panel of the Job Options dialog box. Here you can choose a Color Settings file that tells Distiller how to handle any color it encounters. The intimidating part of this is that you have 10 files to choose from (nine in Windows). The reassuring part is that all but one of them are preset and uneditable—that is, you can't customize (read: confuse) them.

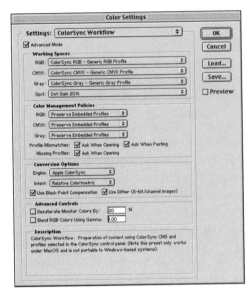
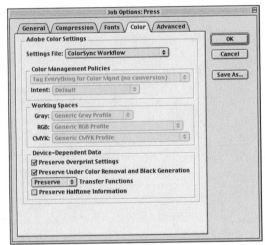

Figure 3-10 Adobe has streamlined the color management interface used in its professional publishing applications. The Color Settings dialog box in Photoshop and the Color panel in Acrobat Distiller's Job Options dialog box, for example, offer the same settings, each of which applies the same policies, working spaces, and conversion options.

If you want to use a PostScript file's existing color management info and only tell Distiller how to manage any unmanaged color in the file, choose None—the only way you're allowed to choose from among Distiller's Color Management Policies (Figure 3-11). You can leave the color unchanged; you can tag it but not convert it; or you can convert color to sRGB, a color space associated with Web publishing. You obviously wouldn't want to choose the latter for prepress, and if you opted to tag unmanaged color, Acrobat would alter the unmanaged color onscreen but wouldn't actually change the color values of any pixels in the file. Instead, it would calibrate color according to the profiles it tagged (or embedded), which are specified in the Working Spaces area of the dialog box. You can't edit the RGB, CMYK, and Grayscale working spaces that Distiller makes use of—but that's OK because they're perfectly suitable for high-end prepress (in fact, most of them are designed for that purpose).

All of Distiller's default Job Options files—Press, Print, eBook, and Screen—use None; Press leaves color unchanged. This is confusing because Distiller will calibrate color based on the working spaces defined in the panel, but it won't embed the profiles in the file or convert the actual pixels.

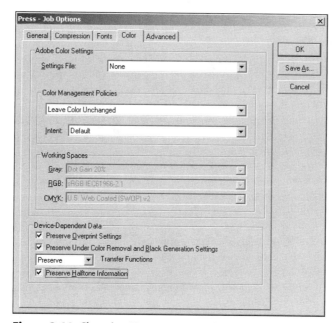

Figure 3-11 Choosing None as your Color Settings file in the Distiller Color panel tells the software to defer to any color management it encounters in a PostScript file and lets you decide how to manage unmanaged color. This is the only time you can choose the policies you want to apply. You should either tag it or leave it unchanged; don't convert to sRGB.

Color Caveat

You must talk to your prepress partner about what color settings file to use in Distiller. The company may want untagged files because it doesn't use ICC color management, or it might prefer a particular color settings file, such as U.S. Prepress Defaults, or it may have a job option file with customer profiles that it wants you to use. There are so many junctures at which color management can go awry that it's critical for designers and their service providers to communicate about how it is used.

The other Color Settings files apply color management to all color in the file, overriding any PostScript file specifications. A few of the other settings are suitable for prepress, most obviously U.S. Prepress Default. This setting tags unmanaged color but doesn't convert it, and the Default rendering intent means it leaves the intent up to the output device. The CMYK profile is a SWOP (Specifications for Web Offset Publications) standard, and a standard 20 percent dot gain is applied by the grayscale profile. The ColorSync color settings file, available on the

Mac, uses whatever color engine and profiles are specified in the ColorSync 3.0 Control Panel—appropriate when you're in an all-Mac but not all-Adobe work environment.

Whatever you do, don't choose Color Management Off (Figure 3-12), which tells Distiller not to tag any color in the PostScript file. If you check this option, Distiller will still use the working spaces grayed out in the panel to convert colors between color spaces, but it won't tag or convert any color in the file. You should only turn color management off if you are distilling files from applications that didn't support ICC color management and whose contents were destined for video or onscreen presentation.

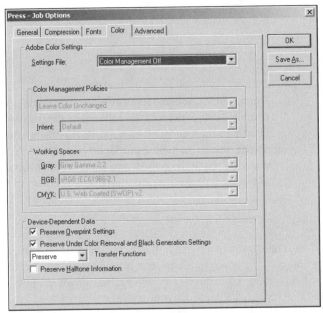

Figure 3-12 Don't turn color management off! This option is for content that originated in applications that don't support ICC color management and is destined for video or onscreen presentation.

Finally, regardless of what Color Settings file you choose, you need to make some decisions about device-dependent data. It's a good idea to discuss the following options with your prepress partner so that you understand what information it wants you to include (as compared to the information it can generate itself when it RIPs to film or plate).

- **Preserve Overprint Settings.** If you've specified overprinting in Illustrator (or another authoring application) so that two or more unscreened inks will be printed on top of each other to create a unique color, check this box to preserve them. Although you can specify this for any PDF version after Acrobat 3.0 (PDF 1.2), only Acrobat 5.0 (PDF 1.4) files let you see the effect both onscreen and in a composite proof.

- **Preserve Under Color Removal (UCR) and Black Generation.** These two processes—which work in tandem to reduce the amount of ink required to produce black on a page—are commonly used to lay less ink down on newsprint and other uncoated stocks. For any black dot on the page, UCR reduces the amount of cyan, magenta, and yellow inks laid down, while black generation increases the amount of black ink. These values are built into CMYK output profiles and can also be edited and saved in a custom profile in Photoshop. Either way, they're saved with the PostScript file, and you should check this box to preserve the information in your PDF files.

- **Preserve, Remove, or Apply Transfer Functions.** Transfer functions provide a means of managing dot gain and loss. The former occurs when ink spreads on paper larger than specified by the halftone screen; the latter occurs when dots of ink print smaller. In Photoshop, you can specify transfer functions in the Print Options dialog box and include them when you save images as EPS. These days, however, most people ignore transfer functions and control image color using Levels and Curves, and specify dot gain as part of their grayscale output profile. Although transfer functions are very precise, you must know exactly how your output device is calibrated and how to compensate for color shifts to use them effectively. Plus, there's no obvious indication for your downstream partner that the file includes transfer functions—a fact that can cause problems at output. If you create transfer functions and opt to preserve or apply them, be sure to alert your prepress partners.

- **Preserve Halftone Information.** This is another option where it helps to know what your prepress partner plans to do with your PDF file. As you learned in Chapter 2, you can specify all kinds of screening options in Photoshop, QuarkXPress, and other applications (halftone screen frequencies, angles, and dot shapes); however, this information will only remain in the PDF file if you check this box.

Many prepress providers and printers prefer that you leave such parameters as overprint settings, UCR/GCR, transfer functions, and halftone information out of your PDF files. One reason is that these settings make the file device-specific instead of device-independent, another is that they'd rather make these decisions themselves. After all, they're the prepress experts, and they know how their devices image files better than you do. Before specifying such functions and including them in your PDF file, check with your prepress and print partners to be sure they want them, and that you can create them correctly.

Advanced

The Advanced panel of Distiller's Job Options dialog box (Figure 3-13) contains a lot of checkboxes that appear dizzyingly complicated. Give yourself a break and accept Adobe's Press defaults in this panel, unless your prepress operator instructs you otherwise. If that's the case, continue reading, and I'll provide a nuts-and-bolts discussion of the essential options presented here.

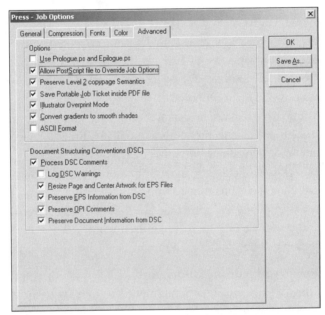

Figure 3-13 The Advanced panel of Distiller's job options dialog box can be daunting; the boxes checked in the generic Press configuration are fine unless your prepress provider tells you otherwise, so don't get too hung up on these things. Be sure to include a job ticket if you're using this type of workflow, to let your prepress partner or printer know what you're up to.

First, notice that this panel is divided into two areas: The top seven checkboxes pertain to options that can be applied to the contents of the PostScript stream; the bottom checkboxes, labeled Document Structuring Conventions, are primarily concerned with preserving metadata about documents destined for print. In other words, they don't apply to Web or eBook publishing.

The first box under Options is Use Prologue.ps and Epilogue.ps. This refers to two files that sandwich every PostScript file. Check this box to make them editable; however, you have to be a real PostScript geek to (a) want to and (b) know how to do this yourself. Still, a number of third-party Acrobat utilities use these files and require that this box be checked. The last box is ASCII Format. Checking it saves PDF files with binary characters in a readable format for debugging; if you check it for this purpose, you must *not* compress text and line art in the Compression panel. In most cases, leave it unchecked or it just bloats your file.

Most of the other options in this panel are self-explanatory. Check Allow PostScript File to Override Job Options to tell Distiller to disregard job options settings that conflict with what's specified in the PostScript file. This means that any Distiller settings you placed in a file before saving it as PostScript or printing it to PDF (for example, embedding fonts, compressing or resampling images, or specifying a resolution) take precedence over anything that's been specified in Distiller itself.

Check Save Portable Job Ticket inside PDF File if you're working in a job ticket workflow. This preserves PostScript file information about resolution and trapping and can be a good way to keep your prepress provider in the loop. See Chapter 6 for more about job ticketing.

Check Illustrator Overprint Mode to allow CMYK colors to overprint.

Finally, checking "Convert gradients to smooth shades" can improve the quality of the final blend as well as reduce file size.

As for Document Structuring Conventions, they're basically metadata about your file, which Adobe calls "comments." Check Process DSC Comments if you want Distiller to keep them with your PDF file. You can opt to log warnings about problematic comments; center an EPS image on a single page and resize the page to the size of the graphic; or save information on an EPS file or on another document's authoring application (creation date, and so on.) for Acrobat's Document Summary dialog box (File > Document Summary). If you're using an OPI workflow in which you've placed low-resolution proxy images in your page-layout file and your prepress partner is to swap in the high-resolution final image, check

Preserve OPI Comments—and be sure your partner has the proper high-res files for substitution.

If and when you alter a job options file, you can click Save As or OK to save your changed settings as a new, custom file. Distiller prompts you with a modified file name of whatever options you edited (such as Press(1).joboptions), which you can make more intuitive if you prefer. The good news is that Distiller won't let you overwrite its four default options, as you could in past versions.

TEST YOUR PDF FILE

After you distill your PDF, open it on another computer at your office—one that doesn't have the fonts you've used or access to the file server where your artwork resides. If it opens and displays properly on that system, you can feel confident that it will open properly for your service provider.

—Tom Mornini, president, InfoMania, Printing and Prepress, Inc.

SECURITY

Although it's not part of the Job Options dialog box, you can apply security settings to any PDF file that you distill, restricting not only who can open the file but also whether viewers can copy or extract contents, fill in form fields, add comments, print the document, and more. By default, Distiller doesn't apply any password or permissions restrictions to documents. Although you won't want your prepress partner or printer to inadvertently alter your file, keep in mind that these folks need to be able to make last-minute corrections (for example, fixing typos in display ads or changing prices in circular inserts) as well as to print, trap, separate, and impose the document.

Even if you're using PDF files to exchange comps but not for final production, viewers generally need to be able to print and annotate the files. If you're worried about secure file transfer, talk to your prepress partners about what they're already using or discuss using a secure service such as Wamnet. In publishing, it is sometimes more appropriate to use security options for exchanging confidential or sensitive documents (for example, proposals or competitive bids) among office staff or with clients rather than for production. You'll notice, also, that the options are really designed to facilitate the safe and controlled use of PDF-based forms.

Still, if you do decide to invoke password protection or restrict what viewers can do with the PDF file, your security options will be applied to any PDF files you produce until you turn them off. Thus, be careful not to lock your prepress partners out of your files. And be aware that if you require a user password (to open a file), you should also specify a master password (for changing permissions and passwords); otherwise, the person who opens the file will also be able to change the document's security restrictions, which rather defeats the point of security. (Distiller, by the way, requires that you enter different user and master passwords.) Of course, you or anyone else can add security to a PDF file in Acrobat itself if you don't restrict the document when you distill it: Simply choose Document Security from the File menu (Figure 3-14), and change No Security to Acrobat Standard Security to access and edit the same Security dialog box you get when you choose Settings > Security in Distiller. When the PDF file is saved, so are the new security settings.

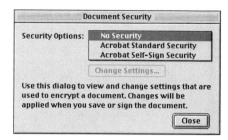

Figure 3-14 If you forget to include (or intentionally omit) security restrictions when you distill a PDF file, anyone can apply them when they open or view the file in Acrobat. Just choose File > Document Security, and change No Security to Acrobat Standard Security to access the same Security dialog box as in Distiller.

Restricting viewer actions on PDF files is called *encrypting* them. If you decide to encrypt PDF files, the permissions that you can specify vary depending on whether you're distilling an Acrobat 5.0 (PDF 1.4) or earlier file. Acrobat 5.0 supports 128-bit encryption, which is harder to crack and gives you finer control over permissions. Acrobat 4.0 (PDF 1.3) and earlier only support 40-bit encryption. Truth be told, both types of encryption are adequate, though 128-bit encryption is currently as good as it gets. Using this type of encryption (Figure 3-15), you can make your content accessible to visually impaired viewers who are using screen readers, and allow it to be copied and extracted. You can choose which of five types of changes

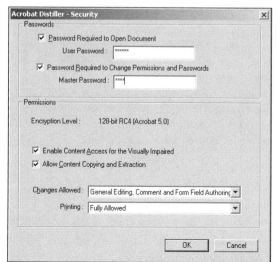

Figure 3-15 Acrobat 5.0 (PDF 1.4) files support 128-bit encryption, which is harder to crack and gives you finer control over permissions. However, it's a good idea to go easy with security: If you do assign passwords, make sure your prepress partners can print and edit the PDF file down the line.

you'll allow to be made to the document: from none, to only filling in fields and signing forms, to performing all types of general editing except extractions and printing. Finally, you can disallow printing; only allow printing at low resolution; or allow full, high-resolution printing.

For prepress, accessibility isn't the issue (that's for giving visually impaired readers access to electronic documents). However, you do want to allow your contents to be copied or extracted. In fact, your partners should be able to fully edit the document and print it at high resolution.

Although the permissions available with 40-bit encryption—for Acrobat 4.0 (PDF 1.3) or earlier files—are less robust, these are the options you'll likely face because PDF 1.3 files are still in common use for prepress (Figure 3-16). You can prevent viewers from printing or changing the document, copying or extracting content, or adding or changing Comments or form fields (other than to fill them in); however, for the reasons described above, you should leave all of these boxes unchecked.

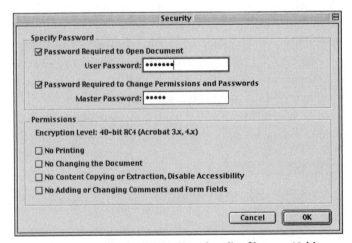

Figure 3-16 Acrobat 4.0 (PDF 1.3) and earlier files use 40-bit encryption. Although options for this type of encryption vary slightly from 128-bit security, aside from password protection, you won't want to restrict files for production anyhow.

HOW DO YOU PREFER TO DISTILL?

Like all software applications, Distiller has a Preferences dialog box where you can tell it how to handle global application issues. Distiller's options here are pretty straightforward (Figure 3-17): You'll want Distiller to notify you when the startup

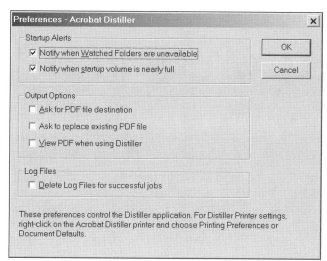

Figure 3-17 Distiller's Preferences are straight-forward: Asking it to tell you when volumes are full or watched folders are unavailable is wise, but keeping log files and asking to restart after crashes can go either way.

volume is nearly full and when watched folders are unavailable. After all, the last thing you want to find out is that your files weren't processed because the free-lancer who worked at your computer while you were on vacation not only changed your directory structure but left a ton of scanned images on your hard drive!

Unless you need a record for a client, you may not need to keep log files for successful jobs. Likewise, I wouldn't bother to check Restart Distiller After PostScript Fatal Error. This type of error is called *fatal* for a reason: You'll probably want to quit other applications and reboot your system in the event of a crash.

On Windows you have a few additional options to specify: First, check "Ask for PDF file destination" to always be prompted by a dialog box that lets you specify a filename and destination when you use drag-and-drop or the Print command. You can also check "Ask to replace existing PDF file" to be prompted by a warning when you're about to overwrite an existing PDF file with a new file of the same name. I like to keep both of these checked even if I just press Enter to bypass them, to make sure I'm saving everything correctly. Finally, you can check "View PDF when using distiller" to automatically open and display a PDF file in Acrobat after it's distilled.

GET IN LINE

As designers continue to bridge the worlds of print and the Web, and custom publishing becomes increasingly essential, so does our need for flexible document production. Imagine this (oversimplified) workflow: Take your widget sales backgrounder, combine it with your widget spec sheet, and—presto!—you have a new widget brochure. Certainly, you could save those files individually as PDF files and then manually mix and match them into a single file in Acrobat as described in Chapter 4. However, you can also save the original files as PostScript and combine them automatically into a single PDF file using Distiller.

Distiller offers two ways to combine PostScript files into one PDF: You can either combine multiple PostScript files that are located in various places on your hard drive, or you can combine all of the PostScript files that are in a single folder. Distiller can do both tasks using two PostScript programs that are available in the Distiller > Xtras folder: Runfilex.ps (Windows) or RunFilEx.ps (Mac) lets you choose and distill multiple PostScript files into one PDF file regardless of their physical location on a hard drive; and RunDirEx.txt distills all PostScript files in a specified folder.

How to Create PostScript Files

Acrobat 5.0 goes a long way toward streamlining the distillation of PDF files by providing predefined job options that meet a wide range of needs for most users, and by letting you print to Distiller directly from the Print dialog boxes in most authoring applications. But knowing how to create good, clean PostScript files can help ensure that your PDF files can be rasterized and separated for printing. Here are some guidelines for ensuring that the PostScript files Distiller intercepts and processes are properly saved.

First, you need to choose a PostScript printer driver and make sure Distiller is your selected PPD (see Chapter 2 for explanations of printer drivers and PPDs). Luckily, Acrobat installs the current version of Adobe's PostScript drivers on your computer, so choose it on your desktop (Mac) or in the Printers Control Panel (Windows). Then make sure the OS is configured with the correct PPD: On the Mac, either go into the Chooser and click Setup or choose Change Setup from the Finder's Printing menu. I actually like to use the Virtual Printer, which I've renamed "PS print to file" so that I know exactly what it's for.

In Windows, choose Distiller as your printer. If you don't do this, you have to set up your printer to print to disk: In the Details tab of the printer's Properties dialog box, choose File as your print-to port.

Next, make sure that your PostScript options are properly configured in your authoring application. That means going into two dialog boxes, Page Setup and Print, and making the following choices (you may have to click through to Properties dialog boxes or navigate through pop-up menus to find them).

continued

---

1. Save data as binary, not ASCII. This results in smaller files that distill more efficiently.

2. Choose PostScript Job as your format, and make it Level 3-compatible. This will produce the smoothest gradient.

3. Don't include fonts. Check the box "Do not send fonts to Distiller." This may seem counter-intuitive after all I've said about embedding fonts, and normally you would include fonts in the PostScript stream, such as when it's headed for a RIP. However, there's an exception to that rule when your PostScript will be run through Distiller 5.0. This is because Acrobat 5.0 drivers use host-based fonts, which means that Acrobat can find the fonts to which the PostScript code refers, and in fact Distiller can embed fonts more efficiently if it is allowed to find the fonts on your system instead of using what's included in the PostScript stream.

4. On the Mac, make sure your Destination is File; in Windows, check Print or Save to File.

5. On the Mac, deselect Substitute Fonts, Smooth Text, and Smooth Graphics in the PostScript options panel of the Page Setup dialog box. Smoothing text and graphics applies anti-aliasing to these page elements, adding numerous unnecessary pixels that bloat the PDF file and make it take a long time to display and print. Distiller gives you a better way to smooth gradient blends in the Advanced panel in Job Options.

6. This resolution setting does not affect image size or downsampling, but if it's too high it can cause problems with reflowed text in PDF files created from Microsoft Office applications and failure to print text from FrameMaker. Adobe recommends PostScript resolution be set at 600 dpi.

7. Give the PostScript file the same name as the original document but with a .ps extension. Distiller will then convert it to .pdf.

Distiller can also convert encapsulated PostScript files, which you can save or export from many design applications, including Illustrator, FreeHand, Photoshop, and QuarkXPress. When exporting EPS files save binary data, *do* include fonts, and save CMYK color. Choose DCS 2.0 as your EPS format: This stands for *desktop color separation*; version 2.0 supports spot color channels. Choose "single file DCS" if the option is there.

Other essentials: Keep in mind that PostScript files are huge—larger than the sum of their parts—so make sure you have enough disk space to generate them. Also, make sure that any screen fonts you're using in the document are loaded, including any fonts used in embedded EPS images. Make sure that all image files in the layout are also available on your computer. And save your settings (if you can), so that you don't have to recheck these options every time you save PostScript. Finally, make sure not to save the file as read-only; if you do, Distiller won't be able to do anything with it.

Although you may find their names off-putting, these programs really aren't that complicated—honest! Think of them as templates: Take the one you want to run, such as RunFilEx.ps, and make a copy of it to actually use (Option-drag it out to the Finder, for example). Give this copy a new name representative of the final concatenated file, being sure to leave the .ps extension intact. (Distiller needs this to recognize the program; it will convert the file to a .pdf when it's finished.) For example, I've named mine "widgetbrochure.ps" (Figure 3-18).

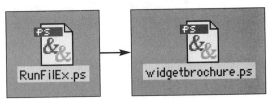

Figure 3-18 To use the PostScript program that comes with Distiller to concatenate multiple PostScript files, copy it to your desktop or Finder and then rename it before you edit it.

Be sure you know the exact names and locations of the PostScript files you want to distill into one PDF file. You may even want to write down this information—low-tech, I know, but very efficient! Once you've done this, open your PostScript program in Word or some other text editor. Don't freak out over what you see (Figure 3-19): Everything preceded by a percent sign is a comment or instruction.

```
%!
% PostScript program for distilling and combining multiple PostScript files.
% When embedding font subsets, it is highly recommended you use this technique
% to distill multiple PS files so only one font subset is used for each font.

/prun { /mysave save def      % Performs a save before running the PS file
        dup = flush           % Shows name of PS file being run
        RunFile               % Calls built in Distiller procedure
        clear cleardictstack  % Cleans up after PS file
        mysave restore        % Restores save level
} def

(Macintosh HD:Folder:Cover.ps) prun
(Macintosh HD:Folder:TOC.ps) prun
(Macintosh HD:Folder:Chapter1.ps) prun
(Macintosh HD:Folder:Chapter2.ps) prun
(Macintosh HD:Folder:Chapter3.ps) prun
(Macintosh HD:Folder:Index.ps) prun


% INSTRUCTIONS
%
% 1. Locate all PostScript files to be distilled.
%
% 2. Make a copy of this file and give it the name you want to have as the prefix
%    for the resulting file. For example, you could name this file MyBook.ps.
%
% 3. Include a line for each PostScript file to be run using the pathname syntax
%    appropriate for the platform running Acrobat Distiller.
%
%       Macintosh pathname syntax:   (Macintosh HD:Folder:File.ps) prun
%       Windows pathname syntax:     (c:/mydir/file.ps) prun
%          UNIX pathname syntax:     (./mydir/File.ps) prun
%
%       Note: The syntax for Windows may look strange, but double escaping the
%             backslash character is required when using filenameforall.
%
% 4. Distill the file on the machine running Acrobat Distiller.
```

Figure 3-19 Distiller's RunFilEx.ps program contains a few lines of code and a lot of lines of comments, all set off with percent signs.

The program itself is only a few lines long, and all you have to do is insert a path using the proper syntax for each PostScript file you want distilled. Each path should be on a separate line and enclosed in parentheses (indicating that they're variables), followed by the PostScript operator "prun." Table 3-2 shows the proper, generic (and case-sensitive) syntax for Mac OS, Windows, and Unix, as well as some sample command lines for my widget brochure example (my hard drive is named Tahoe). Figure 3-20 shows my edited PostScript program.

Platform	Path Syntax	Sample Command Lines
Mac	MacintoshHD:folder:file.ps	(Tahoe:widgetproject:sales.ps) prun
		(Tahoe:widgetproject:specsheet.ps) prun
Windows	c:/mydir/file.ps	(c:/widgetproject/sales.ps) prun
		(c:/widgetproject/specsheet.ps) prun
Unix	./mydir/file.ps	(./widgetproject/sales.ps) prun
		(./widgetproject/specsheet.ps) prun

Table 3-2 The Mac, Windows, and Unix platforms use slightly different syntax to perform the same PostScript commands.

```
%!
% PostScript program for distilling and combining multiple PostScript files.
% When embedding font subsets, it is highly recommended you use this technique
% to distill multiple PS files so only one font subset is used for each font.

/prun { /mysave save def        % Performs a save before running the PS file
        dup = flush             % Shows name of PS file being run
        RunFile                 % Calls built in Distiller procedure
        clear cleardictstack    % Cleans up after PS file
        mysave restore          % Restores save level
} def

(Tahoe:widgetproject:sales.ps) prun
(Tahoe:widgetproject:specsheet.ps) prun


|
```

Figure 3-20 Here's the edited program where I instruct Distiller to concatenate my widget sales and widget spec sheet PostScript files into one brochure.

These runfile PostScript programs contain sample command lines to help you keep the syntax straight. Go ahead and type over them, adding or deleting as necessary. When you're done, save the file and distill it: Drag the file into a watched folder (or launch Distiller), choose your job options, and then select File > Open (Figure 3-21). Choose your PostScript program (widgetbrocure.ps) and then click Open. Confirm the name of the PDF file (widgetbrochure.pdf) and where you want it saved, then click Save. The page order of the final PDF file will reflect the order in which the PostScript files are listed in the program (and the order in

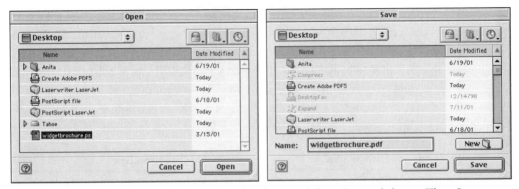

Figure 3-21 To run the program, launch Distiller, choose a job option, and choose File > Open. Browse to select the .ps program file and then click Open. Confirm where you want your PDF file saved and its name, and then click Save.

which Distiller processes them). If necessary, you can change the page sequence in Acrobat. (See Chapter 4 for more about this.)

If you're using RunDirEx.txt to distill the PostScript files into a single folder or directory, the process is almost identical: Copy the program and give it an intutive name; however, this time leave the .txt extension (in case the program itself— should it be in the folder—isn't distilled). Open the program in Word and enter the folder's variable path using the syntax indicated in Table 3-2 but employing the wildcard asterisk character for the file name—that is, *.ps rather than file.ps.

In my example on the Mac the path looks like this:

```
Tahoe:widgetproject:*ps
```

And the entire command line looks like this:

```
/Pathname (Tahoe:widgetproject:*.ps) def
```

Leave the rest of the program unchanged.

A nice benefit of using these programs to combine PostScript files rather than manually adding and deleting pages from existing PDF files into a new one is that Distiller creates only one subset for each font used. Thus, if you use Garamond in both your sales materials and spec sheet, the PDF file has only one subset version of Garamond, not two. Also, note that the PostScript files must be on the same system as Distiller for these programs to work.

Although these programs are written specifically for distilling PostScript files, you can tweak them so that you can distill and combine EPS files, too—a process that takes just three steps. In the copied and renamed RunDirEx.txt or Runfilex.ps file, you'll find the following two lines of code:

```
RunFile
clear cleardictstack
```

Insert an instruction between them as follows:

```
RunFile
showpage % new line
clear cleardictstack
```

Now substitute the .eps extension for the .ps extension for the file names that you list. Finally, set the page size in the General tab of Distiller's Job Options dialog box to accommodate your largest EPS file. Otherwise, it may get cropped.

WATCH OUT

One of Distiller's great productivity features is its ability to create PDF files automatically when they're placed in watched folders—up to 100 folders if you're ambitious as well as organized. These files can be organized by project, client, or whatever system makes sense for your production needs. You must still create a PostScript or EPS file from your authoring application—which is most of the dirty setup work of distilling PDF files through your application's Print dialog box—but depending on your application you can automate the creation of your PostScript files. (See "How to Create PostScript Files," page 110, for more on creating PostScript files.) Then all you have to do is save or move those PostScript files to a folder that you tell Distiller to check periodically. From then on, it does the deed automatically in the background.

Before you set up watched folders (which can be hard drives, directories, or hard drive partitions), there are a couple things you need to be aware of: First, you can't use watched folders over a network. They must reside on the same hard drive as Distiller. You can, however, establish a dedicated production machine on your network that includes Distiller and the watched folders, and then have users drag their PostScript files to that machine (just be sure everyone who puts files in the watched folder is licensed to use Distiller). If your prepress partner will be distilling your PostScript files, a more sophisticated system would be for you to place PostScript files on a secure FTP site and have your partner configure Distiller to watch the site and process your PDF files automatically.

The other thing to keep in mind when setting up watched folders is that you must determine which job options you want applied to the contents of the watched folder *before* you create it. When you've selected the options, choose Settings > Watched Folders. In the Watched Folders dialog box (Figure 3-22), click Add, and then browse to choose the folder you want Distiller to watch. Distiller then automatically places In and Out folders within the folder you chose. You actually have to place queued PostScript files in the In folder (not the one you specified) when you want them to be distilled—annoying, but manageable once you're aware of the idiosyncrasy. Distilled PDF files, along with any error log files, are placed in the Out folder.

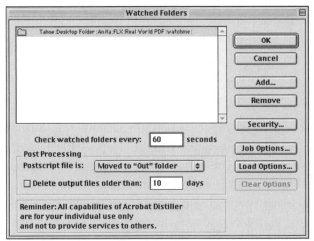

Figure 3-22 To ask Distiller to watch a particular folder for PostScript files to process, choose Settings > Watched Folders. Browse to select the folder, and you're all set. Distiller will apply the Job Option file that was active when you entered the dialog box. If you want to edit the job options that apply to this folder, click the Job Options button; likewise, click the Security button to add encryption.

Distiller will translate every PostScript file dropped into the watched folder based on the job options you chose when you specified the folder. You can, however, edit the job options that apply to the folder by clicking the Job Options button (or double-clicking the folder name in the list), making your changes, and then clicking OK when you're done. In addition, be sure to indicate how frequently (in seconds) you want Distiller to check watched folders and to tell it what to do with processed files (since deleting them can be risky, tell Distiller to move them to the Out folder). Finally, specify when to delete old, processed files. By default, Distiller doesn't apply any security restrictions to the PostScript files it converts in watched folders. To add security such as passwords or permissions, click the Security button, make your choices in the Security dialog box, and click OK.

CHAPTER FOUR

Collaborating, Repurposing, and Proofing

Once you've properly created PDF files, the fun can begin. Acrobat offers numerous tools to facilitate creative workflows before you send files to prepress: You can use them for tasks ranging from simple text touch-ups to sharing comments through a Web server or soft- or hard-proofing using ICC color management. This chapter provides an overview of these varied and useful tools, and shows you how to use them to streamline creative group processes such as editing and proofing cycles.

Note that I will not walk you through Acrobat's entire interface and work area. Instead, I'll assume you have some knowledge of the basics (how to navigate pages, manage toolbars, find hidden tools, and so on). If you're a complete novice, consult the Acrobat manual—a PDF file, not coincidentally, available from the Help menu.

COLLABORATIVE TOOLS

Publishing doesn't occur in a vacuum. It usually involves dozens of people from multiple departments in many companies. Managing and controlling all of these people's input on any given document can be a Herculean task, especially in an age when it's often impossible to assemble all of the players in the same conference room (much less the same time zone) to discuss a comp. If that comp is a PDF file that's been emailed to the relevant players, however, each person can use Acrobat's Comments and Annotations features to mark up the comp, and remain on the same page (pun intended). By the way, you don't even have to launch your email software to send PDF files to your peers: Click the E-Mail button and Acrobat will do it for you, automatically creating a new message and attaching the PDF file for you.

Making Comments

There are basically two ways to comment on a PDF file: You can stick a note on top of the page, or you can mark up the text or graphics with annotations that indicate required changes (explanatory sticky notes can be attached to annotations, too). Obviously, this is not an either/or situation: Reviewers can use whatever combination of tools works best to communicate their wishes. However, as you'll soon see, it can be helpful to make some rules about how you want people to comment on PDF pages. Acrobat includes the following five tools for adding comments on top of a page: Note, Free Text, Stamp, and Sound and File Attachment.

 Note tool. With the Note tool, you simply click on the page or drag a box and write in your comment. Click and drag the note to reposition it anywhere on or off the page; close it by clicking the box in the upper-left corner of the window, leaving just the note's icon visible on the page (you can click and drag to reposition the icon, too); remove it by clicking the icon and pressing Delete.

A sticky note's appearance is dictated by specifications you've made in the Comments section of the Preferences dialog box (Edit > Preferences > General), as shown in Figure 4-1. These include typeface and point size of the text, as well as the opacity of the note and whether notes should be numbered in sequence. If you check Always Use Identity for Author, the note will be labeled with information

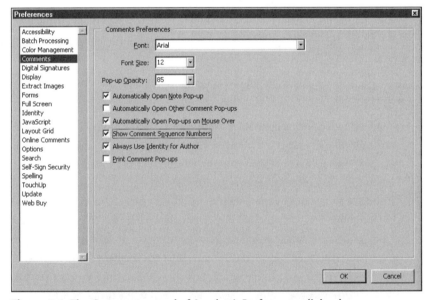

Figure 4-1 The Comments panel of Acrobat's Preferences dialog box.

gleaned from the Identity panel of the General Preferences dialog box. Automatically Open Note Pop-up and Automatically Open Other Comment Pop-ups are helpful options for reviewers or other commentators: Checking these boxes opens sticky-note windows when you create a comment or annotation; you don't have to manually double-click to open one. It's also a good idea to give notes some transparency so that you can see if there's anything (such as another comment or an annotation) beneath them. Keep in mind that the font and opacity preferences you set for the note apply on your computer only; the color, however, travels with the note.

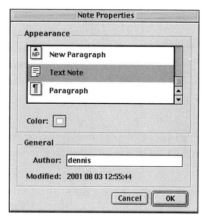

Figure 4-2 The Note tool's Properties dialog box.

You can change the identity, color, and other characteristics of a particular note (as shown in Figure 4-2) by clicking its icon to select it (with the Note tool itself or the Hand tool) and choosing Edit > Properties. You can also choose a different icon for it from the Appearance list (for example, a dialog balloon to indicate a comment, or a triangle to indicate insert text). Changes you make to your notes' appearance remain in effect until you alter them again; however, the author reverts immediately to the user name if you've checked Always Use Identity for Author in Preferences.

Depending on the idiosyncrasies of your particular workgroup and projects, you may want to assign certain colors or type characteristics to certain departments to help make their comments easier to read. For example, you could make marketing notes red, sales notes blue, notes pertaining to copy green, and notes pertaining to art purple. Keep in mind, however, that there's no way to enforce these standards through Acrobat: You must either manually set up the preferences of each member of the workgroup or trust them to adhere to your requested guidelines.

MARK THIS

The way we're using annotations on collateral kits is easy because it's a direct connect. Even if we send a PDF to three people we can compile them easily. And the annotation tools really fit a traditional workflow. Once we pointed out to people they could do it this way, they wanted to; it facilitates changes and saves us money. Our design team used to receive faxes, or wait for interoffice mail, or send a courier to the other building to get the marked-up proofs. Now everyone uses an internal ID number as their log-in, and that rides with their annotations in the PDF file. I've also taught reviewers to use the right tool for the right job: Don't draw a circle and put a note next to it; use the appropriate graphic tool and its associated note as much as possible. Otherwise, we get a lot of empty notes when we summarize comments. And I tell them, don't put editorial changes in quotation marks: say, "Replace with the following text." If I see quote marks I assume they should be in the text.

—Paul Bunyar, senior graphic artist, American Century

 Free Text tool. Hidden beneath the Note tool are several other tools for adding comments to PDF files. Using the Free Text tool, you can add a comment to the page that will always remain visible. It can't be closed like a sticky note; this type of comment, always appears with a bounding box around it. You can, however, drag to resize it or reposition it on a page. With a free-text note selected, choose Edit > Properties to customize the font style, frame appearance, or author (Figure 4-3).

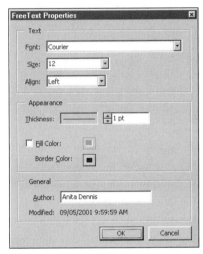

Figure 4-3 The Free Text tool Properties dialog box.

 Stamp tool. Acrobat also ships with a number of graphical stamps which you can either add to a PDF file before sending it out (such as "For Comment" or "Confidential"), or which reviewers can stamp on top of the file as an annotation when they're through reading it (such as "Approved"). To choose a stamp, click to select the Stamp tool, then open its properties (Edit > Properties). In the Stamp Properties dialog box (Figure 4-4), you can choose from four categories of stamps that ship with Acrobat: Faces, Pointers, Standard, and Words. Personally, I find some of them pretty goofy and less than helpful (for example, the smirk face)—not to mention annoying if misused. However, by double-clicking a stamp on a page, you can add a note with clarifying remarks.

You can also create your own stamps: Simply use any image-editing, illustration, or layout application to create a word, icon, or other graphic, and export or distill it as a PDF file. Stamps can also be multipage documents, if you create a series of them. You must save stamps in the Acrobat > Plug-Ins > Annotations > Stamps folder, and they must adhere to a strict naming convention if Acrobat is to properly display their category and name in the Stamp Properties dialog box. (If you see an ENU folder in your Stamps or Sequences folder, don't worry: It means English Universal and refers to the localized version of Acrobat you're using. Other-language versions

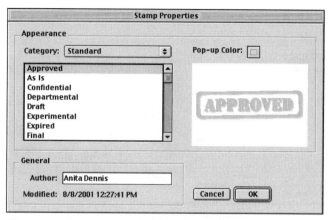

Figure 4-4 The Stamp tool Properties dialog box.

may display different codes, such as FR for French. You can put your stamps or sequences in the ENU folder or in the folder that resides on the level above it.)

With your stamp file open, choose Document Properties > Summary, and enter a descriptive word in the Title field (use the same word as the file name to reduce confusion). This will be what Acrobat uses in the Category pop-up menu of the Stamp Properties dialog box. For the names of the individual stamps as they appear in the scrolling list of the Properties dialog box, you must name each page in your PDF stamp file using a form page template. To do this, view the stamp page onscreen (one at a time for multipage stamp documents) and then choose Tools > Forms > Page Templates. In the Name field, enter the category name followed by the particular stamp name, and set it equal to a label, which should simply be the stamp name.

Say, for example, I wanted to create a custom approval stamp for each member of a sales team that would be reviewing product brochures: I would make the stamp itself the person's name and create a multipage PDF file with five of these named stamps, which I would ultimately share with the sales team. First, however, I would open my five-page PDF file (named SalesStamps) in Acrobat and enter SalesStamps in the Title field of the Document Summary dialog box. Then, with the first salesperson's stamp open, I would choose Tools > Forms > Page Templates. In the Name field I would enter SalesStampsJimSmith=JimSmith, then click Add, then Done. I would then do the same with the second page in my stamp file (Figure 4-5), and so on. When I finished, SalesStamps would be available from the Category pop-up menu, and Jim Smith, Mary Jones, and the rest of the members of the sales team would be able to choose their names from the scrolling list to apply their custom approval stamps to the page.

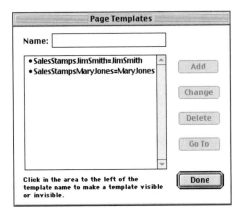

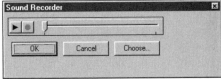

Figure 4-5 The Page Templates dialog box.   **Figure 4-6** The Sound Recorder dialog box.

 Sound Attachment tool. To add a sound annotation, select the Sound Attachment tool and click on the page where you want to place the audio comment. In the Record Sound/Sound Recorder (Mac/Win) box that appears (Figure 4-6), either click Record and speak into your computer's microphone, or click the Choose button and select a prerecorded sound (.WAV in Windows, .AIF on the Mac). A speaker icon indicates a sound annotation; click it to hear the sound play.

If you use sound annotations, they should be explicit: Record yourself saying "Anita approves of this layout" or "Make all quote marks curly." Sounds such as chimes or whistles aren't terribly communicative. Although you can't associate written annotations with sound annotations (as you can with stamps, for example), you can give your sound a short written description (for example, "Approved" or "Fix quotes") in the Sound Properties dialog box (Figure 4-7), which appears automatically once you've selected the sound you wish to attach. This description appears in the Comments palette (see "Managing Comments and Annotations," page 28) and pops up onscreen when you roll the mouse cursor over the sound annotation's speaker icon. Still, if you need to add written text to explain a sound comment, you're not really using sound to convey your message.

 File Attachment tool. Finally, you can attach a file to a PDF document as a way to annotate it: When you use the File Attachment tool to do this, the file comment becomes part of the PDF file itself—that is, it's not just linked. This ensures that the file comment can be viewed on a system other than the one on which it was attached—as long as the person viewing the attachment has the authoring application on his or her computer, a big if. Another downside to file attachments is that

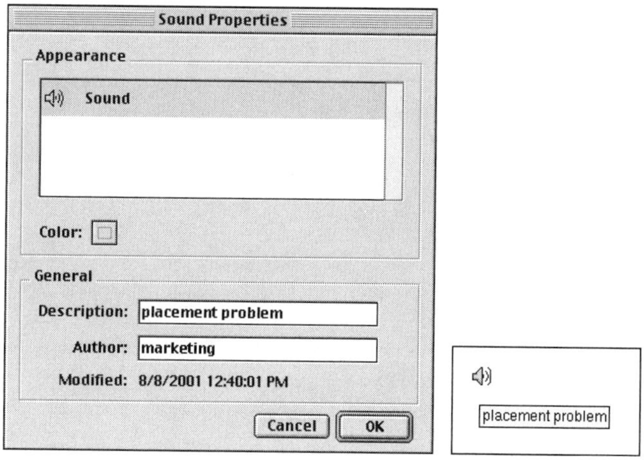

Figure 4-7 The description you enter in the Sound Properties dialog box (a) appears when the mouse cursor hovers over the sound icon on a PDF page (b).

they can easily double or triple your PDF file size if you attach hefty text files or graphics—which, ironically, are the most suitable types of files to attach. If you want to annotate a PDF file with simple instructions about fixing typos or aligning captions with their graphics, a sticky note will suffice. However, to request grander changes, file attachments can be very useful. If, for example, the wrong image is on a page, you can attach the correct one so that the designer or compositor will know which to use: Double-clicking the File Attachment icon in the PDF file will launch the authoring application and open the file, which the designer can then save to the hard drive if necessary. Similarly, if a page layout is incorrect, you can attach an example of how the page should be designed—as a PDF or application file from PageMaker or QuarkXPress, for example. You can also attach text files that your designer can use to repour the layout (and redistill) if the editorial has significantly changed since it was handed over to production.

To attach a file to a PDF document, use the File Attachment tool to click on the page where you want to position it. In the Open dialog box that appears, find the file you want to attach (you may have to choose All Files from the Show pop-up menu to find the one you're looking for). Then click Select. In the File Attachment Properties dialog box, decide what icon and color will represent your attached comment and write a description, that will appear when the mouse cursor hovers over the icon (Figure 4-8).

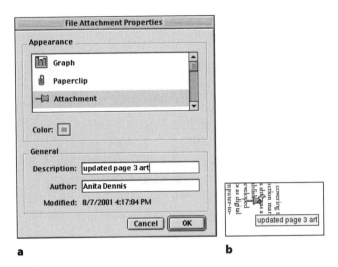

Figure 4-8 The description you enter in the File Attachment Properties dialog box (a) appears when the cursor is positioned over the attachment icon in the PDF file (b).

Marking Up Pages

Pencil, Circle, Square, and Line tools. The first tool for marking up the text or graphics on a PDF page is the Pencil tool. It works, well, just like a pencil. If you have a stylus, it's an easy way to circle a page element or add proofreading marks, such as the delete mark. After clicking and drawing on the page with the Pencil tool, you can add an explanatory sticky note to the mark by clicking it with the Hand tool.

You can also use the Pencil tool to write on the page using a mouse; however, it can't provide the precision or control of a stylus. This is less of a problem with the other graphic markup tools: Circle, Square, and Line. When you draw on the page with the Circle and Square tools, Acrobat automatically creates a sticky-note annotation with any text enclosed by the shape included in it; just double-click the shape to see. This functionality is rather limited, however, since if the text on your page is written in anything other than a simple Roman serif or sans serif face, Acrobat won't be able to capture it to the note correctly. What's more, if you enclose a graphic, Acrobat won't capture anything. In addition, if you resize the mark on the page, the captured text contents of the note won't reflect your change. None of this is necessarily a bad thing, however, since you have to go into the note and explain what to do with the problematic text or graphic anyway. As with the Pencil tool, you have to manually double-click a mark drawn by the Line tool to attach a sticky-note comment. Keep in mind, also, that the sticky notes associated with edits made by graphic markup tools can be hidden: After the note has been written, double-clicking the mark with the tool that created it (or with the Hand tool) toggles the note open and closed. However, it's a good idea to leave notes visible so that the person making your changes doesn't miss any instructions.

By default, the Pencil, Square, Circle, and Line tools draw 1-point marks. You can customize their weight, fill, and border colors, as well as their author, in their Properties dialog boxes. Simply click with the markup tool used to draw the annotation (or with the Hand tool) to select it, then press Command/Ctrl-I. Your specifications will apply to all annotations you create using any of these four tools, as well as to the color of associated sticky notes; however, these specifications will not affect existing marks on the page. (The appearance of the type in the notes is governed by your Acrobat Preferences; see discussion and Figure 4-1 on page 118.) You're better off not using a fill color because you can't control its opacity, and a filled square or circle obscures the text or graphic you're marking up. The Line tool is nice because you can attach arrowheads to the ends (Figure 4-9), which makes for clear callouts. Keep in mind, however, that all of these tools can be used interchangeably to communicate the same types of messages: Delete this, fix this, move that (Figure 4-10). Your choice is really a matter of personal preference or corporate style.

Figure 4-9 The Line tool Properties dialog box.

The Pencil, Circle, Square, and Line tools are considered graphic markup tools even though you can use them, especially the Pencil tool, to mark up text. Acrobat also offers three text-only markup tools: Highlight, Strikeout, and Underline.

For certain tasks, Acrobat's text markup tools are much more efficient than the Pencil tool. Select any one of them and position the cursor over text on a PDF page, and it will change to an I-beam. Click and drag over an area of text—horizontally or vertically—and Acrobat will highlight, strike through, or underline all of the selected words. If you're trying this as you read on a multicolumn page, you'll notice that the selection straddles multiple columns: Press Option (Mac) or Ctrl (Windows) as you drag, and Acrobat will draw a rectangle and mark up individual columns (or portions thereof, depending on how you drag). And if you make mistakes, you can press Command/Ctrl-Z to undo your annotations one at a time.

a

b

c

Figure 4-10 The same edit made using the Pencil (a), Square (b), and Line tools (c). What works best depends on personal preference and corporate guidelines.

You can't, unfortunately, select letters within words, nor can you increase or expand highlight, strike-through, or underline marks by dragging their bounding boxes (as you can with graphic markup annotations). If you select a word and then decide you want to select the neighboring word, too, you must delete the first mark and redraw it to encompass both words—tedious but the only way to avoid having a zillion individual marks, each with an associated sticky note. A word for the wise (from someone who knows firsthand): Think carefully before you mark up text; you save a lot of time if you can get it right the first time.

On the bright side, these tools are nice because you don't have to worry about drawing a perfectly straight line through text (as you do with the Pencil tool); and as with the graphic markup tools, all you have to do is double-click the mark with the tool that created it (or with the Hand tool) to view or edit its associated sticky note. Once again, as long as you've selected text written with a plain serif or sans serif Roman typeface, Acrobat automatically copies the selected text into the note, providing you with a starting point for your comment or editing instructions.

You can change the color and the author (but not the width) of your highlight, strike-through, or underline marks by clicking to select them with the actual markup tool or with the Hand tool and then calling up their properties by pressing Command/Ctrl-I. The graphic markup tools share the same colors and widths; however, text markup tools' colors are independent: By default, highlighted text is yellow; strike-throughs are red; and underlines are green. It doesn't matter what colors you use, as long as they're bright and visible (Figure 4-11).

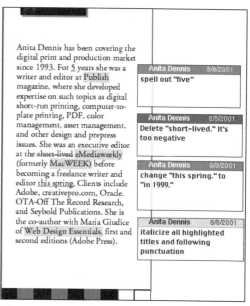

Figure 4-11 A portion of a PDF brochure edited using Acrobat's text markup tools.

If you can devise a system to standardize annotated PDF files, the person actually making your changes (and those of your colleagues) will be eternally grateful. You could, for example, decide that text for deletion should be indicated using the Strikeout tool and marked in the same color by all reviewers. Or you could circulate a style guide within your organization, indicating which departments make comments in which colors, the tools to be used for different types of edits, and even the types of comments various reviewers are allowed to make. When creating a style guide, give as much thought to reviewers' needs as to the requirements of the folks who have to manage the comments and input the changes.

Managing Comments and Annotations

Indeed, managing comments and annotations made to PDF files can be a prodigious task. And getting reviewers to use the markup tools uniformly and effectively is only half the battle. Although Acrobat's comment and annotation features simulate the sticky notes and highlighters of the paper office, users still need to make some adjustments to use them effectively in the digital world. Annotations, for example, can be hard to see on a radiant, low-resolution page—especially if the reviewer doesn't leave sticky notes open for the next viewer. Left open, though, sticky notes can obscure other comments or edit marks on the page. If you're not careful, before you know it, you've lost hours toggling sticky notes open and closed, and panning and zooming around pages to make sure you haven't missed any comments. Luckily, Acrobat offers a few tools that help manage comments and annotations.

Comments Preferences. We visited this dialog box earlier because it contains options for comment authors, such as whether or not sticky notes open automatically when you create an annotation. However, you can also check boxes here that can be helpful for compiling reviewer feedback (Figure 4-12).

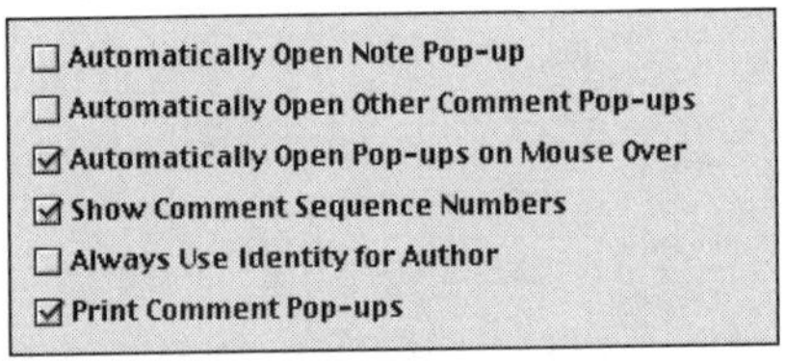

☐ Automatically Open Note Pop-up
☐ Automatically Open Other Comment Pop-ups
☑ Automatically Open Pop-ups on Mouse Over
☑ Show Comment Sequence Numbers
☐ Always Use Identity for Author
☑ Print Comment Pop-ups

Figure 4-12 Checking these boxes in the Comments panel of the Preferences dialog box helps you see viewers' comments onscreen and in print.

To make it easier to pan around a PDF page and view its comments, check "Automatically Open Pop-ups on Mouse Over." If you receive a PDF file and all of the sticky notes are closed, this allows you to see at a glance the comments or descriptions (in the case of sound and file comments) underneath an icon or annotation.

If you select Show Comment Sequence Numbers, Acrobat will place a tiny numeral on top of each comment or annotation that indicates the order in which they were created—a great way to ensure that you catch every comment, especially if you're only viewing them onscreen. Be aware, however, that only the comment and annotation icons are numbered, not their associated sticky notes. Thus, you must still go through each comment and annotation and read each associated note to be sure that you address all concerns. Happily, however, you can select this option even if the person who made the comments and annotations did not, and Acrobat will still number the comments in sequence.

Finally, you can print the comments made in sticky-note pop-ups using a three-step process. First, check Print Comment Pop-ups in Preferences; second, make sure the pop-up sticky notes are open in the PDF file on screen; and third, check the Print: Comments box in the Print dialog box (on the Mac, toggle to Acrobat 5.0 in the General pop-up menu). If either the Comments box in the Print dialog or the Print Comment Pop-ups box in Preferences is unchecked, comments won't print. If both of those boxes are checked but the sticky notes themselves are closed onscreen, only the comment and annotation icons will print.

When it comes to sorting through comments and annotations, I get a bit paranoid about missing one. They can be hard to see in a page onscreen or in print: Sticky notes can hide annotations and get moved away from their associated comment icon, making it difficult to sort out what's what. Thankfully, Acrobat has a few more comment-management features up its sleeve.

Comments palette. Choose Comments from the Window menu or click the Show/Hide Navigation Pane button and then click the Comments tab to display the palette in your document window (Figure 4-13).

If you're like me, you'll love the Comments palette because it shows everything in a nice, neat list—nothing is hidden and comments are in context (because the page itself is right there). By default, comments (and annotations) are listed by page (though, surprisingly, not in

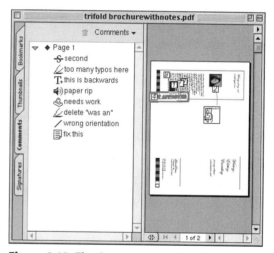

Figure 4-13 The Comments palette allows you to quickly navigate the comments and annotations in a PDF document.

sequential order). You can change the view by clicking the Comments pop-up menu to sort by author, type, or date. Next to the comment or annotation icon, Acrobat displays the item's description or the contents of its associated sticky note: You don't have to slog through them on the page, toggling them on and off.

To move quickly through changes, click to select and view an annotation in the Comments palette (and notice that Acrobat selects it on the PDF page, jumping to that page if necessary). Next, switch to the document's authoring or imaging application to make the corrections (or use one of Acrobat's touch-up tools, if appropriate). Finally, switch back to Acrobat (where your comment is still selected in the

Comments palette and on the page), and press Delete. Make sure you don't save over the PDF file after you've deleted the comments; you need the marked-up file for version control and backup. Instead, use Save As to give the file a new name.

Comment summaries. Another way to get a complete picture of a document's comments is to generate a summary. Acrobat generates a new PDF file for the summary, sorted and filtered as you specify, giving you a clean, text-only view of the comments. To create a summary, choose Tools > Comments > Summarize. In the Summarize Comments dialog box (Figure 4-14), decide how you want to sort the comments. I like to do it by page, but your other options are Type, Author, and Date. If you want to filter out certain types of comments, click Filter. In the Filter

Comments dialog box (Figure 4-17), you can filter comments by time (include those created anytime, in the last 24 hours, or other timeframe), by author (if more than one author made comments, check whose you want to include), or by type (check which comment, graphic, or text markup tools you want to include). Click OK to return to the Summarize Contents dialog box, and click OK again to generate the summary.

Figure 4-14 The Summarize Comments dialog box allows you to summarize the contents of comments and annotations.

Summaries divorce the comments from your view of a PDF page, allowing you to make corrections without the distraction of a marked-up PDF file. Simply print out the summary so that you have the hard copy at your fingertips as you edit the layout or comp in its authoring application. Summaries only work, however, if the comments themselves are well-prepared and explicit, since a summary doesn't include a specific reference for each comment (Figure 4-15). You can see who called out "wrong orientation" and when they did so, for example, but you can't do anything with the information unless it's clear what actually needs to be rotated. This is when it's helpful to remember that Acrobat automatically copies the relevant text into a sticky note when you select it with a graphic or text markup tool: Don't delete the text, but explain what to do with it, if necessary. Likewise, mention the graphic you're referencing in the sticky note when requesting that it be changed.

Finding comments. If you want to find a specific comment or comments in an annotated PDF document, you have two options: You can search for it by choosing Find from the Comments menu in the Comments palette, or by choosing Tools > Comments > Find (Figure 4-16). However, this search feature is fairly limited in that it only searches text strings inside comments or comment descriptions; you

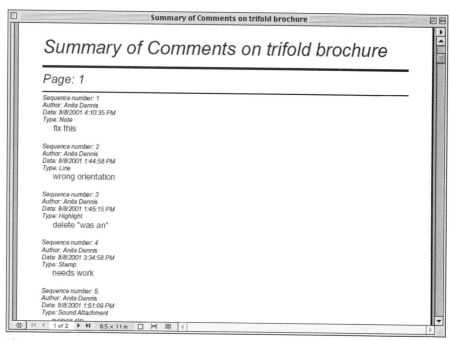

Figure 4-15 A summary of comments in a PDF document.

can't search for types of comments (such as sound or file attachments, or strike-throughs). If a comment is selected on the page, this function will only search that one comment; if no comments or annotations are selected, it will search them all. When it returns a

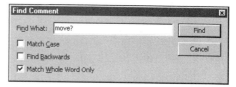

Figure 4-16 You can search comments using the Find Comment dialog box.

result, it highlights the annotation or comment icon on the page, not in the Comments palette and not in its sticky note (even if it's open), which can make it hard to see. Still, if you have a systematic way of calling out certain changes, such as writing "move?" in the note of any comment or annotation related to an image or graphic that may need to be repositioned, you can search for "move" to find all instances of that type of error. After you find one, click Find Again until they have all been uncovered.

Filtering comments. The other way to find specific comments is to filter them (Figure 4-17). In magazine publishing, for example, copy editors may be responsible for editorial changes, while the production department makes changes related to graphics and layout. But what if one PDF file has been circulated among all of the

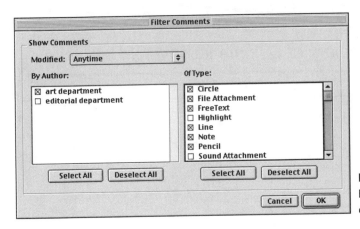

Figure 4-17 The Filter Comments dialog box.

editors and designers, each of whom reviews it in turn? In that case, you can use a filter to sort comments by type or author: Choose Tools > Comments > Filter. In the Filter Comments dialog box, choose whose comments you want to view and what types of comments and annotations to include. Using my magazine example, production might opt to view only comments from the art department, which would be created with either the comments or graphic markup tools. The copy edit department, then, might view only the editorial department's comments, made using the text markup tools. If someone marks up the PDF file once, turns it in, and then says, "Hey wait, I made a couple more changes; here's the file again," you can use the Modified pop-up menu to view only those comments created in the last 30 minutes, the last hour, six hours, or 24 hours, as appropriate. Click OK, and then only those comments you selected will appear on screen or print out in the open PDF file.

Be aware that if you select Deselect All and close the document, you'll hide comments in every PDF file you open thereafter (until you change the setting), including files viewed in a Web browser (more on that in "Sharing Comments Online," in a few paragraphs).

You may have already realized that my magazine example isn't terribly realistic. Given real-world deadline pressure, one proof is rarely circulated sequentially to multiple reviewers. More likely, the production manager would send multiple copies of the same PDF proof to every reviewer simultaneously, and then get back a whole slew of marked up documents—posing a challenge for the lucky folks who need to sort through and resolve conflicting requests. Most of the comment management features covered thus far work well for managing feedback from a single PDF file; however, Acrobat also offers some useful features for managing comments made on multiple PDF files.

Import and Export comments. One way of managing comments on multiple PDF files is to import and export them through a Form Data Format (FDF) document. Don't glaze over yet: It's not as complicated as it sounds. An FDF file, which is an Adobe-specific format, holds the comments as if they were form data and acts as an intermediary between two PDF files. You can't open an FDF file; you simply export comments from one PDF file to it, then import the FDF file into a second PDF file so that the comments can be added to those already in that second file. Assuming the two PDF files are identical except for comments, Acrobat places the comments from the first PDF file on the correct page and in the same location in the second. Acrobat also uses FDF files in other ways, such as digital signatures and especially for forms. See Chapter 7 for more on creating and using PDF forms.

For now, let's imagine a book publisher whose production manager has circulated a PDF file of the first layout of Chapter 1. The author, developmental editor, copy editor, and executive editor will all mark up their own files with comments and annotations. However, to make our example simple, we'll only have them comment on the copy (not the art or layout—yet). One lucky proofreader will be charged with inputting all of these reviewers' changes; to do this, the proofreader will want to see all comments on a single "master" PDF file.

If you were that proofreader, you would start by opening each marked-up PDF file and exporting its comments. Using the author's marked-up PDF file, for example, choose File > Comments. By default Acrobat uses the same document name but appends an FDF file extension. Change the name if you want to use a different convention but keep the FDF extension. Then click Save. Repeat this process until you have an FDF file for each reviewer's comments (that's four in my example).

Then open the original PDF file, sans comments. We'll now import all the comments into that original PDF file: Choose File > Import > Comments, or choose Import from the Comments menu (in the Comments palette). Don't be fooled, however: Even though you can Shift-click to select multiple FDF files simultaneously, Acrobat can't import them simultaneously. You must import from one at a time.

You can also filter comments before exporting them, or wait until they're all on the same page before you use a filter, whichever you prefer. If you filter them first, don't export using the command in the File menu. Instead, choose Export Selected from the Comments menu.

Sharing comments online. Being observant, I'm sure you'll notice that in Figure 4-18 one reviewer stamped the PDF file "Approved" when it still required changes. When you run into conflicting feedback—or even when you simply believe

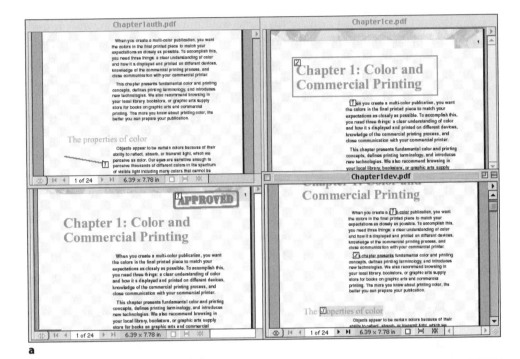

a

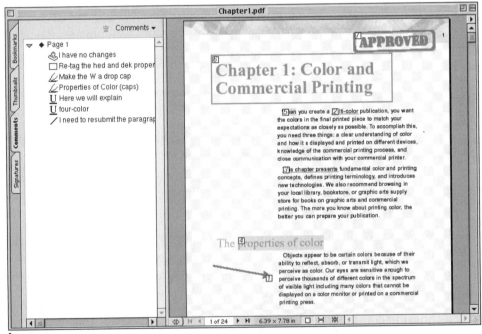

b

Figure 4-18 Using Acrobat's Export and Import Comments commands, you can consolidate comments from multiple PDF files (a) into a single file (b).

comments merit further discussion—Acrobat lets you share comments over a Web server. This way, everyone concerned can view the comments in a Web browser regardless of physical location. You can orchestrate an online session in which everyone views and marks up one PDF file simultaneously, or you can instruct people to review individual PDF files offline and then upload their comments.

Comments shared online are stored as FDF files in a user-specified repository, which can be a network file folder, an HTTP address on a WebDAV server, an ODBC or SQL server database, or an address on a Microsoft Web Discussions server (for real-time, interactive commenting sessions). If you plan to go this route, everyone who will be sharing comments through a server must work in a Web browser with the Acrobat plug-in, and Acrobat must be configured on each reviewer's system to recognize the repository (so that comments can be uploaded and downloaded). I'll explain how to configure Acrobat now; however, you may need help from a network administrator to set up others in the workgroup.

MOVING ONLINE

We're looking at a Web-oriented workflow, where clients review PDF pages on the Web and everything is centrally managed from the server. That's attractive because it keeps the customer in contact with us. When you just email pages you don't know who has it or who's read it. We also want to be sure that everybody has the same version, everybody reviews the same version. That's the beauty of a WebDAV server–based solution.

—Marco Cappuccio, digital technology manager, SS Studios

Start by configuring Acrobat's preferences: Choose Edit > Preferences > General, then click Online Comments from the left-hand list. In this panel (Figure 4-19), change the Server Type from None to whatever you're using—a networked folder in my example. Then identify your Server Settings. If you're using a networked folder, browse to select it. If you're using a Web Discussion server, you'll have to go to Internet Explorer to select the server itself; a network administrator can help if you're using an SQL or WebDAV server. When finished, click OK.

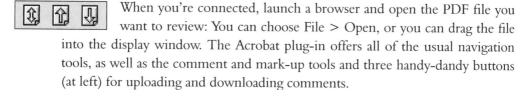

When you're connected, launch a browser and open the PDF file you want to review: You can choose File > Open, or you can drag the file into the display window. The Acrobat plug-in offers all of the usual navigation tools, as well as the comment and mark-up tools and three handy-dandy buttons (at left) for uploading and downloading comments.

After the reviewer has made her comments, she can click the Upload button to save them to the server as an FDF file. Uploaded comments are secure in that no one else can change them—they can only be read and added to but not deleted.

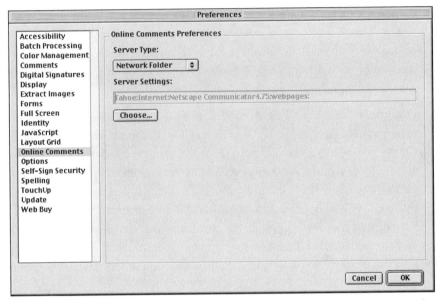

Figure 4-19 In Online Comments Preferences you specify the type and location of the repository for shared comments.

Note also that you can't edit the reviewer's identity in the browser because it's based on the log-in name in the Identity panel of your Preferences.

Now let's return to my book publishing scenario: The proofreader has compiled all of the reviewers' comments into one PDF file, put it on the company intranet, and emailed the executive editor to say, "Please look at this file in your browser." Being a responsive, deadline-conscious manager (whose log-in name just happens to be Anita Dennis), the executive editor promptly opens the PDF file in Internet Explorer. When she sees everyone's edits, she creates a note saying, "By all means, make everyone's changes." Then she clicks the Upload Comments button in the toolbar.

After a reasonable period has elapsed, the proofreader opens the Chapter 1 PDF file—with all of the original comments—again in her browser. She then clicks the Download Comments button, and Acrobat fetches the FDF file with that new comment and adds it to the PDF file in her browser window (Figure 4-20).

In addition to one-way uploading and downloading, Acrobat lets you do both at once, to synchronize the comments you see onscreen with more recent versions on the server. You can also work offline: Simply open the PDF file in your browser and save a copy of it to your hard drive (click the floppy disk icon). Once you've done this, you can annotate the copy at your leisure in Acrobat. When you're

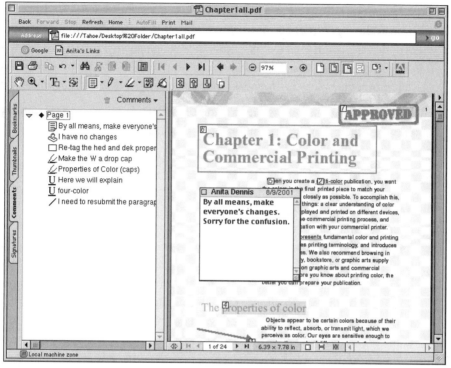

Figure 4-20 Our sample book chapter being viewed in Internet Explorer, after a reviewer has made comments online.

finished, choose File > Upload comments. Click Start when prompted, and Acrobat will upload the comments to the server and switch you over to your default browser to display the file there.

If you're going to share comments online, you'll need to do some planning for the process to work smoothly. Among other things, a network administrator should properly configure server preferences for everyone in the workgroup, as well as make sure that each member has a unique log-in name. JavaScripts can be used to automate the process for people who must frequently log on and off to review documents.

Members of the group may also need to be trained in how to locate files on the server, how to use Microsoft Web discussion threads, and how to follow version control procedures. Because they're saved as FDF files, shared comments exist apart from the original PDF file. If the original is moved or altered between the time it's put out for review and the time you download changes into the FDF file, the shared comments could be misplaced on the page (and that would be just the start of your problems).

In addition, if a reviewer hides comments in the browser, you won't be able to upload those comments. However, if you jump to another Web page or close the browser, the comments will be automatically uploaded. Thus, if they're not careful, reviewers can accidentally delete their comments from the server (luckily, you can't delete other people's comments—even if you hide or delete them while you work).

Finally, sharing comments online won't work if a PDF file has been encrypted to prevent others from annotating it.

Digital Sign-off

Acrobat also includes a digital signatures feature, which is the last link in the digital-collaboration food chain. You don't have to print out the final approved proof and request that the appropriate parties sign hard copies; rather, approval can be authorized digitally. A digital signature is more secure than a generic "Approved" comment stamp; it's even more secure than using password protection to restrict access to sensitive documents. A digital signature freezes the document in a particular state; any changes made after a signature is applied can be identified, tracked, and undone if they turn out to be unauthorized. Digital signatures can be "written" from within Web browsers when sharing comments online, and their authenticity can be verified by anyone who subsequently opens the signed document. In fact, multiple people can sign a PDF document, and the state of the document at the time of each signing can be validated.

Digital signatures can be used for more than just signing off proofs: You can use them to secure confidential documents (allowing only authorized individuals to comment or sign them), and you can employ them for all kinds of online forms and documents (expense reports, contracts, insurance claims, brokerage agreements, tax forms, and so on). In addition, digital signatures for e-commerce transactions and communications represent a burgeoning application. (For more about the legal aspects of digital signatures, see "The Fine Print on Digital Signatures.")

Like its handwritten counterpart, a digital signature provides a means of verifying a person's identity. And just as each written signature has unique characteristics, so do digital signatures. In Acrobat, digital signatures include information about the state of the document at the moment it was signed, as well as the date and time of the signing. This information is encrypted with a *private key,* which travels with the digital signature, as does a *public key,* or certificate. This public key decrypts the private key information and allows others to verify your signature's authenticity.

All of this key information is managed by what Acrobat calls a *handler*. The handler contains a profile of your signature—a password-protected file that determines the appearance and content of your signature and includes all of your key information. Acrobat ships with a default handler called Acrobat Self-Sign Security. Other handlers ship with Acrobat for Windows, and yet more are available from third parties. Signatures themselves can take one of three forms: a digitized version of your handwritten signature imported from a Palm Pilot; a graphic, image, or icon (logo) saved as PDF; or a typewritten name.

The Fine Print on Digital Signatures

Are digital signatures legally binding? The short answer is Yes. For the longer answer, keep reading:

In 2000, the Millennium Digital Commerce Act, also known as the E-Sign Act, became law, conferring on digital signatures the same legal status as the pen-and-ink variety. This federal law superceded legislation in several dozen states, granting legal status to technology that many government and business institutions are eager to adopt because it has the potential to dramatically ease contract management and record-keeping. The law also paves the way for advances in secure e-commerce transactions. Banking, insurance, farm equipment, health supplies, and freight services are just some of the industries that stand to benefit significantly from e-signatures.

Recognizing that many consumers are still nervous that electronic transactions are subject to deception and fraud, however, the E-Sign law includes a provision stating that companies cannot force e-signatures on consumers: Consumers must consent to use them, and companies must make them available in a form that's reasonably accessible. Given the fact that close to 200 million people have Acrobat Reader, one might argue that PDF is an appropriate technology for digital signatures. Although the law exempts many personal and sensitive types of contracts (for example, divorces, adoptions, and wills, as well as court orders, eviction notices, foreclosures, and utility cancellation), digital signatures are allowed (and likely to be legally binding) in work orders, contract proofs, bids, and proposals.

Before you can digitally sign documents, you have to select a handler, log in, and create a profile. Start in the Edit > Preferences > General dialog box. In the Digital Signatures panel (Figure 4-21), choose Acrobat Self-Sign Security as your handler (we'll use this for our example). Acrobat's Self-Sign handler uses a 1,024-bit industry-standard encryption algorithm from RSA for generating key pairs, and it uses the ITT's X.509 standard to encrypt certificates—industry standards used in Netscape Navigator and Internet Explorer, among other applications. (For a list of

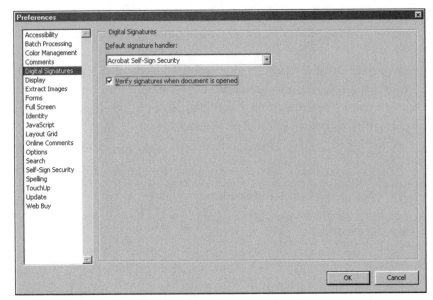

Figure 4-21 The Digital Signatures panel of the General Preferences dialog box.

alternate handlers from third-party developers, see Appendix One, page 293.) Check "Verify signatures when document is opened" if you want signatures on documents that you open to be automatically verified, and click OK.

Next, create a profile. Choose Tools > Self-Sign Security > Log In. (The procedure may vary for third-party plug-in handlers; consult their documentation for instructions.) The first time you log in, the User Profile File pop-up menu in the Self-Sign Security Log In dialog box will be blank: Click New User Profile to create one (Figure 4-22). Your log-in name (per Preferences) will be your user name, though you can change it if you want to. Stick with alphanumeric characters because many punctuation symbols ($, @, %, and &, for example) are off-limits. The user name will appear in the Signatures palette and signature field; I'll get to those shortly. Adding your business information is optional; however, a six-digit (or longer) password is required. You will use this password when you log in and sign documents. All of the information you enter here is encrypted and saved in your private key, and will be decryptable by your public key. When you're finished, click OK. At this point, you'll be prompted to save the profile with your user name and an .apf (Acrobat Self-Sign Security Profile File) extension. Adobe recommends saving the profiles in the Acrobat Preferences folder (Windows) or the Adobe Acrobat 5.0 folder (Mac). Click Save.

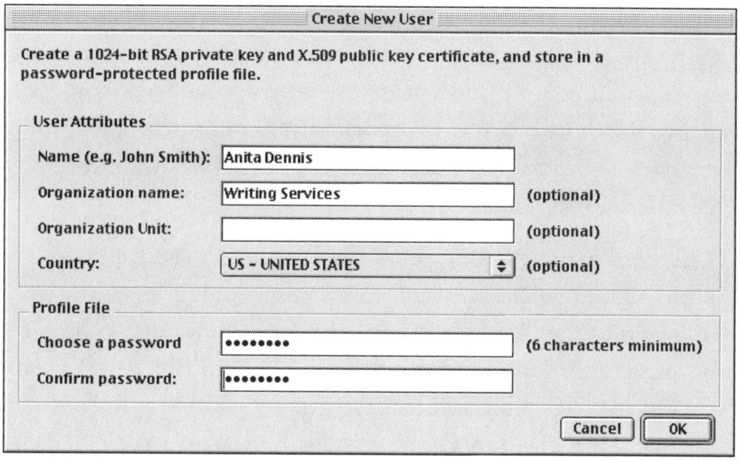

Figure 4-22 The Create New User profile dialog box.

Now you're logged in, but before you can begin to digitally sign documents, you must customize your user settings. Click the User Settings button in the Alert dialog box. If you clicked OK to bypass the alert, choose Tools > Self-Sign Security > User Settings. In the User Information panel (Figure 4-23), you can see your public key (certificate) information. Workgroup members can export their certificate files or email them to other group members so that everyone can build a list of known, trusted signatures, which you can import into the Trusted Certificates panel. It's a good idea to create a backup of your profile from the User Information panel in case it becomes lost or corrupted.

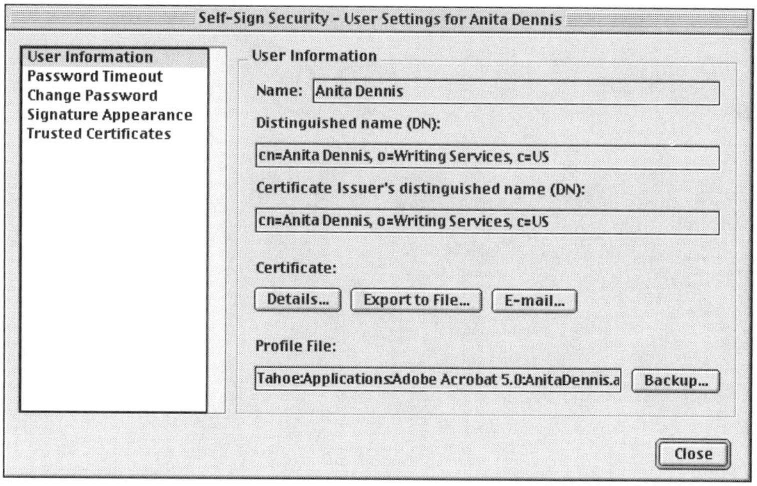

Figure 4-23 The User Information panel of the Self-Sign Security User Settings dialog box.

The password panels of the User Settings dialog box are straightforward: These are where you change your password and apply a "time-out" setting. By default, you must enter your password every time you sign a document; however, you can change that here by saying you never want to be prompted for a password, or that you want to be prompted only after a specified length of time has passed since you last entered your password at log-in.

Click on the Signature Appearance panel to set the appearance of your signature. Until you define the appearance, the list window is empty, so click New. In the Title field of the Configure Signature Appearance dialog box (Figure 4-24), name the appearance something intuitive. (Although this won't be shared with others, you'll want to be able to identify your signatures at a glance.) Under Configure Graphic, click the No Graphic radio button to make your signature a generic checkmark supplied by Acrobat; click Name to add a text version of your user name; or click Imported Graphic to select a custom PDF file or to import a signature from a Palm Pilot. If you use a graphic saved as PDF, Acrobat crops and sizes the file to fit in the signature field. In my example, I created a PDF in

a

b

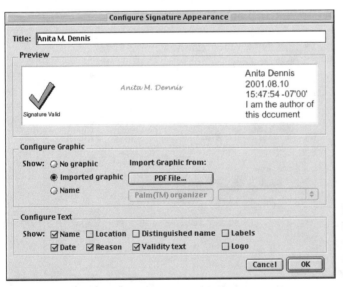

c

Figure 4-24 Your signature can be Acrobat's default checkmark (a), a text version of your user name (b), or an imported graphic (c).

Photoshop using Lucida Handwriting Italic. (Hint: Make your signature large, at least 100 points, so it's clearly visible on the page.) You can choose what key text information (name, date, and so on) you want to show with your signature, and it will appear on the document and in the Signatures palette.

 When you've finished customizing your user settings, you can begin to sign documents. Each time you sign, you have to log in (which you've already done if you've been following my instructions). If you created your handler and user profile previously, choose Tools > Self-Sign Security > Log In. Choose your profile, enter your password, and then click Log-In. To sign a document, either click on the Digital Signature tool and drag an area on the PDF file where you want to sign it, or choose Tools > Digital Signatures > Sign Documents, and you'll be prompted to drag with the mouse.

When you release the mouse button, the Self-Security Sign Document dialog box appears, asking for your password (assuming you haven't specified a time-out in your user profile). Enter it, then click Show Options (Figure 4-25). Now you can specify a reason for your signing the document, some contact information (if desired), and the appearance you wish to use. If you bypass options and just sign the document, Acrobat uses a standard text-based signature. When

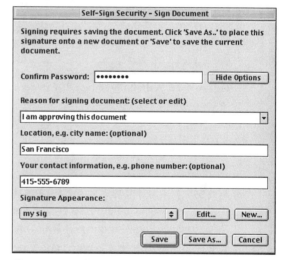

Figure 4-25 The Self-Sign Security Sign Document dialog box, with options showing.

you've finished entering all of the necessary information, either Save to overwrite the existing file or Save As under a new file name, depending on your version-control procedures (perhaps the file was already named for your approval).

Voilà: Your signature appears in the document window and the Signatures palette (Figure 4-26). All of your settings will remain in effect until you change them. You can create and use different appearances for various types of documents and signatures (one for "approved" and another for "changes needed," for example). However, if you sign documents that require different levels of security, you'll need to create multiple log-ins, or profiles. Since each has a unique password, you can

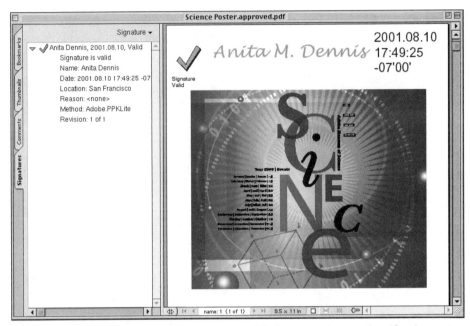

Figure 4-26 A digitally signed PDF document, with the name, date, and verification status in the Signatures palette.

have different log-ins for final versus comp proofs, for documents headed to production versus those headed to editorial, and so on—each with its own password.

You can also use invisible signatures that don't appear on the page but do appear in the Signatures palette. To create this type of signature, choose Tools > Digital Signatures > Sign Document Invisibly. This is useful if you know your document will be printed after it's signed and you don't want the signature to print, too. Keep the following in mind when working with signatures:

- If you delete a page containing a signature, you delete the signature, too.

- The first time a document is signed, you can Save or Save As and give the file a new name. The signature will be appended to the document, but if the document is subsequently re-signed, you must only choose File > Save. Choosing Save As again will invalidate signatures because the command essentially instructs Acrobat to redistill the file.

- When you sign a document in a Web browser, you aren't prompted to save the document; Acrobat saves only the signature data and any comments or annotations you added to the document as an FDF file. If you want to save the signed document on your system, you must click the Save a Copy button after you sign the document, and then specify a location for the file on your hard drive.

- If a PDF file has two signatures, you can compare them to see if they're the same (see next section).

- Signature certificates from multiple vendors aren't necessarily compatible. Thus, it's a good idea to pick one handler with the level of security and features you require, stick with it, and make sure everyone in the workgroup uses it. You can't, for example, import certificates from other applications into Acrobat's Self-Sign Security, but you can use Self-Sign certificates with other applications by encapsulating them in a standard syntax called PKCS#7—as long as the other signature application supports the standard. To make Self-Sign signatures compatible with other applications, go into Preferences and click Self-Sign Security from the list of panels. Before you create a profile, check the Use Certificate Message Syntax box.

The Signatures palette shows a document's signature history: Signatures appear in the order they were written, with the most recent at the bottom. A warning appears if the document was modified between signatures, and invalid signatures are flagged (Figure 4-27). To verify a questionable signature, click to select it with the Hand tool in the palette, then select Verify Signature from the Signature pop-up menu. Acrobat will compare the signature's certificate with those in your trusted list and validate the signature if it finds a match.

Figure 4-27 Signature palette icons, from top to bottom: invalid signature, valid signature, and modification warning.

To view a signature's properties, including its time and date stamp and the version of the document at the time of signing, toggle it open in the palette (click the right arrow on the Mac OS and the plus sign in Windows). You can also access this information (and verify signatures) by selecting the signature and choosing Properties from the Signatures pop-up menu (Figure 4-28). If Acrobat can't verify a signature, click Show Certificate to view all of the information Acrobat can glean about it, including author, serial number, encryption method, and fingerprint data. When you're satisfied that the signature is valid, you can add its certificate to your list of trusted certificates by closing the dialog box and clicking Verify Identity in the Properties dialog box. In the Verify Identities dialog box, click the Add to List button.

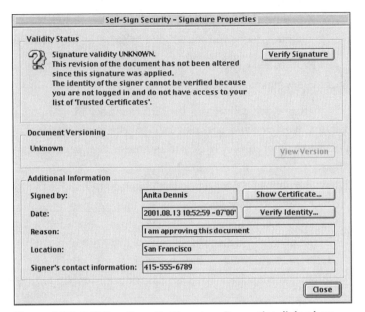

Figure 4-28 Self-Sign Security Signature Properties dialog box.

If you're the one creating and circulating the proof that needs to be signed, you can streamline the process by creating form fields where you want reviewers to sign off—kind of like the old days when you'd smack a red stamp on the page with blank lines for each reviewer's initials. This way, reviewers don't have to drag a signature box on the page, and you can specify that certain actions must occur when the field is signed (for example, making the field read-only). I'll get into forms more in Chapter 7, but creating one signature field is easy: Use the Form tool to drag on the PDF file where you want the

Figure 4-29 The Signature form Field Properties dialog box.

field to be located. When you release the mouse, the Field Properties dialog box will appear (Figure 4-29).

If you select Signature from the Type pop-up menu, Acrobat will offer three tabbed boxes: Appearance, Actions, and Signed. First, give the field a name and description (the former appears in the field when you're editing forms; the latter appears when a reviewer rolls the cursor over the field), then customize its appearance. In the Actions palette you can associate an action with the reviewer's mouse movement (for example, playing a sound when the mouse exits the field). I can't think of many useful applications for these actions when signing off on graphic arts documents, but they do jazz up interactive forms. In the Signed palette, you may want to make fields unalterable (read only) once they've been signed for more security.

If you want a reviewer's signature on every page of a multipage document, use the Duplicate command: Right-click in Windows or Control-click on the Mac, and choose Duplicate to copy the field to multiple pages (or select the field and copy and paste it). Since it's the same field, a reviewer only has to sign once for his or her signature to repeat in all instances of the field. If you want reviewers to actually read each page and sign off independently—and allow for different types of signatures, if one page is approved but another needs work, for example—you must manually create individual signature fields, even if they all have the same properties.

When a reviewer clicks on a signature field, she's prompted to sign it as usual: She'll have to log in and complete the Sign Document dialog box (Figure 4-25).

Comparing Documents

You already know that the Signatures palette can give you a heads-up if a document has been modified between signings. Well, Acrobat can warn you in a different way as well. It allows you to compare two versions of a signed document (or any PDF file) page by page to identify authorized and unauthorized changes. Acrobat can find differences from the page to the pixel level, including different font styles, edited text, moved or altered graphic objects, and changes to entire pages (pages missing or added, out of order, changed orientation).

To see the differences between two versions of a signed document, choose Tools > Compare > Two Versions of a Signed Document. If the document is open, it should appear in the Document pop-up menu of the Compare Document Revisions dialog box (Figure 4-30). Otherwise, click Choose and browse to find the signed document whose versions you want to compare. Acrobat automatically recognizes the states of the document at each signature, and you can choose which two you want to compare from the Compare and To pop-ups. Now choose the parameters you want to compare: font information, text content, or visual changes to

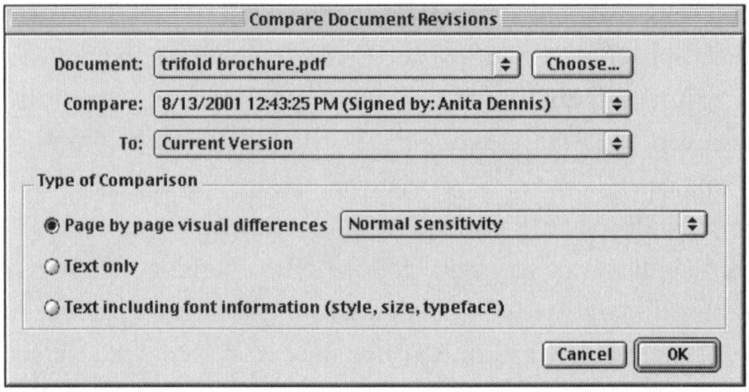

Figure 4-30 The Compare Document Revisions dialog box is the same as the Compare Documents dialog box.

pages. If you choose the last, you must specify how closely you want to compare—the more sensitive the comparison, the more slowly the results will be returned. (To compare two different documents, you use a slightly different command—Tools > Compare > Two Documents—but it summons up the same dialog box.)

Acrobat returns results in the form of a new PDF file: This file includes a summary page for each page of the document that changed between versions, and it indicates what types of discrepancies it found—visual differences, text differences, and so on. The comparison PDF file also provides marked-up versions of the pages where it detected changes. These pages are identified with red headers (which are actually Free Text annotations), and changes are marked with magenta Pencil annotations. You can use the Comments palette to navigate them. If a page has been added or deleted between versions, or if the discrete documents are of different page lengths, Acrobat places a blank, placeholder page with the corresponding page in the other document.

Despite all of these indications, you'll still have to study the documents closely to discern changes. Acrobat will circle the block of text where it detected a change; however, you must read it to figure out what was added or deleted. Keep in mind, too, that some changes may not be noticeable: For example, a changed bounding or crop box could well be invisible. Finally, Acrobat's Compare Documents feature won't tell you if the files were distilled differently, though if compression varied significantly between versions, the software might flag the image on the page.

In addition, although Acrobat identifies changes, you still have to figure out where those changes were introduced—Acrobat (an added comment) or the authoring application (which might mean you have to redistill the second version of the file).

Version-control concerns could surface here: If edits were made in different applications at different times, you might ultimately have to return to the authoring application to generate a fresh, final PDF file to serve as your digital master file.

Editing Content

Once you've identified all of the changes that need to be made to a PDF file, you must determine where and how to make them. In most instances, you'll have to return to the authoring application—to retouch images, for example, or to make extensive text edits (that is, anything that affects fit and flow). Acrobat does, however, offer a handful of features for minor touch-ups that can save you the trouble of returning to another application and then redistilling the file. Approach these features with caution, though, because not only are they fairly limited, any changes you make in the PDF file won't be reflected in the original application file used to distill it. Thus, if you ever have to redistill the PDF file, you're liable to either reproduce it with the same mistakes or be forced to reconstruct the edited piece— both of which cost time and money. Use Acrobat's tools to slightly reposition graphics or fix typos in comps, but for more intensive changes, you're safer editing the source files in their original applications and redistilling the PDF file.

Editing Text

Considering Acrobat's myriad collaboration features, its Touch-up Text feature is at first blush disappointing. Although editing text in Acrobat sounds great, you can quickly encounter roadblocks—especially if you don't have the fonts used in the document on your computer, which is essential for maintaining the integrity of page designs from comp through final prepress. If you don't have the document's fonts, performing such routine editing tasks as fixing typos or changing a font from italic to Roman can be an exercise in futility; also, Undo is almost nonexistent. If you're not careful about each change, you'll find yourself forced to close the file without saving and then start up again. (Tip: Back up your file *before* you edit it.) These limitations, however, are forgiveable since Acrobat is not a page-layout application—or an imaging or illustration application. You shouldn't expect its tools to compare with the ones you'd find in those types of applications.

Before you start editing text in Acrobat, it's essential that you do two things: First, as I said, make sure you have all of the fonts used in the document on your hard drive; then, tell Acrobat to display and print them. If you attempt to edit fonts in a PDF file and Acrobat can't access them, all bets are off. At the very least, you won't be able to change their typeface or add or change characters (except to delete them). And at worst, none of the tasks described below will work reliably without generating Multiple Master substitute fonts.

As you learned in Chapter 3, you should always embed and subset at 100 percent all fonts contained in PDF files distilled for graphic arts workflows—something Distiller's default job options don't necessarily do. Thus, you may find that fonts are handled differently within a document. The eBook job option, for example, embeds and subsets all fonts except Base 14 fonts; the Screen job option, which you may use to generate onscreen proofs, doesn't embed fonts at all. In any case, you can't tell by glancing at a document what fonts it contains or how they're handled.

For this reason, before you start mucking around with a PDF file's text, open the document and choose File > Document Properties > Fonts. The Document Fonts dialog box, discussed in greater detail in Chapter 3, lists all of the fonts in the currently displayed page; clicking List All Fonts displays all of the fonts in the document. The dialog box specifies whether fonts are embedded or subset, if they're substitutes created from a Multiple Master or simply a version of the typeface found on the hard drive, and how each one was encoded. Once you see what's used, you can determine whether they're installed on your computer before you start editing. Then make sure you've told Acrobat to use them: Choose View > Use Local Fonts. This will save you tremendous headaches once you start editing.

 Touchup Text tool. Acrobat's Touchup Text tool lets you make simple corrections to text in a PDF file without having to return to the page-layout application. It works with rotated and vertical type as well as plain old horizontal type. It even works with text on a path (treating each letter as a line on a path), letting you change font attributes; add, delete, or change characters; and adjust the position of lines of text.

The Touchup Text tool lets you modify text characteristics one line at a time: When you click with it on some text on a page, Acrobat selects the entire line. You can then use the I-beam cursor to select individual letters or words and add, delete, or change text on the page. If you increase the line length, Acrobat expands the bounding box and doesn't rewrap; justified text may require some finessing of tracking and word spacing if you make any significant changes to a line. If your layout has hanging (ragged) columns, you can take advantage of the ability to add a line with the Touchup Text tool by Option/Ctrl-clicking on the page. Place your cursor carefully: Once you click, you're committed to the vertical location. You can, however, adjust the position of the line horizontally by dragging with the bounding box's left handle.

If you're editing vertical or rotated text or text on a path, you'll have to adapt to how the cursor arrows move on the page: The left and right arrows move the selected line to the left and right, respectively; the up and down arrows move the cursor between letters and words. This is the inverse of how the arrow keys work with horizontal text.

Choose Tools > Touchup Text > Text Attributes to access the Text Attributes palette (Figure 4-31). Here, you can make extensive modifications to type characteristics—for example, changing point size, adjusting tracking and word spacing values, tweaking indents and alignments, and editing colors.

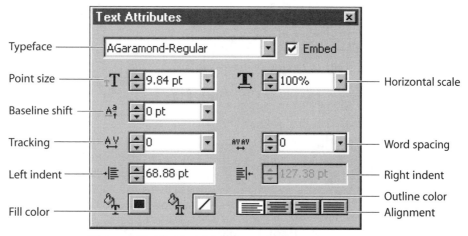

Figure 4-31 The Text Attributes palette.

Notice the Embed checkbox in the Text Attributes palette: If the font on the line you've selected is embedded and/or subset, this box will be checked. If you uncheck this box, Acrobat will change *all* of the characters in your document that use this font. In other words, by unchecking this box, you unembed *all* of the characters in this particular typeface.

If, however, the font (or fonts) of the text on the line is *not* embedded, you can check this box to embed all instances of the font in the file. When you visited the Document Fonts dialog box earlier, you may have wondered what you should do if you received files whose fonts were not embedded; here's your answer: You can embed them by checking this box. Keep in mind, however, that if Acrobat generated a Multiple Master substitute font when it opened the PDF file, you'll be embedding the substitute, not the original typeface. Checking Embed neither subsets the font nor updates the status of the new font in the Document Fonts dialog.

When you add or change text using the Touchup Text tool, Acrobat studies the surrounding text on the line to determine the font for the new characters. If the font of the surrounding text is unembedded (but installed on your hard drive) or substituted with Mac or Windows encoding, you can add or change text with a high degree of confidence that Acrobat will generate the new characters from the installed (but unembedded) font or from a Multiple Master, respectively. The text you add should appear identical to that which is already on the page, even though Acrobat may encode the new characters differently.

Unfortunately, however, if you add or change text in a line of type that's embedded *and/or* subset—even if the font is installed on your hard drive—the way that Acrobat generates the new or changed characters is liable to cause them to appear different from the other text in the line. For example, if the line of text uses an embedded but non-system font, Acrobat will generate a custom-encoded Multiple Master substitution for the new characters. The difference in such substitute fonts can be quite dramatic (Figure 4-32). And even if the line of text is an embedded system font, Acrobat's custom encoding may render the new characters slightly differently from the rest of the text on the line.

Figure 4-32 The word *lazy* on the left is Korinna Regular, embedded in the PDF document. When I added the word *lazy* on the left with the Touchup Text tool, Acrobat created a Multiple Master sans serif version of the typeface. The clipped serifs are especially noticeable at 400 percent (bottom), but the difference is also apparent at 100 percent (top).

Know, too, that when you add or change text on a line, the newly generated characters assume the embedding status of the surrounding text. If you type in new text using an unembedded font, you should manually embed it—and all unembedded fonts—in the Text Attributes palette so that it travels with the document to your service provider.

You're also likely to encounter problems with fonts (embedded or not) when you try to change their typeface. Basically, any time you attempt to change a font to a face that's not used in the file, you'll get a warning box telling you that Acrobat will custom-encode with the new font, which may well be a Multiple Master substitute even if you have the desired font installed. And, in case you didn't notice, you can't change a Roman typeface to italic, bold, or another style in the Text Attributes palette; if you attempt to do so here, you're liable to render a substitute italic or bold font. If you do manage to change a Roman face to italic or bold (or a stylized face back to Roman), be sure to adjust word spacing on the line to avoid crashing letters and unsightly gaps.

What all of this amounts to is that the only time Acrobat makes new characters that are *exactly* the same as the other characters on the line is when they're non-embedded system fonts—which you probably don't use too often. For this reason, you may want to make your text changes in the authoring application you used to generate the PDF file, or use a suitable plug-in (see Appendix One for a list of plug-ins that can be used to edit PDF files).

The Touchup Text feature does, however, have one other trick up its sleeve: Called Fit Text to Selection, this command is located under the Tools > Touchup Text menu on the Mac or in the tool's context menu (right-click) in Windows. This command expands or contracts edited text to fit a particular selection on the line. You could use it, for example, to spell out abbreviations or abbreviate full words. To use the command, drag with the Touchup Text tool to select the space allotted for the edited text (perhaps a word or the whole line), and choose the Fit Text to Selection command, then type in your new text. The text you input will fit in the selected space without affecting other words on the line.

More Touchup Text Tidbits

A couple of other commands to notice in the Tools > Touchup Text submenu: Text Breaks; Insert Line Break, Soft-Hyphen, Non-breaking Space, and Em-Dash; Show Capture Suspects; and Find First Suspect.

- Text Breaks and the ability to insert such characters as soft hyphens and line breaks are used in conjunction with reflowing tagged PDF files.
- Finding and showing capture suspects are for reviewing and correcting pages that have been scanned into a bitmapped PDF page and then captured to editable text. If Acrobat can't decide how to convert an area of bitmapped text into editable characters, you can search for those "suspects" and correct or accept Acrobat's suggested text.

Finally, the 1-2-3 Touchup Order tool on the toolbar is used to reflow tagged PDF files: You can click on tagged elements, which appear numbered (like sequential comments), and rearrange their order. To learn more on creating and using tagged PDF files, see Chapter 7, page 247.

When you begin working with the Touchup Text tool, you may also notice that your fonts' point size is sometimes smaller than what you specified in your authoring application (for example, 9.84 instead of 10 points) in the Text Attributes palette. Don't blame it on Acrobat! This sometimes occurs when the authoring application goes through GDI or QuickDraw to define its fonts en route to Distiller. (This tends to happen with Microsoft Word but not with page-layout applications.)

In addition, you may notice that sometimes the Embed checkbox is grayed out when you edit text, or that after you check it, it grays out, making your embedding decision irreversible. This occurs when you're working with system fonts or elaborate display or script typefaces.

Editing Graphics

Although they're fairly limited, at least Acrobat's graphics editing capabilities won't surprise you by substituting approximations! You can add, delete, and reposition graphics, images, and line art (though not with the precision of a page-layout application), and you can quickly and easily jump to Photoshop or Illustrator for further editing. You still have to be careful about editing within Acrobat or even jumping to an imaging application for touch-up: If the image was placed in and distilled from a page-layout application, that file won't reflect your changes. Thus, you need to pay attention to where changes are made during the design and proofing phases, so that you can produce a final PDF file from the authoring application using the most current versions of images, text, and graphics.

 Touchup Object tool. Acrobat's Touchup Object tool is the key to the program's graphics editing capabilities. Use it to select an object on a PDF page, and you can employ all the commands and tricks you'd expect for routine positioning tasks such as cutting and copying graphics to the Clipboard and pasting them elsewhere in the page or document. Shift-click lets you select multiple objects; Select All selects all of the graphic objects—including text objects—on the PDF page. Any command you then apply, including Delete, affects all selected objects.

You can drag to reposition selected objects or use the arrow keys to nudge objects by 1-pixel increments (in whatever direction the arrow is pointing). Although Acrobat doesn't include rulers, you can toggle on a grid to help with positioning: Choose View > Grid to see it, and toggle on Snap to Grid to prevent objects from being slightly askew if you drag them around the page. (Define the grid in the Layout Grid panel of the General Preferences dialog box.)

The Touchup Object tool also includes some useful commands in its context menu (right-click the mouse in Windows or Control-click on the Mac). You can Paste in Front or Paste in Back of other objects selected on a page. If an object has been clipped, such as an EPS object by a clipping path or a text object by a clip box, you can remove it and view the unclipped object by choosing Delete Clip.

To actually touch up the pixels or vectors in an image or graphic object in Acrobat, you must return to an appropriate application, such as Photoshop or Illustrator. As long as those applications directly read and write PDF files (which Photoshop and Illustrator do), you can link to them from within Acrobat. Remember what I said earlier, however, about maintaining version control: Changes you make to a PDF object in one of these other applications are not automatically saved to the raw image, and they're definitely not saved to the image as it may be placed in a page layout file. So even though it's convenient to jump to Photoshop from within Acrobat to quickly fix red-eye or erase a dust speck from a scan, you must pay attention to which files are edited and make sure you don't introduce mistakes (or actually fail to correct them) for later—and especially final—versions of layouts.

That said, configure Acrobat to recognize your desired image and page or object editor by choosing Edit > Preferences > General, and selecting the TouchUp panel (Figure 4-33). I've chosen Photoshop as my image editor and Illustrator as

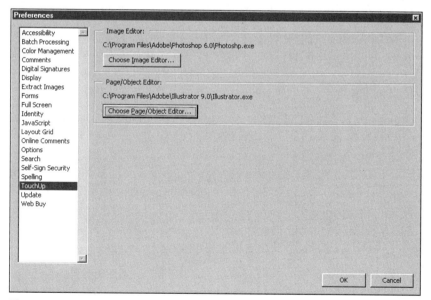

Figure 4-33 In the TouchUp Preferences dialog box, choose the image and graphics applications to which you want to link Acrobat objects.

my object editor. (QuarkXPress is not an option because it can't directly read or write to PDF.) Photoshop must be version 5.0 or later; Illustrator must be 7.0 or later. If you're still using Photoshop 5.0 or 5.5, make sure the PDFFormat plug-in that came with the application is installed, so that the image you edit can be saved back into the PDF document. (Otherwise, it will be saved to disk in its original format.) Better yet, upgrade: You're also restricted to editing the image as a single layer if you jump to Photoshop 5.0 from within Acrobat.

After you've chosen an application, select an image object on a PDF page using the Touchup Object tool. Then choose Edit Image from the context menu. Acrobat launches Photoshop and displays the object there: In the title bar you can see that the object is a temporary PDF file. You're *not* editing the original image; rather, you're viewing and editing distilled color data on the image. This means that if you instructed Distiller (in the Color panel of your job options) to convert images from RGB to CMYK or you applied any color profiles, the color in this temporary PDF file might appear different than the original image file. If you're prompted by a Profile Mismatch warning dialog box when Photoshop opens the image, opt to use the embedded profile; don't convert it. And if your goal is to edit the color values of pixels, just be aware that the color values you're seeing and applying may differ from those in the original file—which means you may ultimately have to redo your work there. (Although you can change color modes, you begin to compromise image integrity if you do this multiple times.)

Color concerns aside, as long as you're using Photoshop 6.0, you can change the image in just about any way you want to: You can add text, apply filters, use brushes, and so on. The only thing you can't do is apply masks. And if you resize an image, be aware that its alignment on the PDF page may be affected.

The process is pretty much the same for accessing Illustrator from within Acrobat: Select an object with the Touchup Object tool and choose Edit Object from the context menu. Acrobat will launch Illustrator and display the graphic there, letting you edit it as desired: make transformations, edit type, and apply filters and effects. If you distilled the original PDF file out of Illustrator as an Acrobat 5.0 (PDF 1.4) file and maintained transparency, you can go back and edit the transparency of the objects now. If you didn't maintain transparency, however, you won't be able to edit blends, gradients, or other transparent effects.

After you've made your changes to the image or graphic, choose File > Save. Then, hop back over to Acrobat, and you'll see the changes in the image or graphic in the PDF document. You can go back and forth between the applications as often as necessary until you're satisfied with your changes.

You can also choose Save As to save a version of the touched-up image or graphic in another format, or to save a copy of it. Choosing Save As does *not* apply the changes to the object in the PDF file. Be careful about overwriting the original image or graphic: Your safest bet is to keep the original image intact in case you need it later.

EXTRACTING CONTENT

In addition to being able to edit page content in Acrobat, the software also offers a few ways to export text and graphics into other applications. If, for example, you make changes to a PDF file and want to go back and preserve them in the application file, you can take advantage of Acrobat's ability to extract content and use it in other files. I'd argue, however, that it's much easier to make the changes in the original application (be it Photoshop or InDesign) in the first place. Acrobat's text and image extraction capabilities are much better suited to repurposing content—that is, when you want to use pages or contents of specific PDF files for new projects destined for print or the Web. However, since these capabilities are often mentioned in the same breath as Acrobat's editing tools, I'll explain them to you now.

You can move PDF text and graphics into another app in one of two ways: copy it or export it.

To copy all of the text from a PDF file, choose File > Save As, then choose Rich Text Format as your format. The RTF file, stripped of graphic objects, can be opened by any standard word processing application or placed in any professional page-layout application. If the PDF file was tagged, formatting (such as tabbed tables) is preserved; if not, formatting is lost. (Windows users have a work-around with the Table/Formatted Text Select tool; see below.)

You can also use Save As to save a PDF document in a common image file format, such as JPEG, TIFF, or even EPS. In multipage PDF documents, each page becomes its own image file. Acrobat pops up a Save As dialog box where you can name the file and choose a destination; click the Settings button to choose interlace, compression, resolution, color space, and other options specific to each format. (If you forget, it's not a big deal; the default options should suffice.)

To extract the graphics in a PDF document (rather than save PDF pages as graphics), choose File > Export > Extract Images As, and choose the format you'd like to save them as (TIFF, JPEG, or PNG). In the Extract Images and Save As dialog box, you're also prompted with a Settings button so that you can customize the resulting image files' parameters. In the Extract Images panel of the General Preferences dialog box, you can specify the smallest size image to extract.

To extract small amounts of text or individual graphics, you can use the **Text Select** and **Graphic Select** tools, respectively (top and middle icons). Click and drag with the tool over the content you want to select, and then use the Copy and Paste commands to save the text or object to the Clipboard before you open it in another application. In addition, you can use the **Column Select** tool (bottom icon) and drag to select entire column, and you can choose Edit > Select All to select all text (or all of the graphics, depending on which tool is selected) on the viewable page or pages.

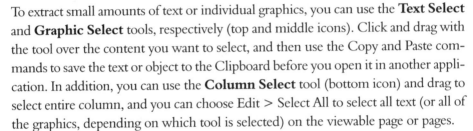

Windows users have one other option: the **Table/Formatted Text Select** tool, which lets you extract selected text while maintaining formatting and tabbed tables. Use it to drag and select an area of text or a table, and then either drag and drop the selection into another application (such as Word), copy it to the Clipboard for pasting elsewhere, or save it as RTF or ANSI text. With the text selected, use the context menu to specify whether to disregard line breaks (Text > Flow), to maintain them (Text > Preserve Line Breaks), or to retain table formatting, including rows and columns (Table). Horizontal is for tables using Roman fonts; Vertical is for Japanese fonts.

After you specify the type of formatting you want to apply, choose what to do with the text: Copy it or choose Save As, and specify the file type. ANSI, Unicode, or RTF are the safest options, especially if you've used symbols; ANSI is also good for Japanese text.

In the Table/Formatted Text Preferences dialog box, click the General tab to set global preferences for the Table/Formatted Text Select tool (Figure 4-34). Choose whether it recognizes selected text by default as a table or as text, how line breaks are recognized, how table cells are formatted, and how characters and paragraphs are formatted for RTF export.

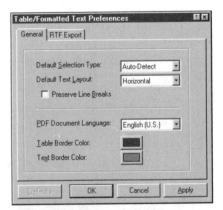

Figure 4-34 Table/Formatted Text Select Preferences dialog.

Managing Pages

Imagine we just zoomed out on the screen so that we're now looking at entire pages in a PDF document. Acrobat has a number of tools for managing PDF pages in one or more files—all of which you'll find useful for repurposing PDF files. These tools provide you with ways to edit pages (crop and rotate) and reconfigure files (by adding, deleting, and otherwise shuffling pages). If you string individual files together to create large PDF documents (as described in Chapter 3), you'll also find many of these commands handy—you may need these tools to move pages, crop or rotate them (to make them uniform), or renumber them. Note that all of the following commands are accessible from both the Document menu and the Thumbnail menu on the Thumbnails palette.

SECURE EXCHANGE

We use PDF to put some of our maps in electronic form, either on the Web, on CD-ROMs, or just to email to government agencies that need our maps for one reason or another. We don't want to give them editable files, so almost every time a PDF goes out of here I make sure it is secured so that they can't go back and open it in Illustrator. We put a lot of energy and time into the production of our product and we don't want someone to grab it and start producing it as their own. It's a matter of copyright.

—Richard Dey, senior cartographer, California State Automobile Association

Extract Pages. We talked earlier about extracting text from PDF pages, as well as extracting graphics and entire pages as graphics files. You can also extract pages from a PDF document and save them as individual PDF page files—useful for repurposing PDF content as well as for circulating pages of documents that have undergone changes since the last round of review.

Although you can use Save As to extract text or graphics in other file formats, this is *not* the way you extract pages of a PDF document: If you Save As and choose Adobe PDF Files as your format or type, you'll get a new saved version of the entire PDF document, including any changes you've made to it or notes you've slapped on. To extract individual pages, use the Extract Pages command. In the Extract Pages dialog box (Figure 4-35), specify the range of pages you wish to extract, as well as whether you want to delete them from the original. (Yes, the pages must be consecutive.) When you click OK, Acrobat displays the page or pages in a new file, appropriately named "Pages from_.pdf," where the blank is the name of the original file.

Figure 4-35 The Extract Pages dialog box.

You must then manually save this file, being sure to choose .pdf as your file format or type.

Insert Pages. Once you've extracted pages from one file, you may want to place them into another. Not a problem: Simply open the PDF file that you want to add the pages to, and choose Insert Pages. Acrobat will prompt you to select the file you want to insert (Shift-click to select multiple files); when you click Select, Acrobat gives you the Insert Pages dialog box (Figure 4-36). Here you can specify where you want the new pages to fall in the document—before or after the first, last, or other specific page in the document.

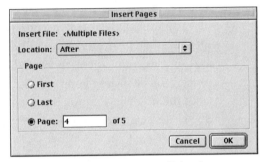

Figure 4-36 The Insert Pages dialog box.

Move and copy thumbnails. You can also put pages from one PDF file into another by moving or copying their thumbnails (another good reason to create thumbnails when you distill files). In addition, you can use thumbnails to reorder pages within a document. Choose Thumbnails from the Window menu. With the Thumbnails palette displayed, click to select one or Shift-click to select multiple pages. Although you can select the entire thumbnail, it's easier to select the page-number icon at the bottom. Drag to move the pages to a new position in the Thumbnails palette in the same document, watching the position bar to see where they're placed. Copy pages the same way by pressing Option (Mac) or Ctrl (Windows) as you drag. Use thumbnails to copy or move pages to another document by having it open onscreen, too, and dragging into the target document's Thumbnails palette. Acrobat automatically updates the page numbers on the thumbnails in all documents when you release the mouse.

Replace Pages. When you copy or move page thumbnails to another PDF file, you add them to that document. If you want to replace a page (or pages) in one PDF file with a page (or pages) from another, use the Replace Pages command. Open and display the document containing the pages you want to replace, and choose Replace Pages from the Thumbnails or Document menu. Acrobat will prompt you to select a file or files that you want to place in the open one. Make your selection and click Select. Acrobat will display the Replace Pages dialog box (Figure 4-37), confirming your request and prompting you to specify which pages in the original should be replaced by the pages in the selected PDF file. After you click OK, Acrobat prompts you again to confirm. Be certain of your choices here: There's no undo.

You can also use thumbnails to replace pages by dragging and dropping them onto page thumbnails in a second document. This isn't quite the same as moving them:

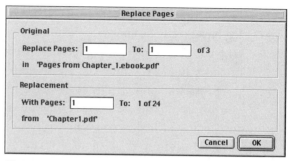

Figure 4-37 The Replace Pages dialog box.

Drag the thumbnail directly onto the page you want to replace (rather than position it between two pages). Release the mouse, and Acrobat replaces the old pages with those you dragged on top of them.

Delete Pages. Use the Delete Pages command to remove a selected page or range of pages from a PDF document.

Rotate Pages. Once you get the right mix of pages in your PDF file, you may need to tweak them to get them to fit properly. The Rotate Pages command can help. In the Rotate Pages dialog box, you can rotate pages in just about any permutation you desire (Figure 4-38): You can rotate the selected page (Shift-click on page thumbnails to select discrete pages), all pages, or a range of pages. After making your selection, you can apply the rotation to odd- and/or even-numbered pages, and you can opt to rotate by orientation: landscape and/or portrait. However, you can't freely rotate: The transform must be applied in 90-degree increments (clockwise or counterclockwise). It's meant to reorient pages between landscape and portrait modes, nothing fancy.

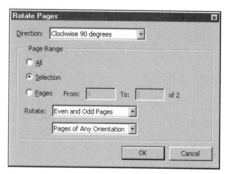

Figure 4-38 The Rotate Pages dialog box.

Crop tool. The Crop tool lets you adjust margins on individual pages or globally—though since you can't see every page onscreen in long documents, it's safer to perform crops on one visible page at a time. Start by making sure you're in Single Page mode (select it from the View menu). Then navigate to the page that you want to crop and drag a bounding box with the Crop tool. (You can drag on corner handles to resize.) When you're satisfied, press Return or double-click inside the crop box to display the Crop Pages dialog box (Figure 4-39). You can also get to this dialog box directly by choosing the Crop Pages command. You can further refine the crop box here: Either enter precise measurements in the various margin text boxes or check Remove White Margins to crop the page to the outermost edges of the page's graphic content. The cropped page size displays interactively as you edit, and you can always click Set to Zero to undo your choices. When you've finished doing this, indicate whether you want to crop a range of pages (specifying odd, even, or both). Unless you're absolutely certain of what the other pages in the document contain, just crop the one visible page. Click OK to apply the crop.

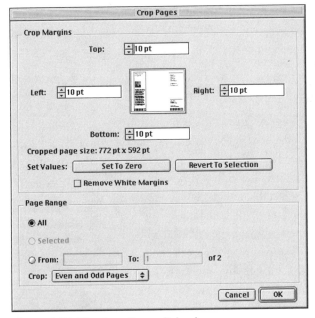

Figure 4-39 The Crop Pages dialog box.

Plug-ins

Thus far, I've only described what you can accomplish using Acrobat's collaborative editing tools; however, there is a plethora of third-party plug-ins out there that offer complementary—and often more robust—collaboration and editing tools for PDF files. Enfocus' PitStop Professional, for example, lets you edit text, but instead of creating substitutes when Acrobat would, it lets you choose from available alternative fonts. Lantana's Stratify PDF, meanwhile, lets you enhance PDF files with layers, which designers are accustomed to using in page-layout applications.

You can place objects or entire pages on layers, giving added functionality to the editing and printing processes.

PitStop and Stratify PDF are just two of many useful Acrobat plug-ins that facilitate everything including editing, prepress, forms, document management, Web publishing, and more. Some are described in the next chapter. Also see Appendix One at the back of the book for a more complete list of the most popular and useful PDF plug-ins for graphic arts design and production workflows.

PROOFING TOOLS

With Acrobat's built-in support for ICC color management and Adobe's standard implementation of color management across all of its professional publishing applications, soft proofing is becoming an increasingly viable activity in Acrobat. Even if you're leery of signing off on onscreen color, you can use Acrobat's proofing features to view color onscreen consistently across Adobe applications, to simulate various CMYK printing conditions onscreen, and to manage the color that's produced in an inkjet comp, for example, as well as in a final contract proof. Hopefully, over time, you'll learn to trust color management and begin working with your prepress partners to create reliable profiles for your workflow. This way, you can closely approximate onscreen what will actually be printed on the press.

Color Management Preferences

You may recall from Chapter 3 that your first opportunity to apply color management to PDF files comes when they're distilled. However, before you view any PDF file onscreen with an eye toward color, you should find out from the document creator whether and how color management was applied (you won't find this info in Acrobat). The options you specify in Preferences affect the way unmanaged color PDF files are displayed; any color management applied to the file when it was distilled takes precedence over specifications you make when viewing the PDF file in Acrobat.

Since there's so much overlap among color controls across Adobe applications, it's easy (though not essential) to use consistent color preferences—the same working spaces and color engine—in all programs, thereby dramatically reducing surprising color shifts. Equally important is making certain that everyone in a workgroup viewing color-managed documents uses the same settings. If all of your team members have calibrated monitors, use the same engine to make color conversions, and apply the same profiles; it goes a long way toward establishing confidence in the color you see and print.

In Acrobat, choose Preferences > General from the Edit menu, then choose the Color Management panel (Figure 4-40). From the Settings pop-up menu you can choose from the same nine color settings available in Photoshop 6, Illustrator 9 and 10, and InDesign 2.0, including generic prepress defaults for the United States, Europe, and Japan; a Custom option; or Color Management Off. On a Mac, you can also choose a tenth settings file, ColorSync workflow, which applies to Mac-only workflows that make use of applications from companies other than Adobe. The various prepress settings files use Adobe's internal color engine to convert color between various color devices, as well as Adobe's RGB color space, industry-standard CMYK press profiles (SWOP in the United States, for example), and appropriate dot gain for those printing conditions.

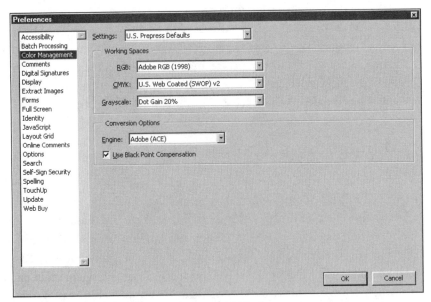

Figure 4-40 The Color Management panel in Preferences.

Choose a prepress setting that's appropriate for your working conditions or create a custom setting if you have a custom output profile from your prepress partner for your final press or contract-proof device. Don't turn color management off, however, because that choice is intended to emulate the color of video and other applications that don't support color management. Checking Use Black Point

Compensation maps the black point of the source color space to the black point of the target color space, resulting in a full dynamic range of colors in the target device. In geek-speak, this is a relative (rather than absolute) transformation, and it reduces the likelihood of washed-out blacks or clipped shadows. Black-point compensation affects the way color is displayed onscreen and in printed documents—though only when the application, not the RIP, manages printed color.

Proof Setup and Proof Colors

Once you've set your Preferences, you can specify proofing conditions. Happily, in addition to using the same color settings as Photoshop, Illustrator, and InDesign, Acrobat has identical proofing tools: Proof Setup and Proof Colors, both of which reside in the View menu (as they do in Acrobat's sibling applications). You can use these features to determine how your onscreen (RGB) colors will look when printed (CMYK).

By using the Proof Setup command, you can choose from a number of predefined output profiles—the same ones available in Photoshop, Illustrator, and InDesign, of course—to simulate CMYK conditions on your monitor. Select View > Proof Setup > Custom, and then choose your desired output profile from the Proofing Space pop-up menu (Figure 4-41).

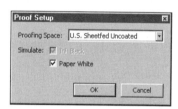

Figure 4-41 The Proof Setup dialog box.

If you have a custom output profile (which should be stored in the ColorSync folder in the System folder on the Mac, or in the System\Color folder in Windows), you can select it from the list or choose one of the myriad proofing devices or printing or prepress options. (You can also choose RGB profiles if you're publishing to the Web from a PC and want to soft-proof viewing conditions on a Mac, or vice versa.)

There are two more choices to make in the Proof Setup dialog box: You can check Simulate Ink Black or Paper White. The former uses a relative colorimetric rendering intent; the latter uses an absolute colorimetric rendering intent. But let me back up a bit: The *rendering intent,* which I mentioned in Chapter 3, describes how the color engine maps colors from one color space to another—in this case, from the CMYK proof space to the RGB monitor space. When you check Simulate Ink Black and use the relative intent, this turns off black-point compensation and provides a more accurate depiction of how true black will print. It maps colors by comparing the white points of the two color spaces and shifting all colors accordingly. It's a good idea to check this box when you're printing under conditions with a small dynamic range, such as to newsprint or to desktop inkjet proofers.

Simulating paper white, in contrast, uses absolute rendering, which theoretically does a better job of representing the entire compressed gamut of the print medium. This makes it a better option for soft proofing. To see the soft proof you've just set up, you must toggle it on: Choose View > Proof Colors (Command/Ctrl-Y).

Despite the tremendous strides Acrobat 5.0 has made in reliable soft proofing, you must still take into account many variables before you can soft-proof with confidence. Above all, you need a high-quality color monitor that has been properly calibrated and profiled (not an 8-year-old CRT, like mine). Viewing conditions, including incandescent versus fluorescent lighting, also dramatically affect the color you see onscreen. Most experts recommend that you view soft proofs in muted, consistent lighting conditions—no glare on the glass, a hood over the monitor, a plain gray desktop (onscreen), and neutral-colored walls.

Printing Managed Color

Most of you would probably rather trust the CMYK values you specify and view in software than resort to soft proofing. That's understandable: It takes time and practice to trust the color you see onscreen—even if that means simply knowing how the color viewed there will differ from the color as it appears in print. As long as you're learning about soft proofing, though, you should also get used to printing proofs from Acrobat using color management—again with the goal of producing color that closely approximates that which your printing press will produce.

As mentioned earlier, you can either let Acrobat apply color management when you print a PDF file (host-based color management), or you can let the PostScript output device's RIP manage color (printer-based color management). However, if you leave color management to a PostScript printer, it will convert an ICC source profile to something called a *color space array* and an output profile to a *color rendering dictionary*. The actual color conversion, based on these files, can occur in one of several ways, either by the driver or the printer, which can lead to unpredictable results. By letting Acrobat manage printed colors, you get more predictability and control because it uses the engine you specified in Preferences and the output profile of your choosing.

Select host-based color management by diving into the bowels of the Print dialog box. On the Mac, choose Acrobat 5.0 from the General pop-up menu, then click

Advanced. In Windows, you can click Advanced directly, without jumping through this hoop. In the Print Settings dialog box (Figure 4-42), go to the Color Profile pop-up menu in the High-End Features area. Choose Printer/PostScript Color Management to cede color control to the printer's RIP, or choose Same as Source if you don't want to apply color management. To use Acrobat's color management, simply choose the desired output profile (for example, U.S. Sheetfed Uncoated v2 or a profile for your desired proofing device).

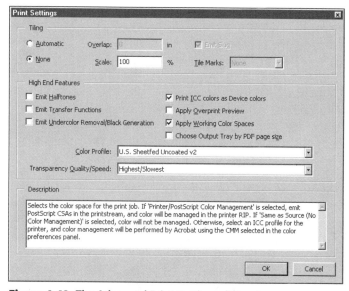

Figure 4-42 The Advanced Print Settings dialog box.

Don't get an itchy clicker finger: You still need to check more boxes before leaving this dialog box! First, check Print ICC colors as Device colors (you would only leave this box unchecked if you planned to let the printer manage your color). If you leave this box unchecked, PostScript will use color space arrays, converted from ICC profiles, to manage color in the RIP.

You'll also want to check Apply Working Color Spaces (which is checked by default). This tells Acrobat to use the RGB and grayscale working spaces defined in Preferences, in conjunction with the CMYK profile you specified in the Color Profile pop-up menu. In Windows you may also have the option to choose an output tray.

Now you're ready to roll: Click OK, then print the document. (See "Advanced Print Options," next page, for more on the other choices in this dialog box.)

Advanced Print Options

The Advanced Print Settings dialog box includes features for much more than just printing color-managed PDF files. Some of them are described here (note, however, that overprints are covered in depth in the following chapter, in the trapping section).

Acrobat's Tiling feature lets you print oversized pages (for example, posters or bill-boards) on multiple sheets of paper rather than scale them to fit on letter-size paper (or smaller). If you choose None (your only option for document pages smaller than those specified in your Print Setup), Acrobat will print the image at 100 percent or let you scale it smaller or larger. Scaling is a good way to print letter-size documents on letter-size paper with trim marks and bleeds. If you print a scaled version of the document that includes printers' marks, your prepress partner will know you've included the information in the file (since it might not be immediately visible in the onscreen PDF file).

For oversized documents, however, you can either scale them or choose Automatic to tile them across multiple pieces of paper. Don't be confused by the term *automatic*, though: You do get to specify how you want the document tiled. For example, to compensate for the small margins that your printer cannot image, you can enter an overlap of up to one-third of the PDF page's width or height, whichever is smaller. If your overlap value equals that of the unprintable margin, you'll be able to trim the white away from the page and the pieces will line up precisely. You can still opt to scale the document should you want to save paper and not print at 100 percent (and you can enlarge the page, too, if you desire). Check Emit Slug to print the file name, date stamp, and tile location on the page, and check the Tile Marks box to help assemble the final printed pieces.

Device-specific parameters—Emit Halftones, Transfer Functions, and Undercolor Removal/Black Generation—tell the printer to use these settings for output (if they're specified in the PDF file) rather than the printer's defaults. You opt to include these settings when you prepare the file in its authoring application. Read more about them in the various applications discussed in Chapter 2. Generally, it's best not to include these specifications and to let your printer control the output for their particular device.

Finally, you can control **transparency** in your printed piece, using the Transparency Quality/Speed pop-up menu. Here you can trade off quality (degree of rasterization) for speed. At the lowest quality level, the entire page is rasterized. The higher the quality setting, the more vector data is preserved. The result is the highest possible resolution-independent output but more time- and memory-intensive processing.

PREPARING FINAL PAGES

Once your PDF files are ready to go, your prepress partners will appreciate it if you take just a few final steps to make sure they're in order.

Renumbering Pages

Acrobat automatically numbers pages in a PDF document consecutively from Page 1. Any time you add or delete pages from multiple PDF documents, it updates automatically. If you're simply proofing pages or producing online documents, Acrobat's generic page-numbering system is probably fine. However, if your pages are destined for prepress, you may need or want to renumber them so that the page numbers in the PDF file reflect actual folio numbers. In book production, for example, you might have one PDF file for each chapter, or in magazine publishing, one PDF file for each feature article in an issue. Or perhaps you're submitting some last-minute changes to a job, and you've received new versions of pages 4, 14, and 404 in a single PDF file, which your prepress provider will swap into his or her imposed signatures. In these scenarios as well as for numbering pages in electronic documents, you can use Acrobat's Number Pages feature to apply numbering styles to all or part of a PDF file, so that the page numbers in the file you hand off to your prepress provider reflect the final folio.

To change page numbers in a PDF file—for example, to make Chapter 3 begin on Page 22 instead of Page 1, open the file and view its Thumbnails palette. First look down at the page number box at the bottom of the document window: In a generically numbered PDF file you'll see 1 of x (Figure 4-43, "before"). Click to select the thumbnail of the first page in the document, and choose Number Pages from the Thumbnail or Document menu. In the Page Numbering dialog box (Figure 4-44), you can renumber the selected page (1, in my example), all of the pages in the document, or a range. Since I'm changing all of the numbers in the file and keeping them as a unified section, I choose Begin New Section, and apply a Roman figure Style (other choices are None; i, ii, iii; I, II, III; a, b, c; or A, B, C).

Before   After

Figure 4-43 The document page number box in Acrobat before the pages are renumbered (left) and after (right).

Choosing Prefix lets you put a prefix before your numbers (for example, to use scientific numbering such as 1-1, 1-2, and so). Finally, enter the page number for the first page in the section in the Start box (22 in my example). Acrobat shows you the styled series in the Sample area of the dialog box so that you can preview your choices before clicking OK.

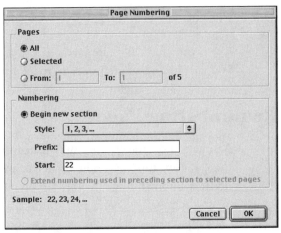

Figure 4-44 The Page Numbering dialog box.

If you're sectioning the document by numbering only selected pages or a range of pages at a time, you can opt to Extend Numbering Used in Preceding Section to Selected Pages. When you check this box, Acrobat automatically applies the same styling to the numbers in the current section, picking up consecutively from the preceding section in the document. After you've renumbered your pages you'll see the new (folio) number in the document page number box, preceding the parenthetical 1 of *x* count (Figure 4-43, "after").

Removing Comments and More

Using Acrobat's PDF Consultant feature, you can run JavaScripts that strip unwanted data from a PDF file or use that data to analyze and repair problematic links, bookmarks, and other metadata associated with electronic documents. To ensure, for example, that all sticky notes have been removed from a PDF file before you send it to your printer, choose Tools > PDF Consultant > Detect and Remove. In the Detect and Remove dialog box (Figure 4-45), check the All Comments box to remove all of the comments and notes attached to the file, including sticky notes and edit marks on the pages of the file, stamps, sound, file attachments, and multimedia clips that could accidentally image or add bulk to the file. Clicking Analyze

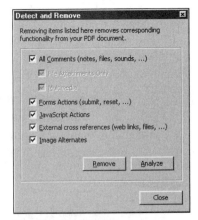

Figure 4-45 The Detect and Remove dialog box.

simply generates a report of the attachments; you might want to click it just to see what's there. To actually remove comments, however, click Remove. The other types of elements you can remove—JavaScripts, form actions, and external cross-references—pertain more to electronic documents and probably don't exist in PDF files created for graphic arts workflows, but check and remove them if necessary.

Don't worry about the Image Alternates checkbox: It's there to let you choose from multiple versions of a single image's dictionary, but as of this writing, no mainstream publishing tool supports the feature yet.

The PDF Consultant feature has another useful function, particularly for electronic documents: Optimize Space (Figure 4-46) lets you remove invalid bookmarks and links, thereby reducing the size of your PDF file. Destination links are links across multiple PDF documents, which—unlike bookmarks—remain intact when pages are added or deleted from the target PDF file.

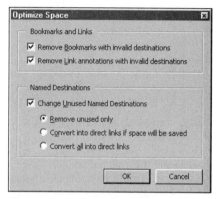

Figure 4-46 The Optimize Space dialog box.

PDF Consultant's final feature is called Space Audit (Figure 4-47). As with the Document Properties dialog boxes (Fonts, Summary, and so on), you can use this feature to glean information about your PDF file. Specifically, Space Audit provides details about what's taking up space in your file—text, images, comments, thumbnails, and more. "Unknown content" refers to any code or data in a PDF file that Acrobat cannot recognize. By clicking Remove Elements, you can jump to the Detect and Remove dialog box, where you can delete any extraneous data. *Extraneous* is the key word here: You can't delete essential or structural data (for example, the PDF cross-reference table or embedded fonts), and you probably won't trim much, if anything, from the file's unknown data.

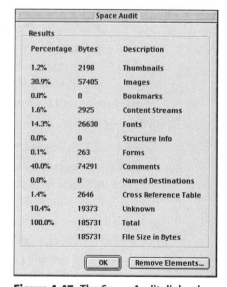

Figure 4-47 The Space Audit dialog box.

Unsecuring Files

Finally, if you've been encrypting files with signatures or security restrictions as you collaborate on or proof them, you probably want to remove these restrictions before you send the file to your prepress shop. Choose File > Document Security and make sure the Security Options pop-up menu is set to No Security. The exception would be if your prepress partners were in your security loop and had the requisite passwords for full file access. If your final file has a signature stamped on it that you don't want to be imaged, you must either delete it or redistill the final file without the signature.

BATCH PROCESSING

No, I'm not talking about micro-brewing. I'm talking about automating and streamlining routine file-preparation tasks (on one or more PDF files) using Acrobat's batch-processing capabilities. The software ships with a number of pre-defined JavaScript processes, including Set Security to No Changes, Save All as RTF, and Remove All Attachments (for example, audio comments). You can edit or create new batch sequences related to page operations (crop and renumber, for example), comments (delete or summarize), document commands (print, extract contents), JavaScript actions (any that you author, or one of several document-level actions that ship with Acrobat, such as close or print), and PDF Consultant capabilities (Space Audit, remove bad links). You can batch-process a single operation or string together a series of processes and apply them to one or more PDF files. And batch sequence files, which have a .sequ extension, can be shared and used by others if they're in the Sequences folder in the Acrobat application folder. In short, batch sequences go a long way toward streamlining all kinds of routine preproduction tasks.

To see the batch processes that ship with Acrobat, choose File > Batch Processing, and the list will appear in a submenu. When you choose one, such as Print 1st Page of All, Acrobat displays a Run Sequence Confirmation dialog box (Figure 4-48): This shows what tasks will be performed before you select the files to be processed (input), and tells you where the processed files will be saved. You can't edit the sequence here (that is, toggle on or off individual operations), though that would certainly be a nice option. The Run Sequence Confirmation dialog box simply provides a visual cue for the tasks that the sequence will perform. An ellipsis in the white box to the left of the gear icon indicates "toggle interactive mode," which means you'll be prompted to modify or confirm the operation when it's executed, so stick around.

Before you learn how to create new batch processes or edit the ones that came with Acrobat, check out the Batch Processing panel of your Preferences dialog box (Edit > Preferences > General). If you want to cancel

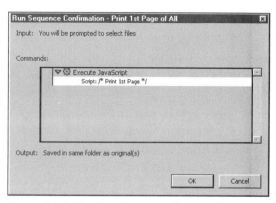

Figure 4-48 The Run Sequence Confirmation dialog box.

the Run Sequence Confirmation prompt that appears whenever you initiate a batch sequence, uncheck the top box (Figure 4-49). And it's always a good idea to check Save Warnings and Errors in Log File so that you can document and fix problems. If you're batch-processing encrypted files, you can select the appropriate handler from the Security Handler pop-up menu. This will prompt you to enter a password when a secured file is opened for processing.

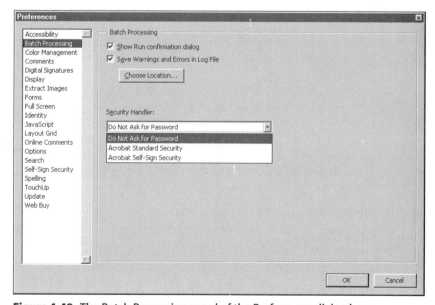

Figure 4-49 The Batch Processing panel of the Preferences dialog box.

Now let's create a sequence that will summarize a PDF document's comments and save them separately for reference. We'll then run PDF Consultant to remove all comments as well as actions, cross-references, and image alternates. Choose File > Batch Processing > Edit Batch Sequences. The Batch Sequences dialog box (Figure 4-50) is where you manage your sequences (for example, deleting, renaming, adding, editing, or running them). Click New Sequence. Enter a name for your sequence— "Summarize and Clean Up," in my example—and then click OK. You should now be in the Batch Edit Sequence dialog box (Figure 4-51).

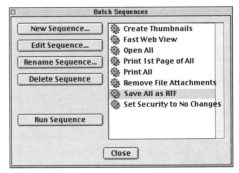

Figure 4-50 The Batch Sequences dialog box.

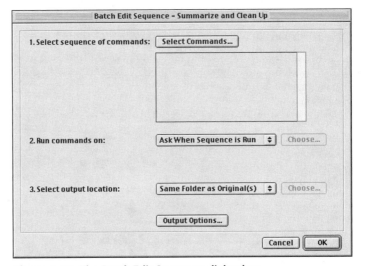

Figure 4-51 The Batch Edit Sequence dialog box.

Defining a batch sequence is a three-step process: First, you must choose the commands, then you must determine how to run the sequence, and finally you need to specify what to do with processed files. Start by clicking Select Commands to open the Edit Sequence dialog box (Figure 4-52). Here you can scroll through the left list of possible batch commands, select one, and click Add to move it to the right and make it part of your sequence. You can rearrange the order of the commands by selecting them individually and clicking Move Up or Move Down. You

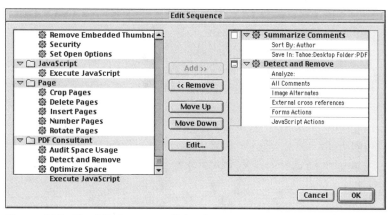

Figure 4-52 The Edit Sequence dialog box.

can remove a command by clicking Remove. And you can edit the options for each command by selecting it and clicking Edit. For my Summarize Comments command, for example, I've opted to sort by author instead of by page, and I've created a special folder where I want to save them. You can toggle the command into interactive mode by clicking the box to the left of the gear icon, as I've done with the Detect and Remove command: This will pause the command and allow you to modify options before it's executed—in case you want to leave some attachments intact. When you're satisfied with your sequence, click OK to return to the Batch Edit Sequence dialog box.

The commands you've selected should appear in the Sequence Preview box. Now determine when you want the sequence to run: You can run it on any currently open files (Files Open in Acrobat); you can let the user determine when to run it (Ask When Sequence is Run); or you can choose specific files or folders (Selected Files, Selected Folder, respectively) to process.

In all but the first case, you can also choose how you want to handle processed files: From the Select Output Location pop-up menu, you can choose Same as Original(s) to save the new file with the same name and in the same location as the unprocessed file (bad idea). If you choose to save in the same location as the original file, be sure to click Output Options and indicate that you want to rename the processed file—by adding, in my example, the suffix "cleanedup" between the original file name and its extension (Figure 4-53). Check "Do not overwrite existing files" to be extra cautious, and specify the file format of the new file: PDF, EPS, JPEG, PNG, RTF, TIFF, or raw PostScript. You'll want some of those file formats if your batch sequence extracts text or graphic content.

You can also select Specific Folder and click Choose to browse and save processed files in a folder other than the source folder; or you can choose Ask When Sequence is Run if you want to let the user determine where processed files are stored (should the desired location be subject to change, for example).

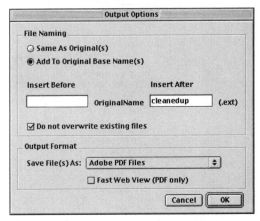

Figure 4-53 The Output Options dialog box.

That's all, folks (Figure 4-54). When you're satisfied, click OK. You can run the sequence immediately from the Batch Sequences dialog box, or you can close out of it and run the sequence anytime by choosing File > Batch Processing > Summarize and Clean Up.

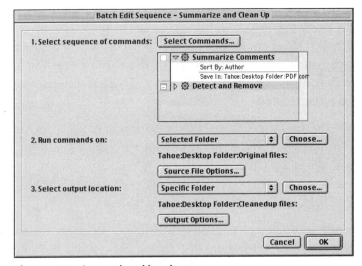

Figure 4-54 A completed batch sequence.

CHAPTER FIVE

PDF in Prepress

Many designers rarely use PDF for anything more than sending proposals and sketches to clients—after this, they say, Acrobat is just "an extra step." As you know, however, this represents just the tip of what you can do with Acrobat and PDF. When you're ready to wade deeper, you can use PDF to review, approve, archive, and produce final files. And in so doing, you may discover advantages—namely savings of time and resources, as well as greater flexibility and control over content use (and reuse).

Keep in mind, however, that by integrating Acrobat into your workflow, you're likely to disrupt existing processes. Cleaner files may well mean quicker processing by your service providers, thus allowing you to lengthen internal lead times. Alternatively, you may need to compress lead times on the front end if you decide to take on preflight steps (for example, checking for unembedded fonts or unconverted RGB images) to save time and money on the back end. Either way, you need to research your options to make sure that proposed changes are productive rather than disruptive—and you must make sure your prepress partners support your decision.

Indeed, many in the prepress world believe that designers should focus on what they do best and leave prepress tasks to the experts (prepress shops). There is, in fact, a great deal to be said for this. Since many printers don't even know which press they'll be running a job on until the last minute, how can you as a designer correctly apply traps, dot gain, and other specifications? You can't—unless you're working under very controlled and closed circumstances. For this reason, you should leave device-dependent considerations (trapping, separations, and so on) to your printing providers—which means omitting these parameters from your distilled PDF files.

Designers may wish to read this chapter with an eye toward gaining a better understanding of what happens after PDF files are handed off for print production. Prepress shops and commercial printers, on the other hand, can get ideas about the types of PDF workflows they can develop. Whatever your situation, you should come away with a better understanding of where you can reap the greatest benefits from a PDF prepress workflow.

HOMEGROWN PDF WORKFLOWS

There are as many prepress workflows as there are prepress shops, if not more. Although the steps required to get PDF-file pixels into spots of ink on a page vary from job to job, there are a few basic tasks that are typically completed:

- Files are preflighted to find and fix problems that will prevent the job from rasterizing

- Files are trapped to compensate for potential ink misregistration on press

- Files are imposed (that is, pages of a document must be placed in order on large press sheets so that when they're printed, folded, and bound, they fall into order)

- Files are separated into their grayscale channels to be imaged

Some jobs also require an OPI (Open Prepress Interface) swap, which means replacing low-resolution placeholders with full, high-resolution images. Typically, various proofs (such as film-based halftone Matchprints, digital proofs, and paginated bluelines) must be generated along the way, and last-minute edits may need to be performed. Finally, files must be rasterized to film, plate, or press (Figure 5-1).

Aside from preflighting first and rasterizing last, steps and processes may vary. However, because PDF workflows often fall into the above-described order, this chapter is organized around that workflow. This chapter will walk you through the processes that comprise a "homegrown" PDF prepress workflow—so called because you can pick and choose from among off-the-shelf, prepackaged software to perform specific tasks.

In addition to this type of homegrown workflow, many major manufacturers of prepress and printing equipment (including Agfa and CreoScitex) offer more complete and automated workflow systems, many of which are based on Adobe's

Typical PDF workflow

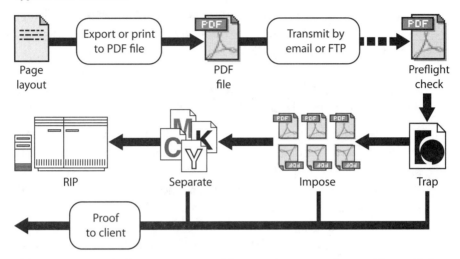

Figure 5-1 In a typical PDF prepress workflow, a printer or service provider preflights a composite PDF file from a client, then prepares it for print by trapping, imposing, and separating it into its four color channels (plus any spot colors) for film or print. The PDF file can be proofed and edited throughout these prepress tasks. If the output is destined for a digital printer, the separation stage is omitted. PDF files can also be archived and repurposed for publication to other media or recomposed into new documents for print.

Extreme architecture. Those systems—which represent a class of products directed at high-volume sites—are described in detail in Chapter 6. If your print partners use any of these systems, there aren't many prepress tasks you can easily take on yourself. However, if you're interested in doing your own PDF production, Acrobat and PDF have been around long enough that there are now tools for almost every conceivable task—no matter how big or small.

If you're a small or midsize prepress shop or printer, you may be interested in many of the products described here because you can integrate them with high-end prepress systems and digital front ends (the software and hardware that drive imaging equipment, including RIPs). Although these systems weren't developed with PDF in mind, they have since been adapted to support and leverage it. Examples of such systems include Scitex Brisque, Dalim Twist, and Heidelberg Delta. In other words, just because you have a long-standing investment in particular prepress hardware and software technologies doesn't mean you can't take advantage of various third-party tools to serve customers who want to submit PDF files or to take advantage of PDF on the back end.

If you're printing to four-color printing devices (for example, a Heidelberg direct-imaging press or a Xeikon electrophotographic digital press), many of these prepress steps are addressed by the front-end software that drive those devices. For example, such devices typically include software for setting trapping, imposition, and screening, and the tasks themselves are typically preformed inside the RIP. However, you still need to preflight PDF files for digital printing, and the printer's digital front end must be able to accept PDF input. Most can.

Keep in mind that although a variety of products are covered here, this is by no means a complete listing of what's available. Instead, this chapter is intended to present a wide spectrum of options—everything from low-cost plug-ins (for solo shops) to automated client/server-based applications (for larger workgroups, prepress shops, and small commercial printers). Because the costs of such products vary greatly (and change frequently), you should check vendor Web sites for the most current compatibility and pricing info. (To find any of the companies listed in this chapter online, sandwich the company name between "www" and ".com" unless otherwise noted. Also, all products run on both Mac and Windows unless otherwise noted.) You'll also find that many vendors offer tool suites that dovetail and interact nicely with one another, as well as bundles with complementary products from other vendors. Additional products are listed in Appendix One and other online resources are in Appendix Two.

PDF ASSURANCES

We have a custom PDF workflow that we created ourselves, in which our designers export to PDF using custom preferences that Home Depot has specified. Those preferences exist on every designer's computer. Everyone does the exact same thing. Their files are sent to a hot folder on an NT workstation, which watches the network, grabs the PostScript, and distills and preflights using PitStop Server. We're now 99.9% sure that our catalog, ads, and tabloid pages will print. We've had a huge gain in quality assurance and cost savings.

—Sean Sullivan, support center systems analyst, Home Depot

PREFLIGHTING

PDF is, in one sense, a pre-preflighted file format: Although it can be separated and printed in a number of ways, it represents an already-structured file containing normalized PostScript, which means it provides a more reliable foundation for turning onscreen pixels into ink on paper than do application files. In fact, it's not uncommon for prepress operators to convert application files to PDF in order to troubleshoot them even if they ultimately plan to convert them to PostScript, EPS, or some other format for processing.

Whatever the case, the PDF file itself still needs to be preflighted. Prepress providers shouldn't make any assumptions about the quality of a file even if it opens and appears to display correctly onscreen. Failure to assess problems up front can lead to wasted time and materials, not to mention costly bottlenecks if plates or film can't be rasterized from the electronic data—costs that are likely to be charged back to you as content creator. Even worse, errors can make it onto the printed page, and you may find you lose a client.

In addition to helping you assess problems with PDF files, preflighting often entails editing those files—to fix typos, for example, or to add or view printers' marks and bleeds if the PDF was distilled to its trim size and those marks were removed or hidden beyond the page's bounding box. Preflighting is kind of like putting on a pair of pants: Slip on one leg to check the file; slip on the other to fix it. Your file isn't dressed and ready to go out the door until you've done both.

PAINLESS PREFLIGHTING

Department stores used to send us four-color ads by film, and it would take hours on the stripping table. PDF has allowed us to paginate four-color files instead of having to scan negatives. And preflighting a PDF file is nothing like working up an application file. It takes 15 to 20 seconds to work up a PDF file so that it's ready for pagination; it would take 20 minutes to work up a Quark file.

—Gianna Tabuena-Frolli, digital team supervisor, San Jose Mercury News

Features to Find

If you plan to take on the task of preflighting PDF files yourself, you need to approach it with common sense. First, talk to your prepress provider about what to look for—not only obvious problems like unembedded fonts but also things your prepress partner commonly fixes but you might not necessarily notice. By the same token, you don't want to spend a lot of time on tasks that aren't significant to your prepress partners (for example, collecting a list of all font and image data in the file) and in the process fail to find more serious problems (for example, missing pages).

You also need to search for the right mix of products from the huge range of pre-flight tools available today (everything from Acrobat plug-ins to stand-alone applications and online services). Some of these products offer soup-to-nuts functionality (preflighting, text editing, *and* image resampling), while others are one-trick ponies (preflight only, no editing). You'll see later in this chapter that the same is true for various trapping, separation, and imposition tools. As you delve into PDF prepress, you need to consider your entire workflow so that you can figure out which tasks you should take on. More than likely, you'll find a product or mix of products that let you do just what you need at a price you can afford; you'll probably even be able to glue it all together with job or workflow management tools.

Preflight products and services always boast about the number of types of problems the software can identify: 150, 400, 600! Keep your feet on the ground: Not all of these conditions are earth shattering or RIP busting. For example, Courier just might be used intentionally, and the lack of a .pdf extension doesn't necessarily spell disaster. When considering your preflight software needs, ask the following questions:

- **Does the software preflight the types of files you use?** Obviously, whatever product you choose should preflight PDF, but does it also preflight various application or image file formats? If you're migrating to a complete PDF workflow, you might need a tool that preflights only PDF files and is capable of identifying a laundry list of problems that are targeted and pertinent to PDF. General preflight tools, in contrast, will identify broken links and other problems in application files. If you're still using a variety of file types, you'll need a tool that can analyze them all.

  In addition, if you're taking advantage of Acrobat 5.0 to generate structured, tagged PDF 1.4 files or PDF files with transparency, you'll want your preflight tool to be able to identify problems related to these features. You'll also want to make sure that the preflight program supports older versions of PDF if you're still generating or receiving them.

- **Is the tool able to detect common font problems?** Examples of these include unembedded fonts, unsubset or improperly subset fonts, unlicensed fonts (embedded or not), mixed TrueType and PostScript fonts, and font substitutions. Also, can it detect these font problems inside embedded graphics?

- **Can the software identify common image problems?** Examples of these include RGB or spot colors that need to be managed through the workflow or converted to process or grayscale, under- or oversampled images, use of the DeviceN color space (see "Duotones and DeviceN," page 214), and the presence of color management and the use of ICC profiles.

- **Does the product check for device-dependent parameters such as overprints, screen angles and frequencies, and transfer functions?** Can it detect the use of low-resolution OPI proxy images and comments? What about the presence of trim marks and bleeds? Does it check composite as well as pre-separated PDF files?

- **Will the preflight tool warn you about security settings? How about links and bookmarks, or embedded sound and linked video?** Although it's natural for preflight tools to focus on page composition and the printed document rather than navigational or interactive elements, it can be useful to know whether such elements exist so that you can remove them if desired.

  In addition, you might want to be able to check for comments so that you can ensure that they have been addressed, and delete them so that they don't print.

- **How does the tool return results?** Does the preflight software give you a written report or a visual display of errors? Can you sort, customize, or print the report in a meaningful way?

- **Can you customize your preflight by creating routines or use profiles that look for specific problems in specific jobs?** Also, does the tool offer hot folders or other types of automation?

- **Does the tool hook into Acrobat, Photoshop, and other authoring applications?** You may well need to return to these applications to fix problems. Can you jump to them, or does the software provide its own tools for fixing problems? If so, are those tools sufficient?

- **How does the preflight software repair problems?** Does it do so automatically, or does it let you choose whether and how to fix problems?

- **Do you have the proper system resources for the product?** Does it run on the platform you require, and is it scaled to your needs? Do you need a stand-alone or server-based product? Does it offer the efficiency, scalability, and reliability you require? And does it come in the language version you need?

 MOVE IT UP

We preflight every PDF file that we receive, but I would love it if our customers would preflight before they send them to us. Preflighting should move upstream and customers should be responsible for sending us clean files.

—Melinda Monti, manager of electronic prepress training and development, Vertis, Inc.

Typical Tools

The following represent some of the currently available PDF preflight tools. Most of the packaged products range in cost from a few to several hundred dollars, but check with the companies for accurate pricing. And remember, this is not a comprehensive list, just a starting point.

Callas pdfInspektor

This Acrobat plug-in preflights only PDF files (Figure 5-2). Although the standard package doesn't offer any editing capabilities, the Platinum edition offers some (for example, color conversions and font embedding). The plug-in generates text reports of its findings (in XML if desired) and also provides a visual display of the problem onscreen. If you purchase an even higher-end Auto edition and pair it with another Callas Acrobat plug-in, AutoPilot, you can use hot folders to automatically preflight and execute other tasks, as well as edit PDF files.

Alternatively you can get pdfInspektor as part of Callas's PDF Toolbox, a suite of plug-ins that also includes a batch PDF creation tool (pdfBatchMeister) for automatically creating PDF files from a variety of preset quality "profiles" from EPS or PostScript files; a batch processing tool (pdfBatchProcess Pro) for creating and preflighting PDF files as well as converting them to EPS; a module (pdfCropMarks) for adding crop and registration marks to PDF pages; a module (pdfCrop&Measure) for cropping PDF files; and a module (pdfOutput) for exporting EPS files from multipage PDF files for import into page-layout applications.

You can reach Callas at www.callas.de.

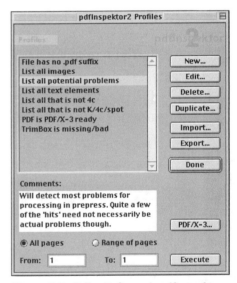

Figure 5-2 Callas Software's pdfInspektor includes predefined routines for inspecting PDF files, which you can modify to suit your conditions. Among the rules pdfInspektor checks are the condition and existence of trim and media boxes; whether the file was created by Distiller; whether transfer functions or smooth shading were applied; and whether the file contains JavaScripts or form elements.

Enfocus PitStop Professional

This product is both a preflight tool and an editing tool. Like pdfInspektor, PitStop is an Acrobat plug-in and a dedicated PDF preflighter (it's actually used in several of the Extreme workflow systems, such as those from Agfa and Fuji). Offering extensive preflighting and editing capabilities, PitStop allows you to identify and remap color spaces for individual images as well as entire PDF documents. In addition, you can edit text and the paragraph will reflow; and you can rotate, resize, and otherwise transform objects on a page.

In the Enfocus workflow, each PDF file has an associated profile that contains metadata that can be used to log changes made to versions of a PDF document. This way, every edit is traceable and accounted for (Figure 5-3), and you can roll back to previous versions if necessary. You can apply profiles at either the creation or preflighting stage: For example, if you want images in your PDF files to have a certain minimum resolution, put that in your profile. If the parameter isn't met,

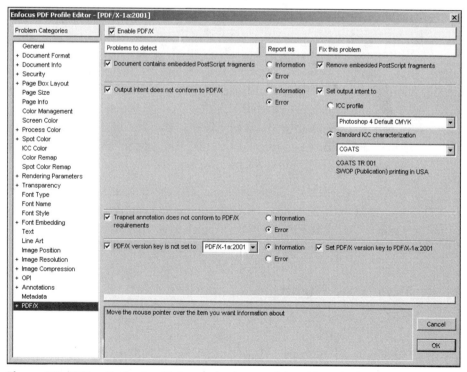

Figure 5-3 PitStop Professional lets you check potential problems in dozens of categories, from document, font, and color info to security, transparency, annotations, and PDF/X compliance (shown).

the distillation will fail or the problem will be reported. PDF files created outside the Enfocus workflow can be preflighted using these profiles to ensure that they meet your quality threshold.

A stand-alone, Windows-based server version of PitStop Professional is also available for high-volume, automated processing.

Extensis Preflight Online and Preflight Pro

The Web-based preflight service Preflight Online began its life as a PDF-only service but now preflights QuarkXPress files as well. By going online, you avoid investing in the hardware and software required to run preflight software yourself—for large commercial establishments, a costly investment that can entail servers and high-bandwidth network connections. Preflight Online also offers features not found in prepackaged software, such as the ability to track customer usage and identify common problems and errors for each customer. In addition, it moves the process upstream, in the sense that it automatically bounces back problematic files to customers. Extensis offers the hosted subscription service to printers, service bureaus, and publishers who can in turn customize it for their Web sites. They pay an upfront fee to have it set up and then a per-document transaction fee. Their customers can submit files 24 hours a day with a Netscape Communicator or Microsoft Internet Explorer plug-in, and the system will check for missing fonts, mixed RGB and CMYK color spaces in a document, optimal image resolution, and so on, depending on the conditions specified by the printer at the back end. Occasional users can also log on and preflight one-off files, though Preflight Online is meant to serve high-volume accounts.

Preflight Pro, meanwhile, is a shrink-wrapped all-purpose preflight package that inspects PDF files as well as numerous application files (Figure 5-4). A Mac-only product, Preflight Pro supports AppleScript automation and hot folders, and allows you to create PDF files using customizable Distiller preferences.

Markzware FlightCheck and MarkzNet

Markzware is another company that offers both online and packaged preflighting for PDF as well as a variety of application files. FlightCheck is the desktop application, a stand-alone program that can check every type of file format from Word to InDesign, CorelDraw, and PDF. Among the conditions it can check for are the presence and use of clipping paths and ICC profiles; the resolution and color space of embedded images; the use of menu-styled and encoded fonts; ink density

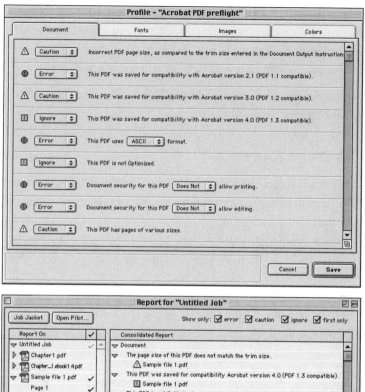

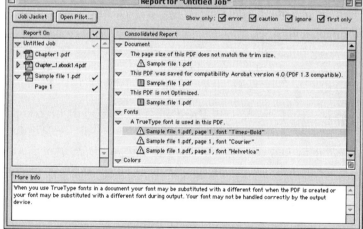

Figure 5-4 After specifying a profile for the file items you want to check in Extensis' Preflight Pro (top), you can preflight files and view reports of their contents (bottom).

values for CMYK images; traps and screen values; and general document information (creator, date, authoring application, and so on). It is not a PDF editor.

MarkzNet is the online equivalent of FlightCheck. Like Preflight Online, this service is geared for printers, prepress shops, publishers, and other large organizations that perform in-house prepress. However, it differs from Preflight Online in that it's not a subscription service; rather, it's installed on your own servers and systems, and checks are performed locally on a client's workstation. If a file doesn't pass inspection, the document creator is notified of the problem, and when it's fixed and the file passes inspection, it's sent to an FTP site for production.

Markzware also makes several QuarkXTensions and a workflow management tool called MarkzScout.

OneVision Asura

OneVision makes the PDF preflight and editing tool Asura as well as two other PDF editing tools, Solvero and Solico. All of these applications interpret PDF files into display PostScript upon opening them—a step that in itself resolves many common PostScript conflicts and errors. Display PostScript, for those of you who aren't familiar with it, uses the same imaging model as PostScript to provide onscreen parity with what will be printed or imaged through the page description language. (However, OneVision is migrating its Mac products to Quartz, the PDF-based 2D imaging model used in Apple's Mac OS X, and is migrating its Windows products to GDI, or graphical design interface, that operating system's model for displaying onscreen graphics.) Once PDF files have been opened in any of these OneVision applications, they become device-independent, object-oriented, layer-based files that can be further edited.

Asura is a stand-alone server-based program that preflights composite and separated PDF files as well as PostScript and EPS. It repairs basic mistakes automatically according to your settings and removes extraneous data such as digital signatures to keep file sizes down. For images, Asura can convert RGB, spot, and other colors to CMYK; apply ICC profiles; measure ink densities; and read OPI comments (Figure 5-5). It can also check and correct hairline rules to make sure they print, as well as detect font substitutions and bitmaps. Finally, Asura can produce multiple versions of one distilled PDF file, each with different output settings—for example, a high-resolution print PDF file and a low-resolution Web PDF file, or a full-color PDF file and a grayscale PDF file.

Files that need further attention can be edited in OneVision's Solvero software, which offers a host of tools for editing and controlling elements in PostScript, EPS, or PDF files or in Solico, a PDF-only editing tool.

OneVision tools have made inroads in newspaper and magazine publishing as well as in financial printing environments.

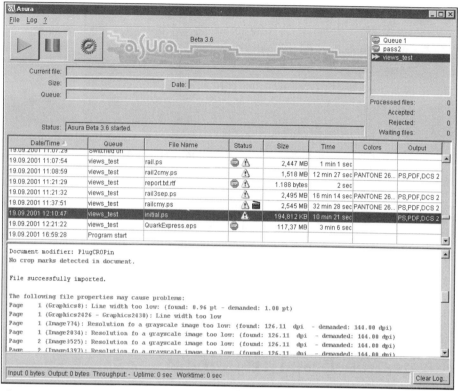

Figure 5-5 OneVision's Asura is a server-based PDF preflight and editing tool.

DON'T WAIT TILL DAWN

We're a 24/7 shop so if at 3 a.m. we're trying to get a page together there may not be a customer to fax it to for approval. We have a policy that we will try to make changes, but we do a lot of coupons and there can be last-minute price changes or someone forgot to change the expiration date, and we'll make those corrections in PDF. We prefer that our customers make changes, but we will use whatever's ready first—ours or theirs. We want pages to come in perfect but in reality they're often wrong.

—Melinda Monti, manager of electronic prepress training and development, Vertis, Inc.

TRAPPING

Trapping, as one printer confided to me, is a printing problem that printers have successfully foisted on designers. At issue here is the way mechanical or physical interactions on press can cause paper to shift or stretch and inks to misregister as the paper rolls through the CMYK printing units. Misregistration manifests itself as unsightly white gaps between adjoining colors or as unwanted underlying colors showing through. Misregistration is especially noticeable with bright or contrasting colors (Figure 5-6).

Figure 5-6 At left, the star is misregistered and not trapped. At right, the trap resolves the ugly white gap.

To prevent such mishaps, you must create traps. Prior to the digital era, you did this by managing the exposure of positive and negative film: In a time-consuming and labor-intensive process, these films were overexposed between two sheets of frosted mylar to distort or diffuse the image and create a trap. Today, however, traps are created in software by specifying that two adjoining colors slightly overprint along their edges. You can specify that a foreground object "spreads" (grows slightly) or that a background "chokes" (shrinks slightly). When properly applied, both tactics eliminate misregistration. The challenge here comes in not producing new artifacts when creating traps.

Application-Based Trapping

In all fairness, the fact that trapping has become an issue for designers isn't really because printers haven't wanted to deal with it. Most printers prefer to trap digital files themselves because they have the knowledge and experience to do so: They know far more than the designer does about the inks, paper, and press that will be used on any given job—the porousness of the paper, the humidity of the air in the pressroom that can cause paper to expand or contract, the speed of the press—and thus they can apply traps much more effectively. But desktop applications such as Illustrator and QuarkXPress have come along and offered trapping capabilities, giving designers the power to specify overprints themselves, even if they haven't been trained in how to do so properly. (Acrobat, too, now allows some control and previewing of overprints, which I'll get to in a moment.)

With application-based trapping, you usually apply traps at the object or page level. In Illustrator and InDesign, for example, you can overprint stroked elements; you can also trap by zone in InDesign. In QuarkXPress, you can trap by color (specifying trap conditions for pairs of colors) or by object (so that you can change trap values for various types of objects, such as having a particular rule overprint on one color but knockout, or replace, it when it's on another). The advantage of application-based trapping is that the default settings usually suffice, which means it's easy for designers to apply. Another advantage is cost: You don't have to buy additional software or pay a fee to your service provider to perform the task.

However, because you must set application-based traps manually, it can be a time-consuming process. And once they're set and flowed into a distilled PDF file, your digital "master" is no longer device-independent—a factor that may limit what you can do with the files down the line. Application-based trapping is also limited (you can't trap imported objects, EPS files, or images), and it's not infallible. And if you make decisions based on guesswork (perhaps because you don't know the final press conditions, which is often the case), you'll more than likely end up paying for your prepress partner to undo your mistakes.

In-RIP Trapping

Many printers and prepress shops dislike application-based trapping, instead preferring to control the process themselves through a process called in-RIP trapping, which is offered in PostScript 3 and as part of Extreme workflows. In this process, trapping occurs when a file is interpreted but before it's rasterized into a bitmap and sent to a marking engine such as a platesetter. The advantages to in-RIP trapping are many: Most importantly, it keeps the PDF file flexible and device-independent until the last possible moment. (In industry parlance, this is called *late binding*: You don't make any binding decisions earlier than absolutely necessary.) In-RIP trapping is also an automated process that requires little operator intervention. Trap styles, like page-layout or cascading style sheets, can be applied to entire documents and reused. And depending on implementation, previews are available.

With in-RIP trapping, the actual traps are specified by software that interfaces with the RIP, or in an application file or independent trapping program. In the case of the latter two options, the information travels with the PDF file in a portable job ticket but isn't applied until just before the file is rasterized.

Dedicated Trapping

Dedicated trapping programs represent a third way to trap—a sort of middle-of-the-road approach. Trapping programs like Ultimate Technographics' Trapeze and ScenicSoft's TrapWise have the advantage of offering in-RIP trapping (in that they can trap entire documents and offer some automation, such as batch processing) while still letting you apply custom traps to individual pages or zones. Most such programs trap a variety of file formats (from DCS to EPS and PDF, including imported graphics) and also offer previews. However, they also share some of the drawbacks of application-based trapping in that they can be brought into the workflow too early, limiting the flexibility of the PDF document down the line. They also entail an extra step in the workflow and sometimes require dedicated hardware.

READY TO TRAP

We trap both in Illustrator and in Scitex Presstouch. The advantage of application trapping is that you can pick up elements and repeat them. We also have a library of graphics that have been trapped so when we get artwork from customers we might take the trapped version of the logo and put it into the artwork. They don't even know it. That's a nice use of application trapping.

—Marco Cappuccio, digital technology manager, SS Studios

The PDF Trap-22

PDF workflows present some trapping conundrums: The good news is that because PDF is a composite format, you can see traps in color, in context. The bad news is that if you've applied traps in an application file that you've distilled to a composite PDF file, the traps may or may not be intact or immediately apparent to your service provider. Happily, Acrobat 5.0 offers some features to help you manage traps in PDF documents.

Certain applications—albeit older ones—can't preserve trapping information when distilled to PDF. QuarkXPress 4.0 and earlier versions, for example, only preserve trap specifications when creating pre-separated PostScript files—in other words, when you create PostScript files of each color-separated channel. And there's little point in distilling those files to PDF; the advantage of PDF is working with composite files. With newer applications you can create your traps in an authoring application and instruct Distiller to preserve them (in the Color panel of the Job Options settings, check Preserve Overprint Settings). To view those overprints in a PDF file in Acrobat, however, you must also distill a PDF 1.4 file.

Assuming you make it this far and that you've got overprints in your PDF file, you can inform your service provider or printer that your traps are there by "declaring" them. In this way, you can help prevent your service provider from undoing your work or adding conflicting traps. With the PDF file open in Acrobat, choose File > Document Properties > Trapping Key. By default, all PDF files declare traps as Unknown. To tell the next person who opens the file and checks the key that trapping has been applied, choose Yes from the pop-up menu. If you wish to alert them that trapping *has not* been applied, choose No (Figure 5-7). Finally, click OK and save the PDF.

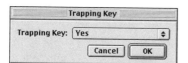

Figure 5-7 The Trapping Key dialog box, where you can tell service providers or printers that you've applied traps to the PDF file.

Figure 5-8 With Overprint Preview off (left), the top object obscures the bottom object. With Overprint preview on (right), the overprinted color is visible.

In Acrobat 5.0, you can also preview overprints created in applications like Illustrator—as long as they were distilled to PDF 1.4. To toggle on the preview, which is also available in Illustrator 9 and 10 and InDesign 2.0, choose View > Overprint Preview. A checkmark indicates you're viewing the overprinted colors, which means you can see how the colors look when the top ink blends with the underlying inks (Figure 5-8). A more accurate preview can be obtained in a color proof. To proof overprints on hard copy, check the Apply Overprint Preview box in the Advanced print settings dialog box.

An Overprinting Primer

Backing up a step, let's talk for a minute about how to create good traps. The first thing you need to know is when they're needed—that is, when two colors adjoin one another. However, you also need to know that you should only apply traps to artwork with areas of color that don't share common inks—for example, spot colors printed on CMYK colors, or vice versa. In addition, you'll usually want to trap 100 percent black objects, lines, or text against color backgrounds.

You don't, however, normally need to trap two process colors when they share at least one ink within a 30 percent tint of each other (for example, for an orange that uses 50 percent magenta and a blue that uses 60 percent magenta). Nor do you need to trap two process colors when the tints of each of the four inks in the foreground color are all either lighter or darker than those in the background color. In these instances, the common inks obscure potential misregistration. And finally, you never need to trap continuous-tone images, such as photographs.

When creating traps, keep in mind that darker colors hold their shapes on press better than lighter colors—which means the lighter color should be trapped because its distortion will be less visible to the human eye. In some cases it will be obvious which of two colors is lighter—pale yellow, for example, is clearly lighter than dark blue—because one color reflects back more light. (Another way to say this is that it has a higher luminance, or *neutral density*.) Other times, however, it can be difficult to gauge the lighter of two colors. In such cases, Photoshop's Color Picker comes in handy: Simply select the HSB color mode readout from the Info palette's options and then move the Eyedropper over the desired color in your art. The B value corresponds to brightness (or luminance), the H value to hue, and the S value to saturation. When comparing two colors, the one with the higher B value is lighter.

When you overprint (which, by the way, can create effects as well as compensate for misregistration), the topmost ink blends with underlying inks. If the two colors have no common inks, all of the colors' ink values will be in the overprinted color. For example, if one color is a 70 percent cyan tint and the other is a 30 percent yellow, the overprinted color will be 70 percent cyan and 30 percent yellow (or green). If the two colors share some common inks, they're *not* added together. Instead, only the values of the overprinted ink will appear in the overprint area. In other words, the overprinted ink *knocks out* the underlying ink or inks.

Spreads should be used to trap a light foreground object to a dark background, making it appear to expand into the background. Chokes, in contrast, should be used to trap a light background to a dark object, making the object appear squeezed.

You can trap rich blacks—blacks that also contain some process colors (a common version is 100 percent black plus 40 percent cyan)—by choking the process colors (sometimes called *undercolors)* in the rich-black objects. This way, you guarantee that misregistration won't cause any process color to show along the edge of the object. This is especially important on fine type, which should not comprise multiple colors because misregistration will show the undercolors. Type that's smaller than 10 points should be only one color; type from 10 to about 24 can be up to two colors; type larger than 24 points or so can be four.

Trap size depends on printing method and substrate. The more refined the process—sheet-fed waterless printing on coated stock, for example—the more stable the paper path and the stronger the medium itself is likely to be, making smaller traps sufficient. However, the less refined the printing process and the more porous the substrate, the larger the trap needs to be. Traps can range from 0.1 to 0.3 point for sheet-fed offset printing on coated paper, to 0.4 to 1.0 point for web offset on newsprint, to 1.0 to 5.0 points for screen printing on fabrics. Talk to your printer to determine the appropriate trap size for your job. You may even find out that your printer wants to do the trapping; most prefer to.

Dedicated Trapping Tools

You can see how trapping can quickly become complex: How do you trap small black type against a blend? Or worse yet, small rich-black type? The more elaborate your artwork, page composition, and inks, the more sophisticated your trapping needs. Also remember that many of the vendors who make dedicated trapping programs also offer OPI or other dedicated prepress packages (such as imposition software). Depending on the tasks you require, you may want to consider a package deal. If you opt to go with a dedicated trapping program, the following represent some of your choices (all of which accept native PDF files for input, as well as output PDF files).

ScenicSoft TrapWise

ScenicSoft's TrapWise (formerly from Adobe) now supports PDF 1.4 files (in addition to EPS and other formats), which means it can maintain existing overprint settings. And because it allows you to specify trap parameters by zones, you have finer control for traps that involve complex color relationships such as blends and vignettes (Figure 5-9). TrapWise also allows you to compare neutral densities so that you can determine whether to create a spread or a choke, and you can apply traps to individual inks, including metallics. In addition to these fine controls, TrapWise can detect existing traps in a file, and it allows you to automate trapping with batch processes, creating preferences for handling inks, fonts, and zone and print options. TrapWise ties into ScenicSoft's OPI and imposition programs, ColorCentral and Preps, respectively.

Ultimate Technographics Trapeze Artist

Like TrapWise, Trapeze Artist offers zone-based trapping for dozens of file types, including PDF. Because it supports Heidelberg Delta documents—which are produced from one of that company's RIPs—Trapeze Artist is sometimes bundled with hardware and sold as part of prepress systems. Using zones, you can create almost any type of trap on a page or in a document—from a trap for text over images and duotones to trap pairs for as many as 32 inks. Trapeze Artist, which only runs on Windows NT, can display up to 16 inks onscreen, in a composite or separated preview.

Figure 5-9 ScenicSoft's TrapWise traps composite PDF files without converting them to PostScript.

Heidelberg Supertrap

German press manufacturer Heidelberg sells its Prinergy trapping technology in a shrink-wrapped product called Supertrap (for more on Prinergy, see Chapter 6, page 222), which is based on trapping algorithms the company uses in its Delta workflow system and RIP. In contrast to the stand-alone applications Trapeze Artist and TrapWise, Supertrap is an Acrobat plug-in: In other words, it only traps PDF files. But as with the other programs, Supertrap allows trapping to be performed automatically (based on predefined rules) or interactively (based on pages or zones), giving you complete control over trap color and type. It also lets you map spot colors to CMYK, edit trap paths, and manage traps for continuous-tone artwork that abuts vector objects (Figure 5-10).

A version called Supertrap Plus is available for the packaging industry, with additional trapping options for controlling the geometry of join lines (making them beveled, round, or mitered, for example) as well as for three-color joins.

OPI

OPI, or Open Prepress Interface, is a set of PostScript commands that lets you design pages with low-resolution *proxy,* or FPO (for position only), images, and then swap in high-resolution versions when it's time to produce separations. Developed by Aldus before it was acquired by Adobe, the specification originally only supported TIFF images. However, the current version, OPI 2.0, supports EPS, PDF, and DCS images as well. Although OPI is an Adobe specification, many non-Adobe products support it, and some vendors have developed their own proprietary implementations, such as Scitex's APR, or automatic picture replacement.

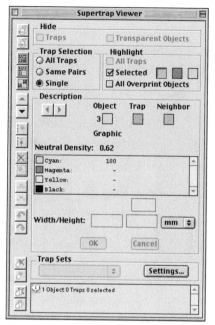

Figure 5-10 Heidelberg's Supertrap is an Acrobat plug-in that lets you trap by zone, individual pages, or an entire document.

The advantage of OPI workflows is fairly obvious: Until the high-resolution file is swapped in (either by the RIP or just before the file hits the RIP), the layout file and its distilled PDF file remain small and flexible. In addition, OPI facilitates a multi-processing workflow: A page designer can work with the placeholder image at the same time another designer is editing and refining the high-resolution equivalent. OPI can be particularly advantageous in magazine and catalog publishing where ads may not be ready until after the editorial page is final, and pages include lots of images, which would otherwise result in extremely large files.

Keep in mind, though, that OPI was developed at a time when disk space, processing power, and bandwidth were at much more of a premium than they are today. Now that all of those technologies have improved, some people believe OPI has outlived its usefulness. And indeed many prepress shops consider it out of place in composite PDF workflows, where files are already small and PDF is being used to view accurate representations of designed pages. Viewing low-resolution proxies in PDF files pretty much defeats the purpose of the file format. In addition, OPI minimizes the effectiveness of Distiller as well as the preflight step if problematic or corrupt images are added later in the process. And finally, OPI limits your ability to repurpose PDF files if you aren't working from high-resolution original content. You could, of course, swap in high-resolution images when layout is complete but before the file has been distilled, but then you haven't really benefited from OPI's advantages.

OPI IS A NO-GO

We don't support OPI in a PDF workflow. What if you have a big photographic book? If you use low-res images in the PDF file, most of the content of the files isn't being tested. If we have an OPI PostScript file that crashes our RIP, the first thing we do is strip out the images and try again, and nine times out of ten it works. You don't want to send a job to a printer and then find out that half of your art is corrupted.

—Justine Trubey, digital prepress product manager, RR Donnelley Print Solutions

While the problem that OPI was created to address may have been solved and PDF does change the playing field somewhat, there are still plenty of ways that OPI—or at least the concept of using low-resolution images in design and swapping in high-resolution images later—can benefit PDF-based print production. Although bandwidth has increased, so has our capacity to fill it. Publications have become increasingly image rich, and design and production have become more distributed, thanks in no small part to the Internet. Indeed, the Internet and a growing need to publish to wireless devices mean there's greater demand for versions of images in varying sizes and resolutions. This makes a technology like OPI, which can manage all of these images (including their locations, versions, and usage) in a database, a boon. This is especially true if the technology can pair different versions of one image with appropriate-quality PDF files: For example, a medium-resolution RGB image for an eBook, a high-resolution CMYK version for print, and so on. Keep in mind, however, that OPI might not be the only way to streamline such a publishing scenario. (See "OPI Alternatives," page 200.)

If you plan to use an OPI workflow, not only do you need specialized software such as ScenicSoft's ColorCentral to produce the proxies and make the final swaps, you also need to make sure that all of the other applications in your workflow support

OPI—from your page-layout program and Acrobat through whatever trapping, imposition, and separation tools you use. Some of these applications may even perform the final swap for you. Helios' PDF Handshake, for example, will swap high-resolution images into composite PDF files as they're imposed and then separate them (Figure 5-11).

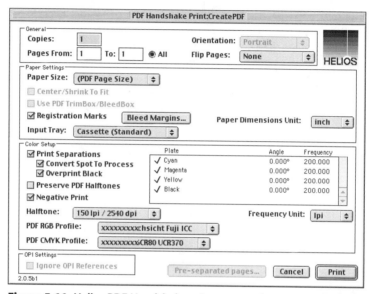

Figure 5-11 Helios PDF Handshake prints composite or separated PDF files to any PostScript printer, recognizing OPI comments in the file.

All of Adobe's page-layout applications, as well as Acrobat, support OPI, as do most of the plug-ins, third-party tools, and automated workflow systems available today. If you use OPI, be sure to activate the proper settings in Distiller when you generate PDF files: Check Preserve OPI Comments in the Advanced panel of the Job Options dialog box (see Chapter 3). If you're not using OPI, you might think it's harmless to leave this box checked, but it does make a difference. Some applications generate OPI comments even if they're not used, which can prevent preflight tools from analyzing the images in your PDF file. If you don't use OPI, uncheck this box to make sure Distiller deletes any irrelevant OPI comments from the PostScript stream.

OPI Alternatives

If you're making major changes to your workflow, such as moving to composite PDF files for prepress, you may want to think a bit more about whether and how you want to incorporate OPI technology. Consider, for example, the case of Eddie Bauer (part of The Spiegel Group).

According to Larisa Sheckler, director of operations for the creative services department of Eddie Bauer, as her company migrates to a direct-to-plate workflow based on composite PDF pages, they're considering also changing from Scitex's APR picture replacement technology to a server-based OPI solution. But Sheckler isn't yet ready to introduce the variable of a new image-swapping technology into the mix." We are in the process of taking out safety nets and building accountability into the workflow," she says. "We need to continue to test and improve our ability to send our vendor clean, error-free files. Once we can do that, we can move from APR to OPI and a true ship-and-RIP workflow."

And by the time Eddie Bauer is ready to consider OPI, Sheckler says, there may be another practical alternative: JPEG 2000. "Our workflow is still being perfected," she says. "When we get to a place internally where we put all the right processes in place, who knows, maybe we'll go OPI, maybe JPEG 2000."

The file format Sheckler is talking about—JPEG 2000—is currently being approved by various international standards committees and uses wavelet-based mathematics to compress and decompress images. Since the decompression step occurs in a series of passes (each of which improves the quality and color of the displayed image), designers and publishers can theoretically control the bit depth and resolution of the final decompressed image—which means that JPEG 2000 could potentially eliminate the need for OPI, since designers could use the file format to output images for a variety of media and hardware devices.

Another alternative to OPI is XML. As publishers grow comfortable using publishing technology to incorporate XML tags into their documents (for example, by creating structured and tagged PDF files), XML could be used to swap low-resolution images for high. In this scenario, PDF acts like a container for content, and XML specifies how the content is used. For more on ways that XML can be used to enhance and complement PDF workflows, see the discussion on JDF in Chapter 6 (page 229) and the section on PDF and XML in Chapter 7 (page 242).

IMPOSITION

When you lay out pages in an application like InDesign or QuarkXPress, they're placed in linear, sequential order. When you distill them to PDF, they stay in that order—fine for electronic documents, where you can scroll through the pages onscreen. However, that page order doesn't translate to printing on an offset or digital press, where a single large sheet of paper holds many different individual pages in specific placement. That's where imposition comes in. Just as page design means arranging text and image elements in a page layout, imposition is the process of arranging the pages of an electronic document in a layout for the press so that when the printed sheet is folded, cut, and bound, the pages fall into the correct reading order.

Imposition Lingo

Before computers entered the picture, the analogous process—called *stripping*—involved manually creating a press layout by cutting film and taping it into position on a flat of paper or plastic, which would be photomechanically imaged onto a plate by exposing it to light. In digital production, however, software can create press layouts automatically, and physical flats of film are falling by the wayside as layouts are imaged directly to plate with lasers. A group of imposed pages that will be imaged to a single plate is called a *form*, and when two forms are printed back to back on a press sheet that will be folded, that's called a *signature*.

Forms are expressed in "*n*-up" terminology, depending on how many pages are on one side of the signature: 2-up, 4-up, 8-up, 16-up, and 32-up, for a maximum signature of 64 pages. Form and signature sizes are determined by document page size, press size, and paper size. Depending on how the paper is turned to be printed on the second side, the layout is called "work and turn" or "work and tumble." You can get a quick idea of how pages are ordered in these configurations by folding a piece of paper at right angles until you have the desired publication length and then number the pages while the sheet is still folded. Unfold them, and you'll see how the pages are positioned in a form (Figure 5-12).

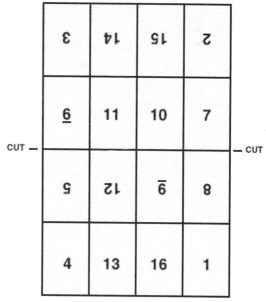

Figure 5-12 An 8-up, 16-page, work-and-turn form.

In certain types of publication printing, signatures must also accommodate a phenomenon called *creep,* which occurs when the inner pages of a publication project out slightly from the outer pages because of the way saddle-stitch binding pushes them. Ultimately, pages are trimmed to smooth the edges; however, imposition software must adjust the content's position on the page so that all pages appear equidistant from the gutter.

In packaging printing, signatures aren't so methodical. Imposition for packaging and other commercial print jobs requires a process called "step and repeat," in which one image or file is duplicated and offset from the original to maximize the number of copies that can be printed on a single press sheet. In this way, printers can also gang multiple jobs on a single press sheet.

What to Look for

While digital imposition isn't the most heart-pounding of technologies, it is an area of prepress that significantly benefits from a PDF workflow. In traditional PostScript workflows, imposition was a monolithic job: The imposition software had to take PostScript data from an entire document file (which could be anywhere from two to thousands of pages long) and configure signatures from that one long, continuous stream (or, more accurately, river) of data. Sure, files could be broken down into shorter segments or reconfigured, but imposing PostScript pages means processing them consecutively and by entire flats—a computationally intensive task that requires a great deal of storage. And since there's a signature for each color plate, any time one page has to be re-imaged, four or more entire forms must be reimposed. If you're working with 8-up or larger layouts, this can slow production to a crawl.

Compared with the above scenario, PDF-based imposition offers a number of advantages. For one, composite files are much smaller and thus faster to impose. In addition, because PDF files are object oriented, you get accurate onscreen previews that you can use to check positioning, creep, and so on. And finally, because these files are page-independent, you can easily swap individual pages in and out of forms for greater flexibility and control over press layouts—which also mitigates the need to generate entire plates or sheets of film when typos or other errors require new separations.

The first thing you'll want to seek out in an imposition package is true, or *native,* support for PDF. By this, I mean the ability to accept PDF files as input, to arrange PDF files on forms, and to spit out PDF forms that will in turn be color separated and editable. Some such packages import and export raw PostScript and/or EPS files; in fact, many have only recently added support for PDF. While such packages initially worked backwards, converting PDF into PostScript and then processing and saving the raw PostScript, more and more are using PDF for actual imposition functions.

Since digital imposition packages do more than simply create press-sheet templates, there are other things to consider when selecting such packages. One important feature to look for is OPI support: If you're using an OPI workflow, your imposition software should be able to read OPI comments and maintain placeholder images so that the high-resolution replacements can be swapped in. Usually this is not much of an issue since many vendors of imposition packages also make OPI server software. You'll also want to look for the correct balance of automation and manual control. For example, using actions or macros to save and reuse page templates can speed jobs, as can the ability to drop files into hot folders for processing. It's also nice to be able to automatically forward press forms to output devices for proofs or final imaging (which means such devices will require PPDs) or to other folders for processing by another application, as well as to offer job queue management.

As operator, however, you'll also want to be able to intervene to edit printers' marks and bleeds, adjust page placement and positioning, add page numbers to sheets, rotate pages, and so on. Many packages let you perform these tasks on individual pages or groups of pages. Another highly touted feature these days is *page pairing,* which allows forms or signatures to be configured in advance so that pages can be dropped into place as they arrive in hot folders or job queues. This is useful in newspaper and magazine publishing, where document files arrive out of order and at different times.

PDF versus EPS

Until imposition and separation packages began to support PDF, many prepress providers had to jump through hoops to impose and separate their PDF files. It was not and still isn't uncommon for these providers to import preflighted PDF files into QuarkXPress and save them as EPS for imposition, or export PDF files from Acrobat as EPS and then place them in QuarkXPress to create DCS files. Such methods have routinely been employed in publication printing workflows, where ads received in PDF needed to be placed as EPS into pages designed in a layout application. Today, however, such acrobatics are unnecessary since third-party imposition and separation products can now process composite PDF files. In addition, Acrobat editing tools (as well as those from third parties, such as CreoScitex's Pagelet) make it feasible to place those PDF ads in PDF files of page layouts.

Imposition Tools

There are about a dozen PDF imposition programs available today, ranging from Acrobat plug-ins to stand-alone applications that can cost anywhere from a few hundred to several thousand dollars. As is the case with so many things, you get what you pay for—which is not to say that the lower-priced products are inferior in quality; they simply don't do as much, which means they're suited for different markets than server-based stand-alone products like Krause Imposition Manager (KIM) PDF Auto Plus. The Quite Imposing Acrobat plug-in, for example, has a handy Create Booklet feature for imposing 2-up booklets for printing to copiers or other digital devices (Figure 5-13), while Krause's KIM offers extensive job control functions and load-balancing for high-volume production environments. As you're researching any of these products, be sure to find out if the vendor offers hands-on training in addition to online tutorials or help services.

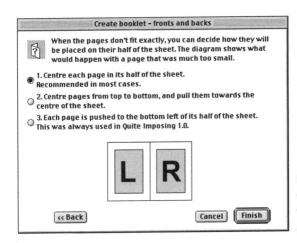

Figure 5-13 Quite Imposing's Create Booklet feature walks you through the process of creating an *n*-up booklet.

Following are brief descriptions of some of the many available PDF imposition programs.

DK&A INposition

In addition to being able to impose PostScript, EPS, and PDF files, INposition prides itself on being able to impose native QuarkXPress and PageMaker files and a variety of image file formats, from PICT to TIFF. This Mac-only program works synergistically with DK&A's (www.dka.com) Mac-based Trapper software, an object-oriented trapping program that also performs color separations and includes an XTension to control trapping within XPress. This program does not trap native PDF files.

Dynagram DynaStrip

DynaStrip's latest and greatest is a versioning module that creates multiple templates of the same layout to accommodate multilanguage editions of publications, publications with localized content, and direct marketing. The software, which performs native PDF imposition, employs a modular architecture that allows it to tie into a variety of prepress systems, applications, and RIPs, such as Scitex Brisque, PCC Artwork's PageFlow and Nexus, and CreoScitex Prinergy. DynaStrip is available for both Mac and Windows.

IPTech ImpozeIt

This Windows-based client/server product imposes PDF files and outputs PDF or PostScript forms, including PostScript 3. It includes wizards to help set up workflows, load balancing (by performing partial output and partial impositioning), and client-side job monitoring and status bars.

OneVision Secare

Secare, which is Latin for "to cut, divide, or slice," is a digital imposition package that accepts, processes, and outputs PDF, PostScript, and EPS files.

Quite Imposing

Quite Imposing differs from the other imposition packages listed here in that it's an Acrobat plug-in—which means it works only with PDF files. All of the other imposition applications listed here are stand-alone programs that can accept a multitude of file formats. Quite Imposing and Quite Imposing Plus are well suited to imposing PDF pages for digital printing (Figure 5-13).

ScenicSoft Preps

ScenicSoft has been around for ages by technology standards: Founded in 1985, it began offering Preps in 1992. In addition to being sold as a stand-alone imposition package, Preps (Figure 5-14) is integrated with numerous prepress workflow systems, including Agfa Apogee, CreoScitex Prinergy, Scitex Brisque, and Rampage. It offers mixing and matching of file types on any job, support for OPI, and support for the XML-based Job Definition Format in the CIP4 standard (see Chapter 6, page 230) as well as portable job tickets. The Windows version can output to digital printing devices. Pandora, ScenicSoft's PDF imposition program for packaging and labeling, includes support for die-cutting.

Figure 5-14 ScenicSoft Preps imposes native PDF files and provides a full, interactive preview of the press form.

Shira PDF Organizer

Developed by the Polish company AC&C, PDF Organizer is a complete PDF imposition package that uses Distiller to convert incoming files (such as EPS, TIFF, JPEG, and PostScript) to PDF/X format for processing (see Chapter 6, page 234 for a discussion of PDF/X). In addition, the program can produce imposed PDF files with or without job tickets (see Chapter 6 for more on job tickets). This Windows-based product works with sibling application PDF Merge-It, an OPI server, to handle OPI workflows.

Ultimate Technographics Impostrip and Impress

Ultimate Technographics (www.ultimate-tech.com) offers two imposition programs: Impostrip, a kitchen-sink program, imposes *n*-up and step-and-repeat layouts for sheetfed and web offset press runs; Impress imposes PDF and PostScript files for digital presses.

SEPARATIONS

The fundamental concept behind PDF-based graphic arts workflows is that the files are composite—that is, all of the color-channel data resides in one file, and what you see onscreen represents the color and content of the printed document. For the greatest flexibility (smallest file sizes, greatest editability, and most accurate color previews), PDF files should remain composite until as late as possible in the production process—usually until after trapping, imposition, and OPI swaps have occurred and just before the pages are rasterized to film or plate. In other words, until you perform color separations—the point of no return.

Whatever your digital file contains at this point will be imaged and printed—which means color, fonts, and traps must all be properly applied. In Extreme workflows (as well as in some other digital prepress workflows), trapping and separations are performed in the RIP; however, in our homegrown workflow, you perform these tasks before final rasterization. Even if the RIP performs the separations, a prepress operator must still specify how to handle them (for example, what screening, dot gain, and other parameters to apply) in a third-party application.

TAKING RESPONSIBILITY

We're starting to send our printer composite PDF files for direct to plate printing, putting more responsibility on us, but that's a better choice. If there's a duotone in there, we have to make sure it's specified correctly. If there's a spot color in a chart, we have to convert it to process color in Illustrator before we make the PDF. So even though it's more responsibility, we do want to go to PDF because it gives us more control over our final files. And if we're building electronic files, why not go as far as we can to cut out couriers and intermediate steps? Plus, it should give our vendors more time to do what they need to do.

—*Paul Bunyar, senior graphic artist, American Century*

In pure PostScript workflows prior to PDF, separations were often generated before files were imposed because the imposed PostScript files were too big to move and process efficiently. However, the process of separating individual PostScript pages and then creating impositions from four files for each page in a flat is (as you might suspect) highly inefficient and inherently risky: It means producing and managing four times as much data (not including spot colors) earlier in the workflow. And to correct last-minute mistakes on a page, you have to create four new separations and then reimpose the entire four forms.

Keeping PDF files composite through imposition provides a much more practical and reliable solution. By keeping pages independent, you can at the last minute replace bad PDF pages in the imposition with corrected files—and because PDF is composite, you're dealing with only one page file and one imposition file, both of which are smaller and thus more manageable than their PostScript equivalents.

The Magic of Screening

Creating separations is the process of dividing a composite color file, such as CMYK, into its discrete color channels. The reason you need to color-separate files is because of the way printing presses work: Offset lithographic presses comprise multiple printing units, each of which is made up of a series of rollers and cylinders. Around one of these cylinders is a plate that has been imaged from a digital separation. When the paper passes this plate, the ink that corresponds to that separation is applied; in standard four-color printing, that's cyan, magenta, yellow, and black. The paper proceeds successively through one printing unit for each color until all four (or two or six or five) inks have been applied and the final piece has the appearance of continuous-tone color even though only four (or three or seven) inks have been used.

Thus, each separation produced from a composite file corresponds to one sheet of film that will be used to image a printing plate (or to one actual plate in the case of computer-to-plate printing). Extracted from the composite color file, each separation is simply grayscale data that correlates pixel data to drops of ink. (You can see why all of the color data in your file must be CMYK before you get to this point. If RGB or spot colors are mixed in your file, it can wreak havoc with your separations.)

To create the look of continuous-tone color in print, you have to perform a little trick. Presses are capable of printing only four inks (let's say, for the sake of keeping things simple), and they can either print a drop of ink (or toner) or not. It's binary: The ink or toner is there or not. But by applying screening to our files when we separate them, we fool our eyes into being able to see many more colors and subtle transitions than are physically on the page.

The most common screen type is a halftone—a square cell containing a *spot* that's usually round, though it can be elliptical, square, or another shape as well. These halftone spots are themselves made up of smaller *dots*—the actual ink or toner dots that printing devices can lay down or image. The number of dots per inch (dpi) that a device can print represents its resolution, which can range from 300 dpi for some desktop printers (though most don't fall below 600 dpi these days) to 2,400 dpi for imagesetters and platesetters.

Thus, the size of a halftone spot depends on the number of dots it contains This is why halftone screening is sometimes called AM, or amplitude-modulated, screening. The larger the spot, the darker the tint in that printed area; the smaller the spot, the lighter the tint (Figure 5-15). (Remember, because we're separating color data into grayscale channels, tint can also be thought of as gray levels on film or plate.)

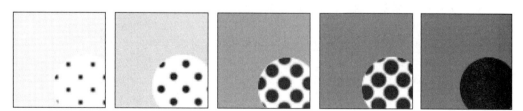

Figure 5-15 Left to right: a 10 percent, 25 percent, 50 percent, 75 percent, and 100 percent tint.

Although the size of halftone ink dots may vary, they're laid on a grid so that their centers are equidistant. The grids are offset at angles from the horizontal in what's called the color's *screen angle* (Table 5-1). If the grids weren't offset, the dots would be apparent and distracting. When offset at angles, the dots form a circular rosette pattern that makes color appear to blend smoothly, especially at high screen frequencies (hold your horses, I'll explain screen frequency in a minute). When grids are too closely spaced, when they are overlaid, or when the paper shifts on press causing misregistration, the result is an interfering moiré pattern that distracts the viewer from the content of the image (Figure 5-16). If your image contains a pattern (such as in fabric) that matches one of the screen angles, it can also produce what's called a "subject moiré."

Ink	Screen angle
Black	45°
Magenta	75°
Yellow	90°
Cyan	105°

Table 5-1 Conventional screen angles for four-color process printing.

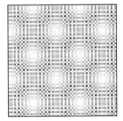

Figure 5-16 A pleasing rosette (left) vs. a distracting moiré pattern.

To recap (because I know this gets confusing), halftone dots can vary in size across an image or a page, but the distance between them remains fixed. This distance is called the halftone's *screen frequency*, or screen ruling. Screen frequency is expressed in terms of lines per inch (lpi), which refers to the number of rows (lines) of halftone dots in each inch. The higher the screen frequency, the smaller the halftone dots (the higher the resolution), which means printed color appears finer and more detailed.

Of course, you can't just slap down any screen frequency you desire—say, 300 lpi just because you think it will look better. Printing press, paper stock, and the capabilities of your imaging device combine to determine the screen frequency you need. For example, newsprint is typically printed at a low screen ruling (85 lpi) because the paper is porous and the press operates at high speeds, which means that finer rulings would lay down too much ink, oversaturating and plugging up color images. Magazines and catalogs, meanwhile, are printed at 133 lpi to 175 lpi because their coated stock can hold the shape of finer dots. Higher line screens, such as 300 lpi, are usually reserved for extremely high-quality reproduction, such as fine-art posters or books being printed on a waterless press.

As for the capabilities of the imaging device, you'll need to balance your line-screen ruling with the resolution that the device can print: The greater the line screen you specify, the fewer levels of gray that are available to it. To maintain close to 256 levels of gray, use the guidelines in Table 5-2.

Output device resolution (dpi)	Maximum line screen (lpi)
600	38
1000	63
2400	150
3600	225

Table 5-2 Use these guidelines to produce separations for PostScript Level 2 devices. Because PostScript 3 offers smooth shading, you can customize these settings by increasing line screens for those devices without necessarily compromising gray levels.

FM Screening

If you plan to print extremely high-quality pieces that require 300 lpi or greater, you may want to consider stochastic, or frequency-modulated (FM), screening. In some ways, this represents the inverse of halftone screening since the dots on the page are the same size but distributed differently: In areas that need to appear dark in tint, the dots are clustered densely, while in lighter areas they're more sparsely distributed (Figure 5-17).

Figure 5-17 Here we see an area of an image as it would be screened by a halftone (top) or stochastic (bottom) algorithm.

Stochastic screening offers a couple of advantages over halftone screening: There's no grid and there are no screen angles, which means there's no chance of moiré patterns appearing in print. And because there are no screen angles to conflict, stochastic screening is also well suited to printing with more than four colors. Stochastic screening is also more tolerant of press misregistration, and because its dots are so small—under 20 microns in diameter, compared with about 50 microns for halftones—they excel at reproducing fine detail such as fabrics and jewelry.

However, in images that don't have a lot of detail—flat or low-contrast areas, or images with lots of highlights—FM screening can cause graininess or noise. And because this type of screen uses such a fine dot, you need greater process control to ensure that dots are imaged cleanly. Most importantly, FM screens require specialized separation software and RIPs (as well as imaging devices that can produce a fine enough dot); they can't be produced from either of the two Acrobat separation plug-ins discussed in the following pages. Agfa, Heidelberg, CreoScitex, and Harlequin, however, all have stochastic screening algorithms that can be applied when in-RIP separations are produced with their software.

Whichever screening method you use, you must also compensate for *dot gain,* which occurs when ink spreads slightly into the paper it's printed on. (Gain can also occur when dot sizes increase as they're transferred from film to plate, but this isn't as big an issue, especially in these days of CTP and digital printing.) Dot gain depends largely on printing conditions—the type of press and inks being used, and the porousness of the paper—but it ranges from 12 to 15 percent for sheet-fed presses printing on coated stock to 30 to 40 percent on newsprint. Dot gain is measured from the midtone, where it has the greatest effect: Thus, 15 percent gain means a 50 percent dot prints at 65 percent, so you must anticipate and compensate for that gain by creating a 35 percent dot on film or plate, for example, instead of 50 percent. (FM screening algorithms build in dot gain compensation; you can't manually control it.)

Color Separating Software

Dot gain—as well as screen frequencies, angles, spot shapes, and other settings (such as whether and how to convert spot colors to process, so you don't end up with any unwanted plates)—can and should be addressed in separation software. Although designers can include all of this information in their distilled PDF files if they specify it in application software, screening information (like that of trapping and imposition) is device specific. Unless your printer tells you exactly what to put in all of the separation and trapping dialog boxes in PageMaker, InDesign, or QuarkXPress, you're better off leaving those fields empty (or at their default settings) or specifying in-RIP separations (if that option is available, such as in InDesign). Your prepress partner can take it from there.

Because separations require a sophisticated understanding of both digital imaging and four-color printing, and because the process of creating them is so integrally tied to rasterizing the final page and sending it to a marking engine, it's little wonder that there are only two off-the-shelf Acrobat tools for creating them: Lantana Crackerjack and Callas pdfOutputPro. These products are rather like David to the Extreme workflow systems' Goliath: As low-cost tools that do a fine job of separating PDF files, they're in hundreds, if not thousands, more print shops—small commercial printers and prepress providers that don't need mammoth, automated Extreme workflow systems.

Crackerjack (Figure 5-18) is the more robust of the two tools; it produces four-color halftone separations complete with spot color mapping to CMYK or other spot color definitions, and it offers separation previews that display overprints, knockouts, and transparency.

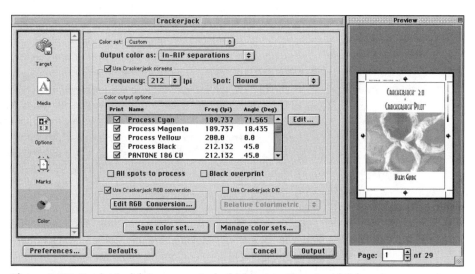

Figure 5-18 Crackerjack lets you control which separations to print, how to map spot colors, line screen and screen angle specifications, and dot-gain compensation.

A few final thoughts on separations in homegrown PDF workflows. You probably already understand that in moving to computer-to-plate production, you lose a couple of your QA checks: If you're used to inspecting film separations for scratches or specks and to make sure that traps, bleeds, and tints are accurately imaged, kiss that step good-bye. Just try to inspect four 32-by-44-inch aluminum plates for every press form; I doubt your printer will want to overnight them to you.

If you design and produce publications, you'll probably also miss your bluelines, the pagination proof used to check image positioning, color breaks, and type as well as front-to-back page registration. Most digital imposition proofers, which are wide-format inkjet plotters, can't print two-sided pages, are low resolution, and aren't well calibrated, so they're not as useful.

As you can see, CTP production requires a bit more trust. However, Crackerjack can help you out here: Use it to perform a preflight separation, if you will, of your PDF files to see if your color channels are in order or to produce a low-cost separation proof on your own output devices using generic screening specifications (or exact specifications, if your printer can provide them). You can even ask your printer to send you the trapped and imposed PDF flat, along with the screening parameters for the job, and then create an in-house imposition or pagination proof if you have the hardware. Of course, you still can't identify specks or scratches that might taint the printing plate, but it gives you a rough equivalent to the proofs you're accustomed to seeing in your film-based workflow.

Duotones and DeviceN

PDF used to get a bum rap for how it handled (or, more accurately, *didn't* handle) certain aspects or types of color reproduction: namely spot colors and duotones. The problem was that these colors couldn't be properly separated from composite PDF files based on PostScript Level 2. However, these problems were resolved with Acrobat 4.0 (PDF 1.3). With this version of Acrobat, PDF began to support PostScript 3, which added the DeviceN color space. As I'm sure you remember from college calculus, n is a variable typically used to express any number greater than or equal to 1, and is often used to raise integers to the nth power (x^n), quickly making it a much bigger number.

The DeviceN color space works analogously to give print publishers an exponential increase in their reproducible gamut of color. It can be used to define the color capabilities of any PostScript 3 device above and beyond CMYK or RGB, whose gamuts are far more limited than what the human eye can see. This means that if any non-RGB or non-CMYK colors have been specified in an application—such as spot Pantone, metallic, or HiFi colors; or multitones, which increase the tonal range of images by printing a grayscale image with two or more inks—PostScript 3 will carry the mathematical descriptions of those colors in the file, be it PostScript or PDF, until it is sent to an imaging device. If that device happens to be an imagesetter or platesetter, a grayscale separation or plate will be rendered for that particular color of ink; if the output device is a proofer, such as an inkjet printer, it will print those colors directly—assuming it has the proper toner or inks to do so.

RIP

RIPs accept data in various formats: Some can process PDF files natively, others require that the PDF first be converted to PostScript 2 or 3. In either case, the RIP is where all of your prepress decision-making is put to the test—I mean, put to rest. After all, if you've successfully trapped, imposed, and separated the PDF file, then the process of rasterizing it to bitmapped data and forwarding it to an image-setter, platesetter, or digital press shouldn't be a nail-biter. And with some time and experience under your belt, it won't be.

In some sense, the PDF workflow ends here, but if you read the next chapter you'll learn about a variety of standards efforts that incorporate PDF into an even larger workflow picture, all the way through post-processing steps such as trimming and binding printed pieces.

PDF FULL STEAM AHEAD

For four years, every job that has gone through our DI press has been PDF. We drew the line and decided to use PDF for the whole process. The benefits were the ability to electronically exchange proofs, to RIP the file, and to send off a low-res copy for customers who were in a hurry and couldn't wait for us to mail them one. It also made it easier to step-and-repeat and impose artwork. We believed that PDF was the future, so we used it for this new service.

—Tom Mornini, president, InfoMania Printing & Prepress, Inc.

CHAPTER SIX

Workflow Systems and Alphabet Soup

After reading the title of this chapter, you may be wondering what two such disparate concepts have to do with one another. Let me assure you, they're integrally tied, as I'll make clear over the course of this chapter.

Adobe Extreme workflow systems take the processes outlined in the previous chapter and wrap them up in a big fat bow that automates and streamlines PDF print production. Now imagine, if you will, that this ribbon is covered with bold, black letters—PJTF, JDF, PDF/X-3, PPML. The technologies represented by this alphabet soup of acronyms not only help drive automated workflow systems, in many ways they're driving the future of PDF workflows as a whole. Read on to see how.

WHAT'S EXTREME?

Any product or technology branded Extreme brings to my mind at least images of snowboarders, skateboarders, and motocross riders. Although managing PDF workflows isn't nearly as exhilarating as such x-sports, Extreme PDF workflows do have something in common with them: speed and fluidity. Rooted in PDF, Extreme workflow systems take advantage of the format's complete and compact nature as well as its page independence to modularize and streamline prepress tasks and rasterization. Such systems also provide process control, coordination, and automation features, such as job tracking and scheduling, error notification, and correction handling. Not surprisingly, the larger the print operation, the greater the benefit of an Extreme workflow.

Also not surprisingly, these systems have price tags to match their capabilities, starting at tens of thousands of dollars—a factor that puts them out of reach for many small and midsize shops. For these types of operations, homegrown systems such as those addressed in the previous chapter probably offer a better balance of affordability and capability.

All Extreme workflows share some common elements (as defined by Adobe): For starters, they're based in PostScript 3 which means they offer rasterization benefits such as smooth shading and in-RIP trapping. They all also process PDF natively. In addition, all such workflows use a common Distiller-based processing module called the Normalizer. And finally, all Extreme workflows use what Adobe calls a *portable job ticket,* which contains processing information and instructions about a PDF file (for example, which prepress tasks should be performed and what device-specific parameters should be applied).

Because processing instructions are separate from processing tasks, Extreme workflows are highly extensible: Users can add or update individual software modules as needed—without investing in entirely new systems.

Process Players

The software modules that perform prepress tasks in Extreme workflows are called *process players* or *job ticket processors.* These modules take their instructions from the job ticket and perform tasks (preflighting, trapping, and so on) on the associated PDF file. Some of these process players are licensed directly from Adobe or other vendors, while others have been developed by Extreme workflow providers themselves. In the end, it's this mix of players (all of which run on standard platforms), the Extreme interface, and final imaging hardware that distinguishes the various systems.

Of the Extreme process players from Adobe, the Normalizer is perhaps the most essential. The Normalizer is a licensed version of Distiller on which OEM vendors put a custom user interface and add features and capabilities that serve their particular market. In Agfa's Apogee PDF workflow, for example, the Normalizer—called the Pilot—serves as the hub of activity by accepting, creating, and even imposing PDF files. It also integrates Enfocus' PitStop Professional to resolve font, color, and other problematic areas based on specified parameters. CreoScitex's Prinergy Normalizer also incorporates preflighting (for example, mapping spot colors to process and performing OPI image swaps) and additionally distributes processing across multiple servers to speed file creation. If you, as content creator, distill PDF files from your application documents before handing them off, your prepress partner or printer will skip to the preflight step in an Extreme workflow. Don't think this gets you off the hook, however. It's still your responsibility to provide your prepress partners with high-quality final PDF files.

One of the benefits of Extreme workflows is that you can perform processing tasks in whatever sequence makes the most sense for a given shop or job. Such tasks can be performed in tandem or consecutively, and you can omit steps that aren't pertinent. Because the pages remain in PDF throughout the process, you can visually check and edit them at any time prior to rasterization.

Process Management

If you think of process players as the rooms of a house, job tickets would be the beams and girders holding the structure together. Portable job tickets—written in the Portable Job Ticket Format (PJTF), an extension of the PDF language—outline the tasks that need to be performed on print jobs in Extreme workflows. This includes prepress instructions such as how jobs should be trapped, screened, and imposed. Once these tickets have been defined, jobs can move through prepress with a minimum of human intervention (though the operator can step in to resolve errors or reroute jobs or tasks as necessary).

Extreme Systems

The Extreme workflow systems offered by vendors such as Agfa and Heidelberg are closely tied to their manufacturers' output hardware: CreoScitex's Prinergy, for example, is most commonly used with computer-to-plate systems, while Agfa Apogee drives imagesetters and platesetters. IBM Printing Systems, meanwhile, uses it to drive high-speed digital printers. In this way, the various systems are closed; however, they're also open in that they'll generally accept many file formats (such as EPS or TIFF/IT) and convert them to PDF for processing.

Make Room to RIP

Always an issue in Extreme and high-end prepress workflows is the point at which you rasterize your digital file. As an object-oriented file format, PDF must be rasterized to bitmapped pixels that correspond to the dots imaged on a given output device prior to being screened and imaged. However, when the file is rasterized, its format becomes much more limited—bigger and device dependent—which means you want to put off that step as long as possible to maximize your file's flexibility and editability.

Of course, every time you proof you have to rasterize the file, and the eternal challenge for prepress operators is how to make the press run match the contract proof and how to make clients' digital comps match the contract proof. The problem is, each device's RIP can render colors and dots differently every time a file is rasterized and imaged; plus, there's potential for PostScript or other errors to occur every time the file is interpreted.

During the mid- to late 1990s (a millennium ago in tech time), there was a lot of hype about ROOM (RIP once, output many) workflows. The idea here is to break up the rasterization process into two components: interpreting the PostScript into a device-independent file format and then rendering or rasterizing that interim file format to any number of devices. Since interpretation represents the most variable part of the process, ROOM proponents reasoned that if you did that just once, you would theoretically be outputting the same data to all output devices (screening and other device-specific parameters aside). ROOM workflows are especially attractive in computer-to-plate production and digital printing environments, where printers are expected to turn jobs around quickly and minimize proofing cycles.

As one of ROOM's biggest proponents, Heidelberg offered this type of workflow in its Delta RIP. Here, PostScript data is interpreted to a DeltaList—a flat, compressed file that describes the objects on a PostScript page—which is trapped and then rasterized and screened. In addition, RIP vendor Scitex (now CreoScitex) has long interpreted PostScript data into its CTLW format, a raster file that in turn can be trapped, edited if necessary, and screened.

In Extreme and other PDF workflows, PDF becomes that interim file format—even though it's not a raster file. With PDF workflows, each output device must still rasterize the PDF data, which can lead to variance across devices. However, PDF workflows still provide most of the benefits of ROOM: a stable, predictable, editable, and relatively small file for processing. Since some Extreme system manufacturers continue to tout ROOM workflows, however, it raises the question of when in Extreme workflows to rasterize PDF files: before or after imposition? Before or after screening? Rasterized flats are significantly larger than PDF-based flats, so network bandwidth may play a part in your decision. Or you way want to rasterize to screened, separated files as a final step in the process—no sooner. The plain truth is that no one page file, PDF or otherwise, will be rasterized identically on any two devices. The real goals are reliability and flexibility, which PDF workflows provide. For this reason, prepress is moving away from proprietary ROOM workflows and toward open PDF workflows.

Based on a reliable prepress platform and offering built-in job-tracking mechanisms and the potential to tie into external content management systems and Web portals for job submission and management, Extreme systems are ideal for high-volume print production. The following provides an overview of some of these systems, describing what they offer and how they work.

Agfa Apogee

Agfa introduced Apogee—the first PDF workflow system to be released—back in 1997, when many vendors were still ensconced in proprietary ROOM workflows.

- **Components.** Apogee Pilot (Figure 6-1) is the hub of activity in the Apogee workflow. Here, normalization and preflighting take place, job tickets are defined, and two key prepress tasks are executed: imposition and

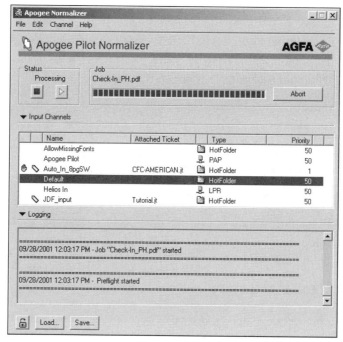

Figure 6-1 The Pilot is where PDF files are normalized in an Apogee workflow system.

OPI image swaps. Imposition is performed through a licensed version of ScenicSoft's Preps; the OPI software is Agfa's own. Through the Pilot, files can be tracked and managed, and files coming from other prepress systems (such as TIFF/IT and Scitex CTLW) can be converted to PDF using a program called CEPSLink.

Apogee also includes a Create module that allows content creators to distill PDF files for use in the Apogee workflow. The software includes Agfa's Normalizer as well as Enfocus PitStop for preflighting, it automatically generates job tickets, and it includes a job ticket editor.

The Apogee RIP performs in-RIP separations and trapping. Screening can employ either Agfa's Balanced (halftone) or CristalRaster (stochastic) technology; trapping can be applied per page or by zone. The RIP, which can also accept raw PostScript Level 1 and Level 2 data, rasterizes screened pages to disk so that you can view them onscreen or print out a proof to check colors, dots, and traps before imaging film or plates.

Once pages are rasterized, Apogee PrintDrive manages their output. It accepts files from any networked RIP and spools them to the various output devices or marking engines, sending them to the shortest queue for the fastest production. Like the RIP, PrintDrive allows you to preview rasterized files, and it will even drive some non-Agfa systems, such as the Polaroid PolaProof halftone contract proofing device.

- **Output.** Apogee connects to Agfa imagesetters (AccuSet, Avantra, Phoenix) and platesetters (Galileo), and to the Agfa Sherpa wide-format inkjet proofer.

- **Distinctions.** Apogee's ability to drive output devices from other companies makes it easy to integrate with printers' legacy imaging hardware.

- **Market.** Commercial printers, small and large.

- **Platform.** Windows NT. Apogee Create is available for both Mac and Windows.

CreoScitex Prinergy

Prinergy was developed jointly by Creo and Heidelberg and then became a product of CreoScitex (though it's still available as an OEM product from Heidelberg). This technology is noteworthy because it's optimized to serve computer-to-plate production environments.

- **Components.** Prinergy stores job ticket information in an Oracle database, which handles job management, archiving, and file storage, and provides feedback and reports on job status and errors (Figure 6-2). In the Prinergy workflow, a *process plan* describes the tasks required for each job and the sequence in which they're executed (as described in the job ticket). As soon as a job is registered in the system, it's sent through a refining process that includes the Prinergy Normalizer, where it's distilled into structured, pre-flighted PDF data that's either composite or separate. (Incoming data can be PostScript, CTLW, TIFF/IT, DCS, and more.) The resulting PDF pages are considered the production "digital masters"—that is, fully normalized, optimized, color managed, trapped, and ready for proofing or final output. The refining process, like all Prinergy processes, can take advantage of distributed processing across a network of servers to optimally balance workloads based on available resources; multiple jobs can also be processed simultaneously.

Prinergy uses its own object-based trapping software, which is built into the refining process and is performed on composite PDF files. You can use an interactive trap editor inside Acrobat to manually create, edit, or delete traps.

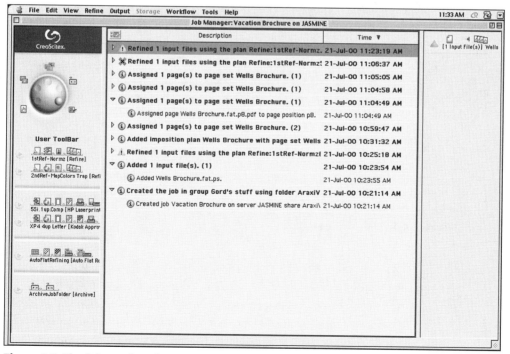

Figure 6-2 The Prinergy interface.

(The trapping software is also available as a stand-alone package called Supertrap, as I mentioned in Chapter 5.)

After these trapped digital-master PDF files have been generated, other pre-press processes can be performed: namely, proofing and imposition, the final steps in the Prinergy system before files are rendered and screened (Figure 6-3). Prinergy uses third-party software (typically ScenicSoft's Preps) for imposition and to create templates. Because files aren't rendered until the last minute, pages and signatures can be edited until the latest possible moment. Screening parameters are applied within the Prinergy rendering engine at the time of output, when a page or signature is sent to an imagesetter or platesetter.

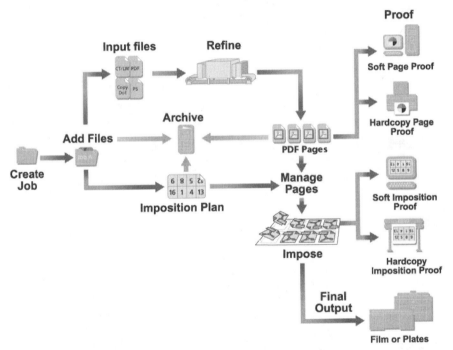

Figure 6-3 The Prinergy workflow.

A recent addition to the Prinergy system is InSite, a Web portal that allows remote proofing of files as well as review, collaboration, and job tracking. Through a Web browser, customers can log on to InSite (which can be password protected) to submit jobs or check job status. They can also view PDF proofs and annotate them with requests for changes or approve them.

- **Output.** Prinergy can drive Creo and Heidelberg imagesetters and plate-setters, as well as a wide variety of proofers from numerous vendors and Heidelberg's direct-imaging press, the DI.

- **Distinctions.** Prinergy's Oracle database can integrate with systems used for scheduling, billing, customer relations, and other tasks—in departments outside prepress.

- **Market.** Commercial printers, especially publication printers that can bene-fit from templated, automated processing. The company makes several ver-sions of Prinergy for different market segments: Connect is the mainstay system with the InSite portal, Direct is a remote plating system for printers with distributed prepress sites, Entro is an entry-level workflow system that drives four- and eight-up Creo platesetters, and Powerpack is for offset and flexographic packaging printers.

- **Platform.** Macintosh and Windows.

PRINERGY POSITIVES

One of the reasons we went with Prinergy is that it works with PDF as single-page elements, so we could pull multiple files together at run time with one job ticket. Using PDF for assembly and imposition saves us time and builds consistency into our process. Each position on a form can be a different file (a card and a label, for example, or a run of three floral tags on one form). It's very efficient that way. Also, Prinergy binds imposition as late as possible, which was very important to us, and it's automated, which is key.

—Mark Martin, The John Henry Co.

Fujifilm CelebraNT

Guess what platform this software RIP from Fujifilm Electronic Imaging runs on? Seriously, though, one of the factors that differentiates CelebraNT from Prinergy and Apogee is the way it handles imposition.

- **Components.** CelebraNT is a straightforward PostScript 3 RIP designed to process PDF page files, using job tickets. Like other Extreme workflow sys-tems, CelebraNT processes jobs into page-independent PDF files that you can edit if necessary. From that point, pages can be rasterized either in-RIP or post-RIP. In one workflow, CelebraNT imposes the high-resolution, ras-terized pages into a signature that can be proofed or sent to a final output device. In this scenario, CelebraNT draws high-resolution images from an OPI server if required. In an alternative workflow, CelebraNT can generate low-resolution EPS files from every normalized PDF page, which can then be imported into an imposition template while their PDF counterparts are rasterized. The RIP then pulls down the high-resolution pages when they're ready. In both scenarios, trapping and screening are performed in-RIP, and CelebraNT can then descreen the rasterized files to proof them to a device other than the final marking engine.

A remote option lets users on client Macintosh and Windows systems access the CelebraNT RIP, and CelebraNT offers a Primer module that can be distributed to clients so that they can distill proper PDF files.

- **Output.** Fujifilm and Hewlett-Packard proofing devices; Fuji imagesetters and platesetters.

- **Distinctions.** CelebraNT is married to Fujifilm input devices (scanners) and output devices.

- **Market.** Large and small prepress and printing environments.

- **Platform.** Windows NT.

Screen Trueflow

Dainippon Screen's Trueflow, like CreoScitex's Prinergy, uses a relational database to manage file processing. However, Trueflow differs from other Extreme systems in that it can process PostScript and other files directly—without going through PDF.

- **Components.** Although Screen doesn't brand Trueflow with an Extreme moniker, the company has worked closely with Adobe to base the system on the PDF file format, and it has all of the elements of a typical Extreme workflow: Trueflow accepts and normalizes incoming files to page-independent PDF files, then performs prepress tasks based on instructions in an accompanying job ticket. Trueflow uses hot folders to automate tasks and a relational database server to store files and manage processes. The system itself is operated through any Java-capable Web browser (Figure 6-4): The browser provides the interface for executing and tracking all jobs, as well as setting up job tickets. Trueflow performs trapping automatically as soon as a file enters the system; however, you can also use a trap editor to customize settings. After trapping, the file is imposed and screened—both of which are performed in-RIP. Imposition, screening, and trapping are all done using Screen's own

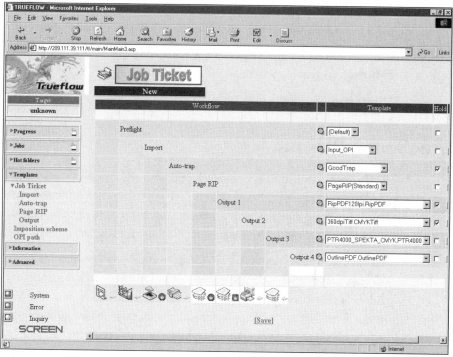

Figure 6-4 All Trueflow processes, including creating job tickets, are driven through Java-enabled Web browsers.

software and algorithms; preflighting is performed by software developed for Screen by Adobe.

Trueflow distinguishes itself from other Extreme workflow systems in a number of ways: First, it uses its own internal job ticket format, not Adobe's, which allows Trueflow to use the same trapping technology that the company developed for its other workflow product, Taigaspace. In addition, although the system can generate a normalized PDF file, it typically creates and uses an internal file called TRP (trapped file) to drive its trapping engine and then go to the RIP. In this way Trueflow can take in a number of file formats—raw PostScript, EPS, separated 1-bit TIFF files, PDF, and PJTF files—and keep their contents intact so that they can be sent straight to an imagesetter or platesetter, for example, without intermediate processing or handling. It also allows the system to generate raster and other files: TIFF/IT, for example, or PostScript.

- **Output.** Trueflow can output to screen imagesetters, platesetters, and digital proofers; various file formats will drive existing legacy equipment.

- **Distinctions.** The Web interface, which allows an unlimited number of users to access the system, is well-suited to cross-platform production environments as well as remote processing.

- **Market.** Midsize printers and four-up and eight-up CTP environments.

- **Platform.** Windows NT.

CreoScitex Brisque

While CreoScitex's Prinergy was developed with PDF workflows in mind, Brisque was created as a Scitex "digital front end" (RIP) using the company's raster CTLW format. It has been subsequently adapted to an Extreme prepress workflow, allowing long-time Scitex users to migrate to PDF from their legacy Scitex systems.

- **Components.** As one of the first high-end prepress systems to automate workflows with job tickets, Brisque uses its own job ticket technology, not Adobe's portable job tickets, but is migrating to JDF job tickets. The system normalizes incoming files (in any number of formats, including PostScript, DCS, CTLW, and more), and then preflights and edits them using Enfocus' PitStop Professional. These normalized PDF files can be returned to clients for approval, then when they're approved, they can take one of two processing routes: Brisque can rasterize PDF files to the CreoScitex linework format and perform all subsequent processing on that raster file, including trapping with CreoScitex's Full Auto Frame software, imposition with Brisque Impose (an OEM version of ScenicSoft's Preps), and screening using any of CreoScitex's screening algorithms. In addition, OPI swaps can be performs with APR (automatic picture replacement) either in the Normalizer or in-RIP.

  Alternatively, Brisque can perform all of the requisite prepress processing tasks on PDF files: Acrobat is a standard component of the system, so customers also have the option of performing such tasks as trapping and imposition (using such programs as Supertrap) before rasterizing.

- **Output.** Brisque can output to CreoScitex imagesetters and platesetters as well as digital printing and proofing devices, including Iris inkjet printers.

- **Distinctions.** Although it wasn't conceived with PDF in mind, Brisque has gone a long way to accommodate PDF workflows, giving users the choice of leveraging PDF for any or all prepress tasks or relying instead on the company's raster CTLW format. For many, it might offer the best of both worlds.

- **Market.** A wide span of graphic arts institutions and workflows, including commercial, publication, and packaging printing, on-demand printing, and in-house printing plants.

- **Platform.** Unix and Macintosh.

ALPHABET SOUP

You can't get very far into a discussion of PDF workflows—especially Extreme workflows—without finding yourself swimming in a sea of acronyms: PJTF, PPML, PDF/X, PDF/X-1, and PDF/X-3 to name a few. I've already touched on one of the big ones—job tickets that fall under the PJTF heading—but not even that one is straightforward, since there's also the emerging acronym JDF. The following section explains the differences between PJTF and JDF, and brings you up to speed on the significance of all the other TLAs—and FLAs and SLAs.

PJTF and JDF

It's hard to accept that workflow systems built within the last five years could already be out of date, but such is the way of technology. Even before PDF had been fully accepted by the market and partially integrated into most prepress workflows, a key element of Extreme was being pushed aside by a newer and more flexible element: PJTF job tickets were taking a backseat to JDF—or job definition format—tickets.

PJTF job tickets contain instructions and descriptions of what needs to be done in prepress: how to trap, screen, and so on. They're used in PDF workflows, and are themselves PDF files. They can take the form of reusable templates, but that's as far as they go.

JDF job tickets, in contrast, are based in XML and address the entire manufacturing process—from design through prepress, press, postpress, and delivery. JDF 1.0, released in spring of 2001, is meant to streamline and automate communication and production in any type of publishing environment, including on-demand printing and e-commerce companies, and especially to help printers produce increasingly complex jobs and shorter run lengths. With JDF, you can define such postpress tasks as binding and cutting as well as bridging the communication gap between actual production machinery and the systems that drive them.

Distiller Clones

The Normalizer that is part of Extreme workflow systems is essentially Distiller with some custom enhancements. Although there are several PDF creation tools on the market besides Acrobat Distiller, few produce PDF files as stable and reliable as those created by Distiller. Many such tools were developed to augment Acrobat, offering ways to convert images or HTML to PDF, or to automate conversion processes from Word or other business applications. As you'll recall from Chapter 2, most of these alternative creation tools do not process PostScript data, and thus the resulting PDF files are not suitable for high-resolution imaging and printing. There are only two bona fide non-Adobe PDF creation tools that interpret PostScript: Aladdin GhostScript and Global Graphics' Jaws PDF Creator.

Jaws PDF Creator, formerly called NikNak, works much like Distiller: It acts like a PostScript print driver so that you can either print to it from an application or drag and drop PostScript or EPS files onto it on the desktop to convert them to PDF. Available for Windows and the Mac, it offers a Distiller-like job options control panel, including a predefined setting for files that will be commercially printed.

GhostScript is a PostScript interpreter available for Windows, OS/2, Linux, and various flavors of Unix. Written in C, GhostScript comes in two versions: AFPL (also known as Aladdin) GhostScript and GNU GhostScript. These versions are essentially the same except that GNU is slightly behind in development, and its licensing policies are subtly different: Both allow free use and copying, but only GNU GhostScript allows commercial distribution, and only under certain conditions. GhostScript is a command-driven program, but graphical interfaces are available that allow you to view and print interpreted pages: Viewing applications include GSview for Windows, OS/2, and Linux; MacGSView for the Mac; and Ghostview on Unix. Although it can produce PDF 1.4 files, GhostScript isn't really a suitable replacement for Distiller because as freeware it doesn't come with a warranty or tech support. In addition, all of the tools required to process and manage PDF files for prepress are integrally tied to Distiller, making GhostScript and PDF Creator secondary players. GhostScript is, however, embedded in many commercial printing devices (licensed through Artifex Software).

Hold onto your boogie boards now, here comes another wave of acronyms: JDF is being developed by the CIP4, an association of industry vendors (including Adobe), printers, organizations, and others who are promoting computer-based integration of graphic arts processes through this standard. CIP4 is also the successor to CIP3, which was founded in 1995 and developed the PPF standard, which I'll get to in a minute. CIP3 stands for the International Cooperation for the Integration of Prepress, Press, and Postpress. CIP4 added a *P*: It's the International Cooperation for the Process Integration of Prepress, Press, and Postpress.

Because JDF job tickets are based in XML, they're much more extensible and open than PJTF job tickets: They can be used by any vendor's hardware and software as well as integrated into multivendor print production workflows. In addition, they can grow to encompass processes and devices not yet anticipated—for example, JDF is already being eyed for integration with e-commerce systems. To better understand what JDF job tickets offer, let's backtrack for a moment to the CIP3 PPF standard.

CIP3 and CIP4

Before it became CIP4, CIP3 developed the print production format (PPF) standard, a PostScript-based wrapper for digital prepress files (like the PTJF). PPF does not contain the high-resolution content itself, but rather the following:

*   Administrative metadata such as job name, copyright info, the application file used, and so on

*   Preview images for each color separation, which allows ink keys to be preset on press

*   Transfer functions, to calculate the area of ink coverage

*   Position and color of color and density measuring strips

*   Position of registration marks

*   Cutting and folding data for imposition

*   Application- and vendor-specific data, such as machine settings for reprints

*   Information about binding, stitching, and trimming

Although PPF is based on PostScript, it's an open standard that any vendor can use to automate processes. In addition to offering quicker setup and production, some of the major benefits of the CIP3 PPF standard are ecological: Less paper, ink, and water are wasted in press setup. In existence since 1995, the format has been implemented in many PDF workflow systems and products such as Prinergy and Apogee (among the Extreme products), as well as ScenicSoft Preps and Global Graphics' ScriptWorks RIP. Many prepress-based CIP3 implementations take the form of support for digital ink-key presetting, so printers don't have to manually retrieve settings from plates using a plate scanner.

The CIP4 JDF standard goes beyond Adobe's PJTF and CIP3's PPF formats: While PJTF addresses the link between design and prepress and PPF addresses the links between prepress, press, and postpress, JDF links all of these processes—in addition to business and production management—under one umbrella (see Table 6-1). It's able to do that because it contains the following:

- Descriptions of tasks to be executed

- Descriptions of resources needed to perform various tasks

- Descriptions of the content that needs to be processed

- Messaging capabilities that communicate across devices and processes

	CIP3	CIP4
File format	PPF	JDF
Technology	PDF	XML
Processes addressed	Prepress, press, postpress	Design, prepress, press, and postpress; business, production, and resource management; communication among all of these processes

Table 6-1 The CIP4 job ticket standard, based on XML, is far more comprehensive and ambitious than CIP3 in its goals of automating print production workflows.

If you think of the JDF specification as an apple tree, the apples would be processes that need to occur, the leaves would be the resources required for those process, and the branches and limbs connecting them would be the communications required to make those processes happen automatically. The trunk, of course, would be the job itself, and the entire tree would be the finished product.

Now imagine a print job such as an annual report. The JDF specification would contain, coded in XML, everything that defines the job: a list of page elements and a description of where they fall on the page; the number of pages in the document and their size; color specifications; trapping, imposition, and screening parameters for the RIP; plate-making parameters (the type of plate being imaged, its size, and so on); printing requirements (ink densities, the length of the print run, scheduling, and so on); and required postpress processes (binding, finishing, and trimming). In addition, the JDF would contain billing, invoicing, and other sales and customer-service data—considered "resource" material in the JDF file. Some of the information may be specified by the designer, some by the printer's sales rep, some by the printer's production manager. Information can be added at different points during the workflow by appropriate parties.

JDF resource information is consumed by what's known in JDF-speak as *nodes—tasks,* in English. So think again of our lovely apple tree: One low-hanging apple is the RIP, which looks at the JDF (a leaf on its stem) and sees not only what needs to be rasterized but also instructions on how it's to be rasterized. When the RIP finishes processing the content, the updated resource information is sent to the next apple up the branch, the platemaker, which reads the resources in the specification and does its job accordingly. Each task is performed based on the preceding task, and each task is provided with all of the resources it needs to do its job.

Although those shiny red apples are pretty spectacular, the branches and limbs are what really hold the tree together. Likewise, the key to the JDF workflow is communication among processes: The RIP says, "I'm done," not only so that the platesetter knows to start imaging those aluminum sheets but also so that the prepress operator knows, too. Thus, the JDF tells us when a job is finished, if an error has occurred, whether it's missing fonts and cannot be rasterized, and so on.

In addition, because JDF is meant to integrate with existing workflows, you shouldn't have to change the way you do things to use it. It can process tasks as your system capabilities and workflow dictate: serially, in parallel, or partially overlapping. In theory at least, JDF can expand and adapt as your needs and practices change (for example, if a print shop were to adopt an e-commerce model of accepting, tracking, and managing jobs). JDF's benefits include cost reductions and faster turnarounds through automation as well as improved collaboration, planning, and follow-through due to better communication across departments.

Keep in mind, though, that PJTF, PPF, and JDF job tickets are not either/or propositions. Products and technologies can and do support more than one standard, at least for the time being (see Table 6-2). In the future, however, this is likely to change, and JDF job tickets will replace their predecessors. But before you go about adopting JDF job tickets *tout de suite*, remember that your workflow—dictated by the types of jobs you handle, as well as by the urgency and complexity of turning them around—will determine when it's time for you and your partners to adopt job tickets. In addition, you should consider JDF to be just one component of many (including moving to CTP or digital printing and migrating to composite PDF files for prepress) in your overall plans to automate manufacturing processes.

	PJTF (PDF)	CIP3 (PPF)	CIP4 (JDF)
Apogee	Y	Y	Y
Prinergy	Y	Y	Y
MetaDimension	Y	Y	Y
Brisque	Proprietary job tickets	Y	Y
CelebraNT	Y	Y	Y
Trueflow	Proprietary job tickets	Y	Y

Table 6-2 Many PDF workflow systems support multiple job ticketing standards.

PDF/X and TIFF/IT

Way back in Chapter 1, I mentioned a raster file format called TIFF/IT used primarily in the production of digital advertising. You may have also noticed that many Extreme workflows input or output TIFF/IT files. Although this format serves a niche market, graphic artists have probably also heard of a related format called PDF/X. Let's take a look at these file formats.

TIFF/IT is also sometimes called TIFF/IT-P1. The P1 version of the file format is a derivative of the larger, ISO-certified standard, and for all practical purposes it's what is actually used today. TIFF/IT-P1 includes three things: a continuous-tone (CT) file, a linework (LW) file for text and line art, and a final page file. This last typically contains low-resolution previews of image content and pointers to the CT and LW files. (Quick quiz: Which prepress vendor jumped on the TIFF/IT bandwagon early on? If you answered Scitex, you're correct!)

PDF/X, meanwhile, is both an alternative and a complementary file format to TIFF/IT, depending on your needs. Unfortunately, PDF/X is confusing because numerous versions exist: PDF/X-1, PDF/X-1a, PDF/X-2, and PDF/X-3. (For a shortcut summary of all of the PDF/X flavors, see Table 6-3.)

The Committee for Graphic Arts Technologies Standards (CGATS) developed the PDF/X standard at the request of DDAP (the digital ad distribution consortium that developed TIFF/IT) and the Newspaper Association of America, both of which wanted a standard for exchanging vector advertising data akin to the TIFF/IT format for raster advertising data. CGATS, by the way, is accredited by the American National Standards Institute (ANSI), which has also ratified the PDF/X standard. But I'm getting ahead of myself.

CGATS decided to use PDF for the task, but since that standard wasn't developed with prepress in mind, the committee narrowed the specification to ensure that everything in the PDF file would be suitable for high-end printing: That meant excluding RGB images, annotations, buttons, form fields, and other page elements that make the final separations either unpredictable or just plain poor. CGATS called this version of PDF PDF/X, and it's like a preflighted PDF file—or at least a partially preflighted file (it doesn't address *all* problems that can arise in a PDF file)—but the label tells you up front that the file should print. CGATS and ANSI both approved PDF/X-1 in 1999, which is why it's sometimes called PDF/X-1:1999.

PDF/X-1 offers what its supporters call *blind exchange:* As a "fat" file that contains everything it needs for accurate printing, PDF/X-1 files can be exchanged by content creators and producers with confidence regardless of the equipment they'll use to image the file. This means PDF/X-1 files can include both vector and raster data and, unlike pure PostScript, can reference external image data such as TIFF/IT files and embed those files in its format. In this sense, PDF/X-1 can serve as a "wrapper" for TIFF/IT files, offering all of TIFF/IT's reliability but with better compression, support for trim and bleed areas, and the ability to be viewed in Acrobat. Current SWOP standards recommend that digital ads be supplied either as TIFF/IT-P1 or PDF/X-1.

The problem, however, is that PDF/X-1 is based on PDF 1.2, which was extremely limited in its handling of spot colors and duotones on pages for print publication. Thus, by the time PDF/X-1 made it to the ISO in 2001, that international standards body had approved a different version, based on PDF 1.3, called PDF/X-1a, or PDF/X-1a:2001 (just rolls off the tongue, I know). PDF/X-1a requires that all color be specified as CMYK or optional spot colors, and that all fonts be embedded. It also prohibits OPI references.

Unfortunately, the story doesn't end there. Adobe continues to develop and update Acrobat and the PDF specification, so the PDF/X standard must adapt as well. That's why PDF/X-2 and PDF/X-3 are in the works.

PDF/X-2 (being developed by CGATS as of this writing) will be based on PDF 1.4 and provide more flexibility. For example, it will support the device-independent LAB color space and ICC color management, as well as OPI workflows, and it will not require that fonts be embedded. While these features will make PDF/X-2 a more open and flexible standard (allowing prepress professionals to perform editing, use their own fonts, and make OPI swaps), they also make it a less reliable file format.

Finally, PDF/X-3 is on the verge of being approved by the ISO. This version of the standard sits somewhere between versions 1 and 2 in terms of openness and flexibility. It is meant, at least in part, to serve digital printing workflows that are not covered by SWOP and SNAP standards. Like PDF/X-2, it will support LAB and other device-independent color spaces, but is based on the PDF 1.3 spec. In most other respects, however, it more closely resembles PDF/X-1a because it's also intended for blind transfer: Fonts and images must be embedded, and no OPI comments are allowed. PDF/X-3 is basically the same as PDF/X-1a except that PDF/X-3 allows you to use both input and output device profiles, allowing a fully ICC-compliant color-managed workflow. PDF/X-1a requires only output profiles.

	Approved by	Based on	Features	Market
PDF/X-1: 1999	CGATS, ANSI	PDF 1.2	CMYK and spot colors allowed; embedded fonts and images; no OPI	U.S. print advertising (now)
PDF/X-1a: 2001	ISO	PDF 1.3	CMYK and spot colors allowed; embedded fonts and images; no OPI	U.S. print advertising (in the future)
PDF/X-2	CGATS*	PDF 1.4	Device-independent and ICC color management supported; unembedded fonts and OPI allowed	Commercial print and packaging, in U.S. and internationally
PDF/X-3: 2002	ISO*	PDF 1.3	LAB and ICC color management; embedded fonts and images; no OPI	European print advertising; digital printing; color-managed workflows

Table 6-3 Two of the four PDF/X standards have actually been approved. The asterisk denotes a standard being reviewed (that is, it hasn't been approved).

THE PDF/X PROMISE

We chose PDF/X-1a: 2001 as our default manufacturing file format because it best suits catalog and advertising publishing and is readily accepted by our CTP printing partners, including those in our own organization. We use AppleScripts and other automated processes to produce them, because it's not yet something you can create out of the box, and we verify our files with Apago's Checkup tool. PDF/X gives us an assurance of quality and excellence, which is worth the do-it-yourself approach that we established to create the files but might be prohibitive to other companies. We see this as a value-added service that we can offer that our competitors can't.

—Scott Tully, workflow specialist, The LTC Group

Standards are approved slowly; thus, existing products only support the 1999 PDF/X-1 standard. These include preflight tools (PitStop Professional), Extreme systems (Apogee, Brisque), and various and sundry RIPs and conversion tools. One product that supports PDF/X-3 has already been released, based on the ISO draft of that standard: Callas Software's pdfInspektor 2, which can preflight PDF/X-3 files. And although you cannot currently simply check a box in Distiller or an application's Export dialog box to make sure your files are /X-compliant, standards bodies envision that you will be able to do so in the future. In the meantime, you must use a verifier such as Apago's PDF/X-1 Checkup to make sure that PDF files comply with the standard; if you don't go the PDF/X route, a good preflight check can go a long way toward ensuring that your PDF files will sail through prepress without a hitch.

Keep in mind also that just as PDF itself isn't a panacea for all prepress workflow woes, neither is PDF/X. Although it allows seamless file exchange, those files must still be well-constructed. PDF/X won't detect typos, nor will it flag the presence of low-resolution images in a file.

 MOVING TOWARD X FILES

PDF/X is my file-exchange goal. It can't be wrong, it can only be right.

—Michael Weinglass, vice president of manufacturing and production, Easyriders, Inc.

PPML / VDX

Now that we're on a roll with CGATS and PDF/X, why stop? Let's look at a related standard passed by a sibling subcommittee, this one for variable data exchange. The PPML/VDX standard—which stands for "personalized print markup language/variable data exchange"—hadn't been approved by ANSI as of this writing; however, PPML 1.5 has already been implemented in numerous short-run digital printing products, including Fiery servers from EFI, front ends such as Xeikon's Emerge, and variable page-layout tools such as Pageflex's Mpower.

As a printer control language, PPML (which is based on XML) provides a standard way to reuse images in print production. Instead of pages being the smallest objects that the language recognizes, PPML can define and recognize individual objects on a page and print them independently. Thus, when those parts of pages are stored independently (such as the same image of a car in blue, yellow, and green), you can print personalized brochures without having to redundantly download images and rasterize them. The result is money saved—and a more targeted brochure. Typically, the reusable image elements are downloaded once and stored in the printer, and pages are designed in PageMaker, QuarkXPress, or another page-layout application. You can then use a plug-in such as Meadows Information Systems' DesignMerge to place the correct variable content with the right page before it's printed.

How does this relate to PDF? Glad you asked! PPML/VDX is a subset of the standard that supports PDF, which means that PPML-enabled software can accept PDF as a variable-data content and also produce final PDF pages that can be sent to any PostScript RIP that drives digital printing devices. In addition, the resulting merged PDF files can be soft-proofed in Acrobat, saving on the cost of individual hard copy proofs. PPML/VDX also allows blind file exchanges; as such, it works only with PDF/X files.

Finally, PPML's authors are working with JDF developers to add variable-data support to JDF job tickets—which will allow PPML systems to be controlled and automated in JDF workflows. Already, PPML/VDX allows you to produce variable-data jobs with a PDF workflow—especially those jobs that are templated and run multiple times with a particular print partner.

NON-EXTREME PDF RIPS

There are, of course, a wagonload of RIPs that support PDF, even though they don't bear the Extreme brand name. In fact, any PostScript 3–based RIP can process native PDF files, and systems and packages from numerous vendors offer varying degrees of automation and customization as well as varying emphasis on PDF's role in the workflow.

Dalim's Litho system, for example, is geared toward the packaging industry with its support for 64 color channels (for mixing CMYK and spot colors on a job), step-and-repeat imposition, and object-oriented trapping and editing. For Litho, as well as for Dalim's Twist production system, PDF is just one of many possible input and output file formats. Dalim also offers Swing, a Linux-based workflow system that supports PDF.

At the other end of the spectrum are RIPs like Heidelberg's MetaDimension, which is actually a completely PDF-based workflow system that uses portable job tickets to streamline processes just like Extreme systems do (Figure 6-5). MetaDimension is modular, allowing users to scale their implementation to suit their needs and to integrate with existing systems. A Preflow version includes Supertrap and Enfocus PitStop, while a DeltaFlow option allows Heidelberg Delta users to migrate to PDF.

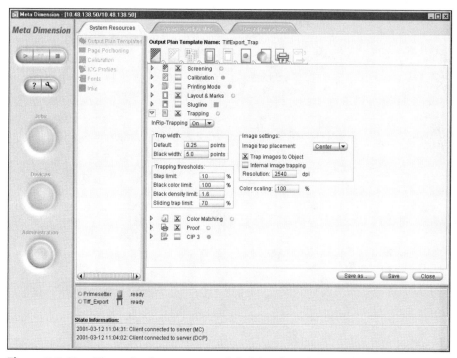

Figure 6-5 MetaDimension lets you create job ticket–based templates to automate prepress processing of files for tasks ranging from trapping (shown) to screening, calibration, proofing, and CIP3 functionality.

You can also integrate Heidelberg's Signastation imposition software. In its more robust capacity, MetaDimension offers JDF job-ticketed workflows that automate every step of PDF production, from preflighting to postpress finishing.

While telling you which PDF RIP to buy is beyond the scope of this book, this chapter should show you what happens to your files once you've handed them off. And that in turn should help you comprehend what the devil your prepress partner means when she says that PDF/X-1a files are being processed through a Brisque RIP.

MAKING ROOM FOR MORE

In the last few years there's been incredible demand on our presses, such as for Harry Potter books, and we've wanted to increase throughput and add to our capacity without having to add RIPs. Much of our work is with reprints and corrections, and being tied to the press form–based PostScript workflow takes too much time. With PDF we can make late-stage changes and re-RIP individual pages in a few minutes instead of a few hours because we don't have to redo all 31 or 63 other pages on the form.

—Justine Trubey, prepress product manager, R.R. Donnelley Print Solutions

CHAPTER SEVEN

Electronic Documents

Up to this point, we've focused on generating and using PDF files in print-centric production environments: That is, how to send application files down a chute that transforms them into perfectly printing PDF files. However, there's more to PDF files (and to publishing processes) than this narrow workflow vision implies. Indeed, PDF offers benefits for more than just printed documents—a good thing since print media isn't always the final destination of today's content. On the Web, eBook readers, handheld devices like personal digital assistants, cell phones, and more, much of today's content takes an electronic form.

Two of the most common types of electronic documents available today are eBooks and forms—applications that have little in common except that both are well served by the PDF file format. PDF's biggest benefit here is in page-design control and integrity. The conundrum of online publishing today is that although you can enhance your print content with interactivity (and thereby potentially reach a different audience), that typically means publishing it through a markup language—and in the process relinquishing control over the way your information is displayed on browsers and smaller, portable devices.

But while markup languages such as XML (and its derivatives) and the page-based PDF file format were once viewed as dichotomous technologies, this has begun to change. Adobe has brought much of the flexibility of markup languages to Acrobat and PDF, adding the ability to save metadata with PDF files and to create structured and tagged files, which is particularly useful for eBook publishing. In addition, the company is employing other powerful technologies, such as JavaScript and connectivity to Web servers and relational databases, for use in PDF-based forms and to manage libraries of digital PDF documents. In this chapter, we'll take a look at how all of these technologies come together to facilitate PDF use in electronic documents.

PDF VERSUS XML

To understand the relationship between XML and PDF, you need to know something about the origins and function of each. PDF, as I've explained throughout this book, provides a structured, object-oriented way to view content. Not surprisingly, since it stems from PostScript, PDF is optimized to represent (in print or onscreen) graphically rich, typeset pages.

XML, however, is a whole different ball game: It provides a means of describing data in a text file. As a markup language, it uses fixed syntax rules to "mark up"—or *tag*—a file's text and data in a format that can vary for different document styles. XML grew out of SGML, the Standard Generalized Markup Language, which is also a system for organizing and tagging document elements, developed by the ISO. While SGML provides a standard way to define and represent text in a device- and system-independent electronic format, XML, developed by the World Wide Web Consortium (W3C), provides a standard format specifically designed for structured documents and data on the Web.

Although XML is a language, it may make more sense to think of it as an alphabet. It's one thing to know the characters that make up an alphabet—*A, B, C, D,* and so on—however, those characters don't have much value until you begin combining them to form words. In XML, tags and their attributes equate to letters: Tags are words bracketed by less-than and greater-than symbols; within these brackets, attributes define the tag more specifically and take the form of something equaling a value in straight quotation marks. Take, for example, the following:

```
<memo author="Sally Smith" date="011002">
```

Here, memo is the tag and author= and date= are its modifying attributes.

Like any alphabet, XML tags and attributes have little meaning until they're organized into greater, structured language systems. In XML-speak this means DTDs (document type definitions) and *schemas*—sets of rules that allow other applications to understand the XML dialect being spoken. (You can think of these rules as XML's grammar.) One DTD might define the <a> tag to mean "anchor this element at the top of the page," while another might define it to mean "this is an address field for my business card." The sky's the limit as long as there are applications that can read and display documents in the language defined by your DTD. Examples of XML schemas include XHTML, which describes how content should be displayed in a Web browser; SVG, for displaying Web-based vector graphics; JDF, for print-production job tickets; PPML for variable-data printing; and OEB (Open eBook), for eBook readers.

Although they're both device independent, PDF and XML couldn't be more opposite in their origins and functions (see Table 7-1). While XML provides a structure that describes how data should be used (often for onscreen display), PDF contains data whose position, size, color, and font are fixed in a graphical form that we associate with printed typeset pages. Until recently, this typically meant two discrete and parallel workflows. In the case of print production, art designed in Photoshop and Illustrator, and pages composed in PageMaker or QuarkXPress yielded graphically rich, PostScript-based files that were ultimately flowed through a RIP. Content destined for onscreen publication was either extracted from finished print pages and reconfigured in HTML or completely reauthored independent of the print path—both of which are inefficient for dual-media publishing.

PDF	XML
Describes elements on a page	Describes elements and their functions
Stable	Adaptive
Stores pages	Organizes and stores content
Uses typesetting-like directives	Uses tag and attribute descriptors
Preserves original design intentions	Styles afford different visual display of information
Places form above function	Places function above form

Table 7-1 PDF and XML, whose features appear to be quite contradictory, can be used in a complementary fashion with some forethought.

Converting print pages into online pages also requires attention to design detail since not all print design considerations translate directly into online or electronic formats—for example, ligatures, drop caps, and small caps. To ensure that your online pages retain the look and feel as well as the design and typographic integrity of your original printed pages, you must do a fair amount of manual finessing: Executing an Export as HTML command won't suffice.

It's likely you'll feel these issues most keenly when you need to digitize a library of legacy paper documents or out-of-print books. Which is better: Converting them to XML or to PDF? The answer to that question depends on what you ultimately plan to do with those documents. If your content needs to be searchable and extractable as well as portable (for viewing on different types of devices), and if function takes precedence over form, XML is the more expedient option. If, however, you need to retain the appearance of the original page and you don't plan to display or reflow your documents on multiple devices, PDF is the better choice—as it is for documents with complex layouts or those with layouts you don't want altered in any way. Finally, although there are ways to search PDF pages and collections of PDF documents on hard drives or over a network (described later in this chapter), commercial Web search engines cannot search PDF files. Thus, if you want your online content to be searchable on the Web, stick to XML.

Although you shouldn't expect PDF to cede its page-centric roots, it is beginning to tap into XML and take advantage of that language's flexibility. One of the ways it's doing so is through an Adobe-developed architecture called XMP.

XMP

XMP (Extensible Metadata Platform) represents a syntax of metadata information that Adobe's applications understand and exchange. XMP metadata, which can describe documents at the page or object level, is part of the larger application or PDF file and thus travels with it (like a wrapper around a candy bar that tells you how many forms of sugar are baked in and the number of calories you're about to consume).

The first products to support XMP metadata are Acrobat 5.0, Illustrator 10.0, and InDesign 2.0. Although each of these applications supports varying metadata, they generally include things like author, creation date, and title, which you would find in a document's Properties dialog box. In Illustrator and InDesign, you can access and enter metadata by choosing File > File Info (Figure 7-1). In the File Info box, which is the same in both applications, you can specify typical document properties as well as such data as copyright information and owner URL. The Summary panel contains document creation and modification dates as well as other information.

To view XMP metadata in Acrobat 5, choose File > Document Properties > Document Metadata (Figure 7-2). The data is grouped by schemas—categories of related information. XMP defines 13 schemas, 3 of which you see in the Document Metadata dialog box. The first, the Standard PDF Properties schema,

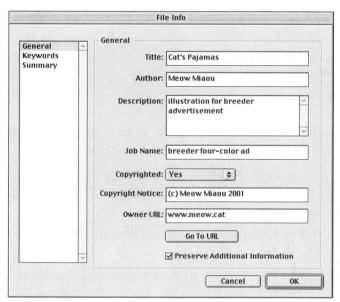

Figure 7-1 Illustrator 10 and InDesign 2.0 metadata includes author and document information such as copyright details.

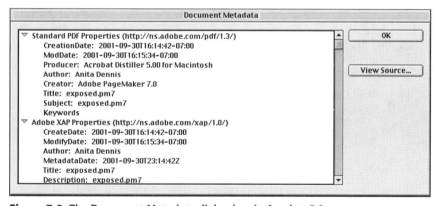

Figure 7-2 The Document Metadata dialog box in Acrobat 5.0.

includes document components that Distiller picks up from the authoring application and the PostScript stream: creation date, modification data, producing application (typically Distiller), author, creating (authoring) software, title, subject, and keywords. In addition, you can edit some PDF Properties metadata in the File > Document Properties > Summary dialog box; changes you make there will be reflected in the Document Metadata dialog box. Alternatively, you can edit the XML directly by clicking the View Source button.

The other two schemas in the Acrobat metadata dialog box are Adobe XAP Properties and Dublin Core Properties—ominous-sounding names, but if you look at the information they contain, you'll see a lot of overlap with Standard PDF Properties. XAP (Extensible Authoring and Publishing) represents document and content metadata in such a way that non-Adobe applications can access PDF metadata. And Dublin Core Properties are based on a standard that defines 15 metadata elements, including title, subject, description, source, language, creator, rights, date, and type, for cross-disciplinary information exchange.

XMP, however, is more a part of publishing's future than its present since the technology isn't fully leveraged today. For example, Illustrator 10.0 can't read XMP metadata saved in Acrobat 5.0 when it opens those PDF files, though this situation is likely to change. Adobe has also opened the specification to third-party software developers. XMP holds great potential—especially in the areas of copyright and digital-asset management, and for such markets as pharmaceuticals and finance, which have highly regulated, custom publishing needs. Imagine, for example, being able to embed copyright and permissions metadata in an image you create in Photoshop, and having that information travel to the page-layout application and the PDF file. With this info intact, users trying to extract the image would know whether and how they could reuse it.

One parting reminder: Don't confuse XMP metadata with job tickets. XMP tags are a different can of worms and would be ignored by a RIP if they were to make it that far downstream.

EBOOKS

Acrobat is also tapping into XML's capability to create structured, tagged PDF files—one of the most exciting applications of which is eBooks—because they preserve the natural reading order of electronic documents, regardless of the device on which they're displayed. A burgeoning market, eBooks require advance planning not just to determine if they make financial sense but also to make the production process flow smoothly. It's especially important to give forethought to the design of eBooks, which falls somewhere between print and Web site design: Readers will approach eBooks expecting a structure and reading experience that's comparable to printed books, but also expecting links and bookmarks much like Web site navigational tools. It is through the marriage of PDF and XML that you can provide a balanced design for eBooks.

Structure and Tags

In their "natural" state, PDF files represent dots, which are to be imaged by a marking engine (in a printer or imagesetter, for example) or onscreen. By itself, PDF doesn't know that dots are parts of letters—which are parts of words, which are parts of sentences, and so on. Structured PDF, however, does recognize this hierarchy, or tree, of information so that you can repurpose print files for electronic delivery. For the same reason, structured PDF files do *not* recognize comments, page numbers and running headers, layout or printing artifacts such as rules separating footnotes from page content, or crop or registration marks.

Tagged PDF files include not only the structure tree but additional information about file content: For example, they can tell whether text is part of a formatted list or table, and they can recognize soft and hard hyphens. As a result, tagged PDF files can be reflowed onscreen—adapting to any aspect ratio with text relationships and reading order intact—and used with screen-reading devices to assist the visually impaired. You can reflow tagged PDF files in Acrobat, Acrobat Reader, Reader for the Palm, and Pocket PC devices.

Creating Tagged PDF Files

The most efficient way to create tagged PDF files is to export the tags from the authoring application when you create the PDF file and then finesse them as needed in Acrobat. By building flexibility into the PDF file upstream in the creation process, you reduce the amount of repurposing required later. Along these lines, when you export a tagged PDF file to RTF (or perhaps to a markup language, using Adobe's Save As XML plug-in), the tags stay in the text file. Planning ahead can thus save you a lot of manual labor.

You can export tagged PDF files from the following applications:

- PageMaker 7.0
- InDesign 2.0
- FrameMaker + SGML 6.0

You can also generate tagged PDF files from Microsoft Office applications in Windows using the PDFMaker plug-in, and when you create PDF files using Acrobat's Web Capture feature. With the former, choose Acrobat > Change Conversion Settings, then select the Embed Tags option in the Office tab of the

Acrobat PDFMaker for Microsoft Office dialog box. After you've done this, click the Convert to Adobe PDF button. If you go the latter route, choose Tools > Web Capture > Open Web Page, then click Conversion Settings, where you can check Add PDF tags. When you're finished, click OK and then click Download.

For all other applications, you must use one of two work-arounds: Either insert "pdfmark" operators into the PostScript stream (the more difficult method) or use the Acrobat Make Accessible plug-in (the easier method). When you export PDF from PageMaker and InDesign (or create PDF files in FrameMaker and Word), the tags are based on the document's paragraph styles. Note that I said "export PDF": To preserve tags in PageMaker and InDesign files, you must export the content to PDF rather than print to Distiller. Because Distiller's eBook job option optimizes content for eBook viewing (downsampling color and grayscale images to 150 dpi, for example, and converting colors to sRGB), it doesn't import tags from PageMaker or InDesign's paragraph styles. The result is a valid eBook that can be read on any device that supports the PDF format; however, it won't reflow from the original page's line breaks, which can make reading hazardous to your eyes.

Exporting Tagged PDF from PageMaker

To generate tagged PDF files from Adobe PageMaker 7.0, start by creating an appropriately formatted document. Most likely your readers will be viewing your eBook on a couple of systems: for example, a desktop PC (where they download it) and a handheld device (where they read it). Unfortunately, a typical letter-size page doesn't translate well to either. Thus, you should use a smaller page size— say 7-by-10 or 6-by-9 inches—that can display nicely on a variety of devices, with room for bookmarks and thumbnails. If you know your eBook will be read only on a computer screen—that is, not printed—consider making it a 640-by-480 landscape (wide) orientation (for viewing on 15-inch or smaller monitors) or 800-by-600 pixels (for viewing on 17-inch or larger monitors). As long as you export the PDF file from InDesign or PageMaker (instead of distilling it), the result will be the page size you specified. If you go through Distiller, not only will you lose your tags but the software will create pages based on your Page Setup, which means you'll have to re-create tags and crop pages in Acrobat.

In the Document Setup dialog box (Figure 7-3), there's no need to make double-sided, facing pages since the book won't be printed and bound. By the same token, you can make margins uniform: eBooks don't have binding, so you don't need to allow for it on the insides of pages. In Windows, choose Distiller from the

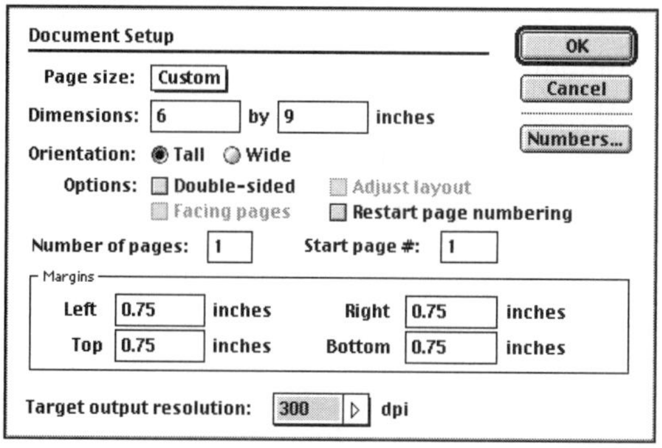

Figure 7-3 In PageMaker's
Document Setup dialog box
(Command/Ctrl-N), specify a smaller
page size for your eBook and equal
margins all the way around.

Compose to Printer pop-up menu, and on the Mac specify a Target output resolution. Don't chintz on resolution: 300 dpi will create sharp enough text and graphics initially, even if you downsample and compress them. Don't worry about page numbers right now: The PageMaker file in my example will have seven pages that translate directly into a seven-page PDF file that's correctly numbered.

By default, PageMaker 7.0 creates single-column documents: Leave your eBook this way. Multicolumn pages don't translate well into electronic documents because they force readers to scroll around the page. Because your eBook is only 6 inches wide and it will be tagged for reflow, readers won't be burdened by such confusing navigation.

As you spec your text (using intuitively named styles such as Title, Subhead, and Body text), avoid delicate serifs and thinly stroked typefaces, which can break up and be difficult to read onscreen. Use solid tints and larger point sizes and leading than for printed pages—at least 12 points for body text with at least 2 points of leading (Figure 7-4). Don't spend much time kerning individual letter pairs: This adds to your file size without significantly improving the screen. Instead, set wider tracking values globally.

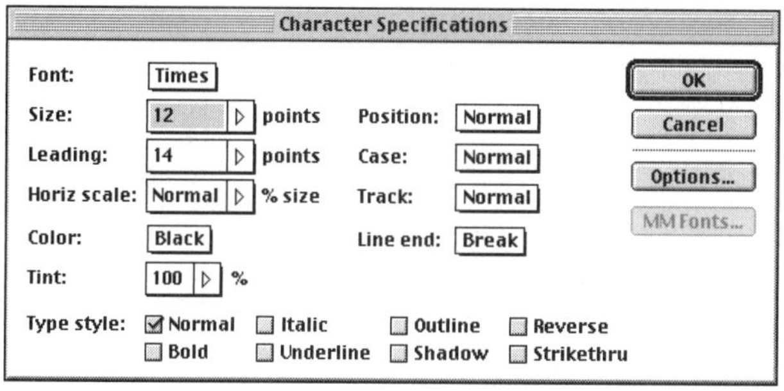

Figure 7-4 Specify text for
eBooks at a larger point
size than you would for
print, and use clear, sharp
typefaces.

As for graphics and images, you face the same challenges in eBook design as you do in Web design: Different monitors and handheld devices have different color and resolution capabilities. A PalmPilot, for example, won't display the same color as a Rocket eBook. To level the playing field, spec your eBook colors in sRGB. Also, think about your audience when you decide how many, and what types of, color graphics you want to include. Color adds heft (bytes) to eBooks, which means you may have to balance portability with graphical richness. And although complex layouts will be maintained in the master PDF file, the position of graphics will change when the PDF is reflowed. Depending on the size and position of the original graphic, sometimes it will move to the bottom of the reflowed page, and sometimes it will move to the top of the page. You might want to create a few layouts and test how they reflow to be sure that they still look right.

When your layout is eBook perfect—a text-only short story, in my example (Figure 7-5)—you are ready to export it. Choose File > Export > Adobe PDF. In the General tab of the PDF Options dialog box (Figure 7-6), choose your job option and check the Embed Tags in PDF box. If necessary, you can create a custom job

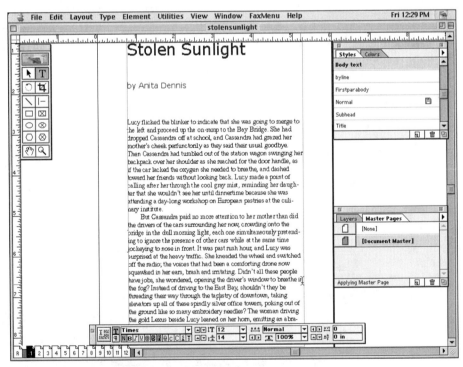

Figure 7-5 A fictional book layout in PageMaker.

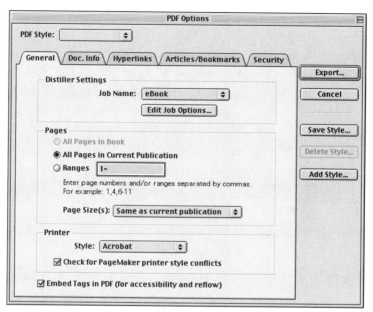

Figure 7-6 To generate tags with a PageMaker document when you export to PDF, check the Embed Tags in PDF button in the General tab of the PDF Options dialog box.

option or use the standard eBook option that Adobe ships with Acrobat. (Many eBook publishers like the eBook setting but tweak it slightly to embed the Base 14 fonts.) Although tagged PDF was introduced with Acrobat 5.0, you can embed tags in versions of PDF earlier than 1.4 when you export from PageMaker. If you've created hyperlinks from a table of contents to individual chapters or from index entries to their corresponding pages, you can embed those and set their appearance in the Hyperlinks tab. To create bookmarks from tables of contents and indexes, use the Articles/Bookmarks tab. (Because this is a book about Acrobat, not Page-Maker or InDesign, I'll explain how to create those navigational elements in Acrobat later in this chapter.)

Exporting Tagged PDF from InDesign

To generate tagged PDF files from InDesign, set up your eBook using the same design guidelines covered in the preceding section. When you're ready to create the PDF file, choose File > Export. In the Export dialog box, choose Adobe PDF as your Format or Type, then click OK. In the General panel of the Export PDF dialog box that appears (Figure 7-7), choose eBook from the Style pop-up menu to apply Distiller eBook job settings for compression and font embedding. This also automatically checks the Include eBook Tags box. It's fine to change your Style or Conversion settings for the eBook, but make sure Include eBook Tags stays checked to produce structured, tagged PDF files that reflow in Acrobat. Check Include Hyperlinks and Include Bookmarks, also, if you've generated those in InDesign and want them to be carried over into your structured PDF file. Otherwise, you can create them in Acrobat (see "Links and Bookmarks," page 256). When you've made your choices, click Export.

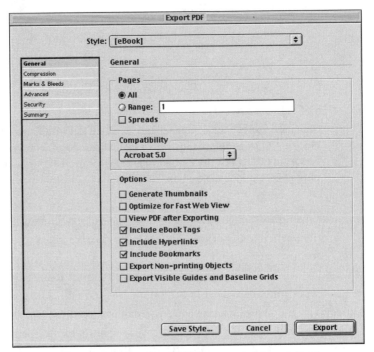

Figure 7-7 To save tags with a PDF file exported from InDesign, check the Include eBook Tags box in the General panel of the Export dialog box.

Reflowing Text

Once your eBook has been generated, you can see how text reflows in Acrobat by choosing View > Reflow or clicking the Reflow button (the one with the squiggly arrow that looks like a loopy *Z*). The PDF file maintains its page construct no matter how you drag (Figure 7-8). In other words, the text reflows and the page changes shape, but the contents remain the same, regardless of page size or shape. A narrow page becomes longer to accommodate the content, and a wide page becomes shorter. The last word on the original page will be the same as the last word on your resized page (which sometimes causes midsentence widows), and the page will always print at 6 by 9 inches (or whatever your specified as your document setup).

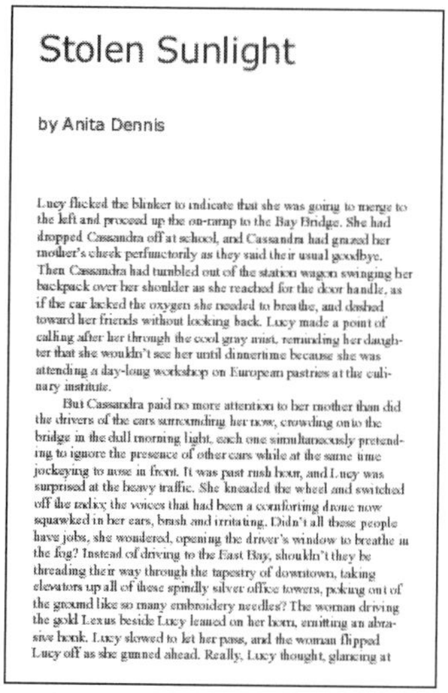

Stolen Sunlight

by Anita Dennis

Lucy flicked the blinker to indicate that she was going to merge to the left and proceed up the on-ramp to the Bay Bridge. She had dropped Cassandra off at school, and Cassandra had grazed her mother's cheek perfunctorily as they said their usual goodbye. Then Cassandra had tumbled out of the station wagon swinging her backpack over her shoulder as she reached for the door handle, as if the car lacked the oxygen she needed to breathe, and dashed toward her friends without looking back. Lucy made a point of calling after her through the cool gray mist, reminding her daugh-ter that she wouldn't see her until dinnertime because she was attending a day-long workshop on European pastries at the culi-nary institute.

But Cassandra paid no more attention to her mother than did the drivers of the cars surrounding her now, crowding on to the bridge in the dull morning light, each one simultaneously pretend-ing to ignore the presence of other cars while at the same time jockeying to nose in front. It was past rush hour, and Lucy was surprised at the heavy traffic. She kneaded the wheel and switched off the radio; the voices that had been a comforting drone now squawked in her ears, brash and irritating. Didn't all these people have jobs, she wondered, opening the driver's window to breathe in the fog? Instead of driving to the East Bay, shouldn't they be threading their way through the tapestry of downtown, taking elevators up all of these spindly silver office towers, poking out of the ground like so many embroidery needles? The woman driving the gold Lexus beside Lucy leaned on her horn, emitting an abra-sive honk. Lucy slowed to let her pass, and the woman flipped Lucy off as she gunned ahead. Really, Lucy thought, glancing at

Original

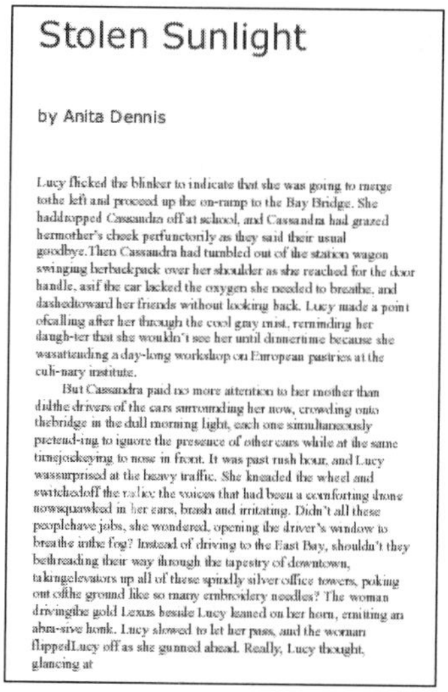

Stolen Sunlight

by Anita Dennis

Lucy flicked the blinker to indicate that she was going to merge tothe left and proceed up the on-ramp to the Bay Bridge. She haddropped Cassandra off at school, and Cassandra had grazed hermother's cheek perfunctorily as they said their usual goodbye.Then Cassandra had tumbled out of the station wagon swinging herbackpack over her shoulder as she reached for the door handle, asif the car lacked the oxygen she needed to breathe, and dashedtoward her friends without looking back. Lucy made a point ofcalling after her through the cool gray mist, reminding her daugh-ter that she wouldn't see her until dinnertime because she wasattending a day-long workshop on European pastries at the culi-nary institute.

But Cassandra paid no more attention to her mother than didthe drivers of the cars surrounding her now, crowding onto thebridge in the dull morning light, each one simultaneously pretend-ing to ignore the presence of other cars while at the same timejockeying to nose in front. It was past rush hour, and Lucy wassurprised at the heavy traffic. She kneaded the wheel and switchedoff the radio; the voices that had been a comforting drone nowsquawked in her ears, brash and irritating. Didn't all these peoplehave jobs, she wondered, opening the driver's window to breathe inthe fog? Instead of driving to the East Bay, shouldn't they bethreading their way through the tapestry of downtown, takingelevators up all of these spindly silver office towers, poking out ofthe ground like so many embroidery needles? The woman drivingthe gold Lexus beside Lucy leaned on her horn, emitting an abra-sive honk. Lucy slowed to let her pass, and the woman flippedLucy off as she gunned ahead. Really, Lucy thought, glancing at

Reflowed to narrower portrait orientation

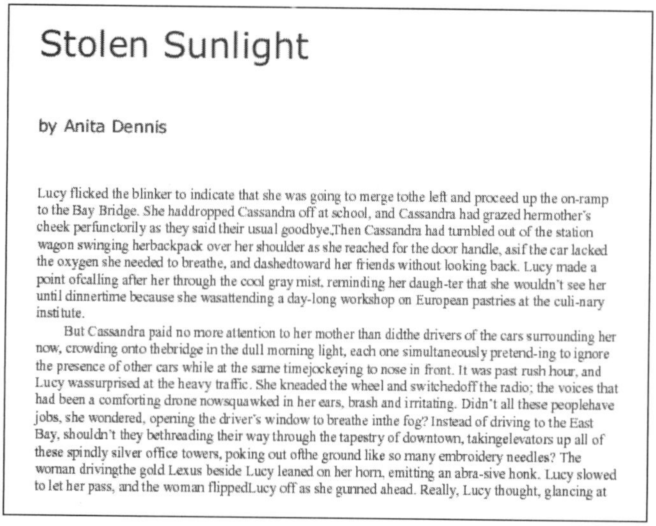

Stolen Sunlight

by Anita Dennis

Lucy flicked the blinker to indicate that she was going to merge tothe left and proceed up the on-ramp to the Bay Bridge. She haddropped Cassandra off at school, and Cassandra had grazed hermother's cheek perfunctorily as they said their usual goodbye.Then Cassandra had tumbled out of the station wagon swinging herbackpack over her shoulder as she reached for the door handle, asif the car lacked the oxygen she needed to breathe, and dashedtoward her friends without looking back. Lucy made a point ofcalling after her through the cool gray mist, reminding her daugh-ter that she wouldn't see her until dinnertime because she wasattending a day-long workshop on European pastries at the culi-nary institute.

But Cassandra paid no more attention to her mother than didthe drivers of the cars surrounding her now, crowding onto thebridge in the dull morning light, each one simultaneously pretend-ing to ignore the presence of other cars while at the same timejockeying to nose in front. It was past rush hour, and Lucy wassurprised at the heavy traffic. She kneaded the wheel and switchedoff the radio; the voices that had been a comforting drone nowsquawked in her ears, brash and irritating. Didn't all these peoplehave jobs, she wondered, opening the driver's window to breathe inthe fog? Instead of driving to the East Bay, shouldn't they bethreading their way through the tapestry of downtown, takingelevators up all of these spindly silver office towers, poking out ofthe ground like so many embroidery needles? The woman drivingthe gold Lexus beside Lucy leaned on her horn, emitting an abra-sive honk. Lucy slowed to let her pass, and the woman flippedLucy off as she gunned ahead. Really, Lucy thought, glancing at

Reflowed to landscape orientation

Figure 7-8 **With the Reflow option checked in Acrobat's View menu, you can drag to resize the document window and the tagged PDF file will reflow on the fly.**

Tagged, reflowable PDF documents are still new—which means they have certain limitations: You can't reflow Asian-language text. And even Roman text occasionally overlaps—another important reason for using clear, simple typefaces to maximize legibility. Finally, even though Acrobat is supposed to recognize soft hyphens, it didn't work in my tests (Figure 7-9). Luckily, Acrobat has a few tools to help you finesse reflowed text. With Reflow mode off (such as in Actual Size or Fit in Window view), use the TouchUp Text tool to select the sequence of characters or words you want to fix, then choose Tools > TouchUp > Text Breaks. Acrobat will parse the selected line of text and return a Text Breaks window that shows where word breaks exist, indicating unrecognizable glyphs with question marks (Figure 7-10).

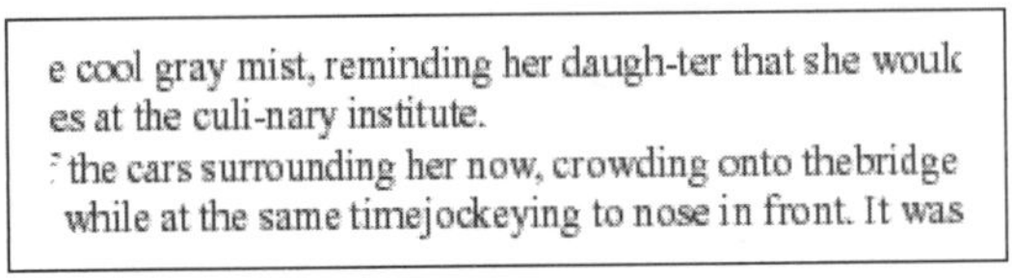

e cool gray mist, reminding her daugh-ter that she woulc
es at the culi-nary institute.
the cars surrounding her now, crowding onto thebridge
while at the same timejockeying to nose in front. It was

Figure 7-9 Reflowed text can crash, and incorrect hyphens can appear where original line breaks occurred.

toward her friends without looking back. Lucy made a point of
calling after her through the cool gray mist, reminding her daugh-
ter that she wouldn't see her until dinnertime because she was
attending a day-long workshop on European pastries at the culi-
nary institute.
Text Breaks
wasattending a day-long workshop on European pastries at the culi-nary

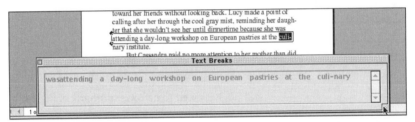

Figure 7-10 The Text Breaks window shows breaks between words, which you can edit with the TouchUp command.

To edit text—add soft hyphens, line breaks, nonbreaking spaces, and em dashes—position the TouchUp Text cursor where you want to add or replace a character, and choose Tools > TouchUp > Insert. Then choose which character you want to insert. Now when you reflow the page, the words will be properly broken (Figure 7-11), and you can save the PDF file with those changes for the next reader.

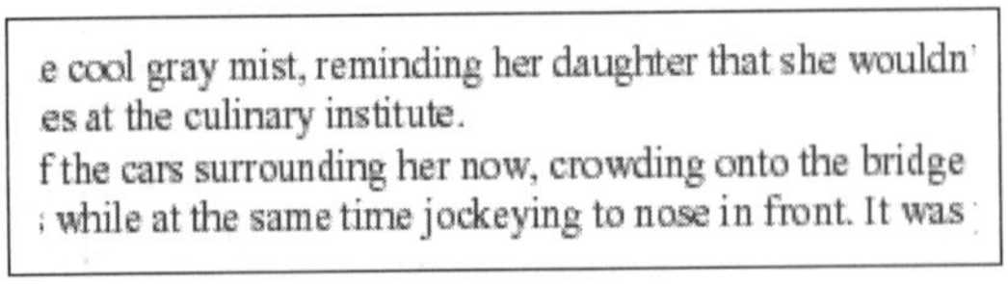

e cool gray mist, reminding her daughter that she wouldn'
es at the culinary institute.
f the cars surrounding her now, crowding onto the bridge
while at the same time jockeying to nose in front. It was

Figure 7-11 Inserted soft hyphens and nonbreaking spaces correct crashed text and hard hyphens.

As with Web publishing, be sure to preview your final eBook on multiple devices to see how color and layout come across when the file is reflowed.

Editing Tags

If tagged content doesn't flow as you'd like—perhaps an image falls to the bottom of the page and you want it to appear in the middle—you can adjust (or create) tags in Acrobat. First, take a look at the document's logical structure tree by choosing Window > Tags. In the Tags palette, click the Tags Root arrow to toggle open a view of the document's tagged content. You can also choose Turn On Associated Content Highlighting from the Tags menu so that when you click to select a tag—such as the story title "Stolen Sunlight" in my example (Figure 7-12)—the associated content is outlined. Click the TouchUp Order tool (the one with the numbers *1-2-3* on it) to view sequentially numbered content.

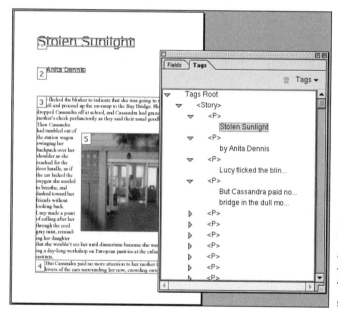

Figure 7-12 A tagged PDF document with associated highlighting turned on and the TouchUp Order tool selected.

To change the reflow order of tagged elements, select the TouchUp Order tool and click the elements' numbers in the order you desire (Figure 7-13). An element's number and outline turn red when the tool is positioned over it, which helps you identify two closely positioned objects. For any element that's highlighted in red, you can also Control-click (Mac) and right-click (Windows) to access the context menu that lets you move the element forward or back in the layer stack (Swap with Previous or Swap with Next). To start over at any time, click another tool on the toolbar and then click the TouchUp Order tool again. To make your changes take effect, save the document and reflow it (Figure 7-14).

Figure 7-13 Use the TouchUp Order tool to click the numbered boxes in any order you desire.

Figure 7-14 The first page of my eBook with the elements reordered so that the picture doesn't appear as the last thing on the page.

For those who are brave enough and familiar enough with XML tagging, the Tags palette offers further editing capabilities, such as creating and editing child elements, and editing role and class maps as well as tag artifacts and comments. To enhance accessibility for visually impaired readers, you can add alternate text to images and specify the language of the tagged elements.

TWO FOR THE PRICE OF ONE

We distill two files from our Quark pages: one for eBooks and one for print. We send the high-resolution (600-dpi) PDF to the printer in Taiwan who separates and prints the file, and we use the low-resolution (72-dpi) PDF for our eBooks. PDF gives us a continuous process; the files are complete; and both versions come out identically.

—Thomas Kuo, vice president of engineering, ComicsOne.com

Links and Bookmarks

My short story is extremely simple; most eBooks will be more complex, with tables of contents, indexes, and multiple chapters. In such cases, you'll need to give more thought to structure and navigation, adding links and bookmarks (for example, from TOC headings to the first page of each chapter and from index entries to the particular subject on the page). For example, to make the most of the eBook form factor and to make eBooks as interactive as possible, you may want to link to relevant Web sites and other PDF files. You may also want to save long books in multiple PDF files, perhaps one for each chapter, to make them smaller, more flexible, and download faster. In addition, if you're forced to repurpose print documents with print-centric layouts (such as, multicolumn pages), you may want to define article threads to make them easier to navigate.

You can create links and bookmarks in many page-layout applications (including PageMaker and InDesign), which you can then export with your PDF file. You can also create them in Acrobat, which I'll explain now. To facilitate that, I've enhanced my eBook to make it a "collection" of two short stories with a table of contents. (Any literary agents out there?)

Creating Links

Links allow a reader to click on text or a graphic and jump to another location in the document—for example, from the title of a short story in a table of contents to the first page of that story, or from a piece of text to an associated figure or illustration. They're easy to create in Acrobat using the Link tool (Figure 7-15). Simply select it, then drag with the cross-hair cursor to mark the area where you want the link—in my example, around the first entry in the TOC. While I like to make it easy for readers by giving them a large target zone—in this case, the entire entry— you can also just marquee the page number, or press Ctrl/Option to select exact text with an I-beam cursor. When you release the mouse button, Acrobat displays the Link Properties dialog box, where you define how you want the link to appear and what you want it to do (Figure 7-16).

Figure 7-15
The Link tool.

I've made my link an invisible rectangle; however, if you want yours to be visible, you can set its color, width, and style (solid or dashed). You can also choose one of the following options to specify the link's appearance when selected: None (no change), Invert (changes the outline color to its opposite), Outline (changes link color to its opposite), or Inset (displays an embossed rectangle). I like a subtle outline.

In the Action section of the dialog box, choose the type of action you want from the pop-up list: If you want the link to take readers to another page in this or another PDF document, choose Go to View. You can also add interactivity to your links by opting to play a movie or sound; by resetting, submitting, or performing other actions relating to forms (see "Electronic Forms," page 266); or by linking to a URL. Whichever action you choose, the dialog box prompts you with how to

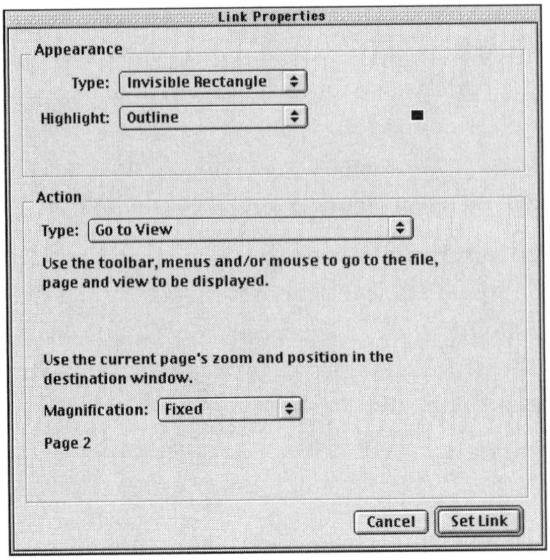

Figure 7-16 The Link Properties dialog box.

proceed in creating your link. For Go to View, you simply navigate to the page that you want to link to—yes, you do so with the dialog box still active—by choosing a command from the Document menu (such as Next Page or Go To Page), or by using the page arrows at the bottom of the document window. The Page flag at the bottom of the dialog box updates to show which one you've chosen (2 in my example). Then all you have to do is choose the view that you want the page to display and click Set Link. Whatever view you choose, make sure it's consistent across all of your links as well as with the opening view (see "Finishing Touches," page 263): You don't want to discombobulate readers by displaying different views of pages.

You can edit links at any time by choosing the Link tool and moving the cursor over the link. You can then click and drag to resize, or double-click to access and redefine its properties. Right/Control-click to follow or clear the link. And to use a link, move the Hand tool over the link and when it turns into a pointing finger, click it to jump to the other page.

Creating Bookmarks

Bookmarks, which are listed in the Bookmarks navigational pane at the left side of the document window, are especially helpful for navigating longer eBooks because they allow you to view and jump to chapter names without accessing the table of contents. Bookmarks are just like links in that they can also perform other actions, such as playing movies. However, I'm going to keep my example simple, just creating bookmarks that link to page views. (If you create a table of contents in PageMaker or InDesign, remember that you can import it as PDF bookmarks automatically.)

Click the left and right arrows at the bottom of the document window to open the navigation pane. Then click the Bookmarks tab (or choose Window > Bookmarks). With your TOC page in the document window, click the New Bookmark button (the page icon) or choose New Bookmark from the Bookmark menu. Change the bookmark's name from Untitled to Table of Contents by typing over the word. Now go to the next page that you want bookmarked—in my example, the first story, "Exposed"—and create and name another bookmark. Make sure that all of your pages are on the same view when you create bookmarks (to ease the reading experience), and that they coincide with your document's opening view (see "Finishing Touches," page 263). Repeat this process until you're finished (Figure 7-17).

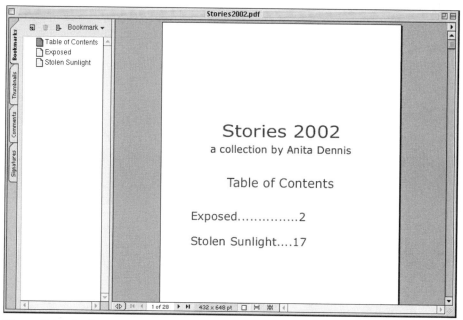

Figure 7-17 Bookmarks allow readers to jump to specific pages of an electronic document from a navigational window pane.

The Bookmark menu provides all sorts of ways to edit bookmarks. For example, you can access a bookmark's properties, where you can change its destination, action, and appearance (Figure 7-18). You can also nest bookmarks—if, for example, you want to link to a section or figure in a chapter—by selecting (highlighting) the *uber*-bookmark before creating a sub-bookmark. Alternatively, you can create a bookmark and then drag it to the proper position (a small line appears under the parent bookmark when you've positioned it properly). You can delete bookmarks by Right/Ctrl-clicking the bookmark and choosing Clear from the context menu, or by dragging the bookmark to the Recycling Bin or Trash. To link a bookmark to a page other than the one that's displayed, create the bookmark, navigate to the correct page, then choose Bookmark > Set Bookmark Destination. Click Yes in the warning box that appears.

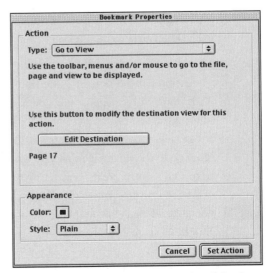

Figure 7-18 The Bookmark Properties dialog box.

Finally, if you're brave, you can create bookmarks from structured PDF files by choosing Bookmark > New Bookmarks from Structure. This will generate a bookmark for every tag in your document (in my short story example, that would mean dozens of paragraph tags). To be useful, these bookmarks generally need further editing—for example, changing the tag (such as <P>) to a more intuitive label.

Creating Article Threads

Article threads, the final navigational device covered in this chapter, are useful for helping readers follow multicolumn electronic documents that require scrolling. They also make it easier for readers to jump over sidebars and unrelated material that might otherwise distract them. You create articles by drawing boxes around pieces of content and creating a path from the end of one box to the top of another, similar to the way text is linked and flowed across multiple pages in a page-layout application.

To define article threads, select the Article tool (Figure 7-19) and use it to draw a marquee around the first section of text. Acrobat wraps the text with a resizable bounding box and labels it "1-1." The first 1 is the article number; the second 1 is the box number.

Figure 7-19
The Article tool.

A plus sign at the bottom of the box indicates that you're going to add more text to this first article. Go to the next block of text in the article and draw a box around it; Acrobat will label it "1-2" (Figure 7-20).

Keep this up until you've marqueed the entire article, then press Enter/Return to complete the thread. In the Article Properties dialog box that appears (Figure 7-21), enter the title, subject, author, and keywords, then click OK. (Actually, you don't need to enter all of this info; however, do enter a title, which will appear in the Articles palette.)

Choose Window > Articles to display the Articles palette, which you can then use to edit the articles or navigate the document. If you wish to change an article's name, click its label; if you wish to delete an article, click its icon and drag it to the Trash or Recycling Bin. You can edit an article's properties by selecting the article in the palette and choosing Properties from the Articles menu. Keep in mind, however, that you can't change the order in which articles are listed in the palette, so make sure to create them in the order you desire.

Figure 7-20 The first two boxes of an article thread.

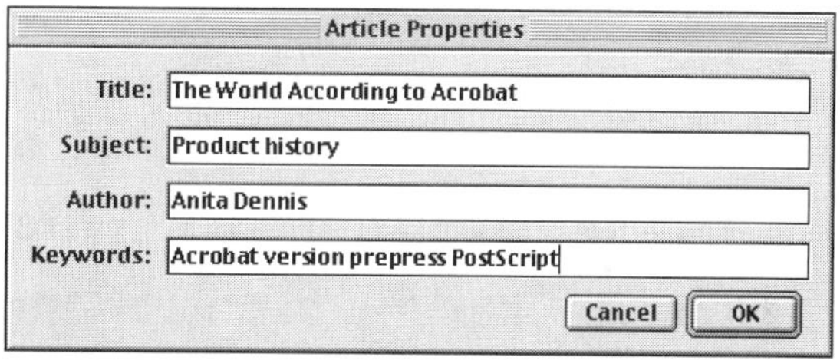

Figure 7-21 The Article Properties dialog box.

To navigate an article, double-click its icon in the Articles palette to jump to the beginning of the thread, which will appear in magnified view in the document window. When you're finished reading that section of the thread, click the Hand tool (which will display a small downward arrow in its palm) to automatically display the next section (Figure 7-22).

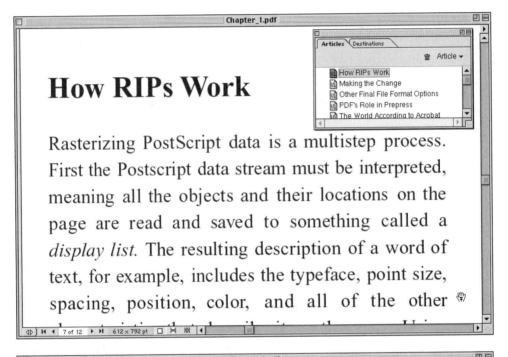

How RIPs Work

Rasterizing PostScript data is a multistep process. First the Postscript data stream must be interpreted, meaning all the objects and their locations on the page are read and saved to something called a *display list.* The resulting description of a word of text, for example, includes the typeface, point size, spacing, position, color, and all of the other

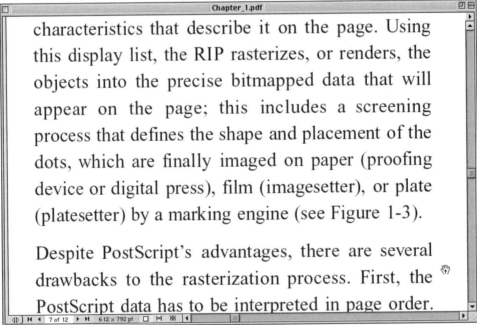

characteristics that describe it on the page. Using this display list, the RIP rasterizes, or renders, the objects into the precise bitmapped data that will appear on the page; this includes a screening process that defines the shape and placement of the dots, which are finally imaged on paper (proofing device or digital press), film (imagesetter), or plate (platesetter) by a marking engine (see Figure 1-3).

Despite PostScript's advantages, there are several drawbacks to the rasterization process. First, the PostScript data has to be interpreted in page order.

Figure 7-22 Use the Articles palette to jump to the beginning of a thread (top). Navigate to adjacent sections of the text by clicking the downward- or upward-pointing hand icons.

Finishing Touches

But wait! You're not finished creating your eBook or electronic document. There are still some details to check and tweak. First, make sure the default page view—the one Acrobat displays every time it opens the document—is appropriate. It's difficult enough adjusting to reading electronic type on radiant displays without being distracted by a different page view each time the page is "turned." Viewers can zoom in and out of an onscreen page, but just as in print, all pages should start out the same "size." (Although all of your eBook pages will be technically the same size, differing page views can make it appear as if they're not.)

To ensure that this is the case, define your opening page view by choosing File > Document Properties > Open Options. In the Document Open Options dialog box (Figure 7-23), you not only specify a Magnification setting but also how you want the document window to appear—with or without thumbnails and bookmarks, with or without menu and toolbars, and so on. When choosing a magnification, make sure it will result in a readable view—you don't want to force your reader to zoom in just to begin reading. For many documents, Fit in Window displays text too small; Fit Width, which magnifies the text and fills gray space, is a better option. Your choice here will be the default display view for all pages in your document (once you've saved your changes). So, make sure your bookmarks display pages at the same view you specify here.

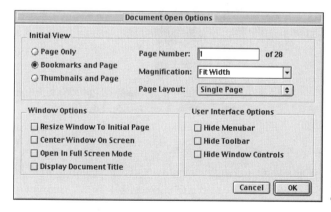

Figure 7-23 The Document Open Options dialog box.

In Document Open Options you can also choose any page of the document as the opening page (using the Page Number field). And Single Page provides the best page layout for eBooks since it's a comfortable way to read eBooks and is how Acrobat eBook Reader displays pages by default.

Next, if you think your readers will be using the Acrobat eBook Reader, make sure your eBook has a well-typeset and -designed cover, because the first page in your PDF file will be displayed as a thumbnail in that software's Library (Figure 7-24)—a gallery of eBook cover thumbnails. You may also want to save a JPEG or GIF thumbnail version of the cover image—approximately 100 pixels wide, 96 dpi, and RGB—for display in eBookstores on Web browsers. You can create the thumbnail in a number of ways—one of which is by extracting the page from the PDF eBook, opening it in Photoshop, resizing and resampling it, and then saving it as a JPEG or GIF.

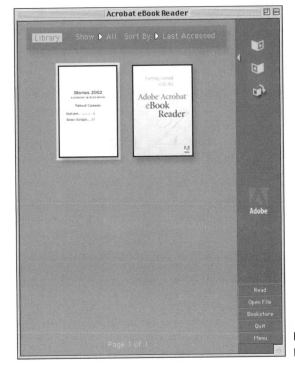

Figure 7-24 The Acrobat eBook Reader Library.

Another issue you may need to resolve in your eBooks is page numbering. Although page numbers and running headers from PageMaker and InDesign files are omitted when you export structured and tagged PDF files, you may find yourself working with nonstructured PDF files generated from legacy page-layout files with their page numbers intact. Or you could be combining various PDF files. There are, in fact, any number of ways you could end up with page numbers that conflict with Acrobat's page numbering scheme (which by default numbers PDF file pages consecutively beginning at 1).

There are a number of ways you can resolve this problem. For starters, it always helps to plan your book's structure in advance; this way, you minimize problems in the production stage. If possible, go into the original page-layout files and either number the eBook with Arabic numerals from page 1 or export structured PDF files that omit page numbers in headers and footers. In addition, consider how your eBook will appear when displayed in two-page view in Acrobat or the eBook Reader: Give your cover a "back"—a blank page—and add a blank page to the front matter (if necessary) so that you end up with an even number of pages. This way, you ensure that spreads will be displayed properly in two-page views: that is, with odd-numbered pages (including the first page of text) on the right. (To add and renumber pages in Acrobat, including sectioning parts of the document to accommodate Roman numerals for front matter, see Chapter 4.) Finally, make sure your table of contents and index entries point to Acrobat page numbers, not the page numbers from your page-layout application.

The final issue we'll touch on here is security. You may want to apply permissions restrictions to your eBook—for example, to prevent unauthorized people from copying or extracting text. You can do this when you distill or export PDF files from most authoring applications, or you can apply them in Acrobat itself. If you're producing Acrobat 5.0 (PDF 1.4) files and invoke 128-bit encryption (File > Document Security, then choose Acrobat Standard Security from the Security Options pop-up menu), you have the option of allowing readers to only print the document at low resolution. If you do this, the books will be printed at 150 dpi, which is suitable for reading a hard-copy version of the text but not for high-resolution reproduction.

Although this chapter should serve as a solid launching pad for designing and producing PDF eBooks, there are many other issues to consider when undertaking such a task—issues that go beyond the scope of this book, such as distribution, planning, copyright protection, promotion, and pricing. Adobe Content Server (see Chapter 1, "The World According to Acrobat") addresses many of these topics, offering packaging, distribution, procurement, and fulfillment services as well as hooks into databases and e-commerce systems that could be good investments for certain eBook ventures.

ONE FOR ALL

In the future, creating eBooks will be a more collaborative process. It won't be just about writers. It will require writers, editors, videographers, and Web producers.

—Jennifer Gold, director of new media, Rough Guides

ELECTRONIC FORMS

Although electronic forms may not be as glamorous as eBooks, they represent a practical, hands-on application for electronic PDF publishing—and one that's already in wide use in businesses and governments everywhere. The IRS, for example, purports to be the largest distributor of PDF documents in the world, with more than 8,000 PDF documents available on its intranet, including more than 3,000 forms. Of these, roughly 900 are available to the public and 500 can be completed online.

Although most businesses don't need to publish electronic forms in the same volume as the IRS, this example demonstrates the incredible potential of electronic forms. When tied to databases, PDF forms can save hours of manual labor in re-keying information. Picture, for example, completing a form to request that your health insurance company reimburse you for a doctor's prescription: You locate the PDF form on your company intranet and open it in your browser to complete it online. Type your social security number into the first field, and the form draws all of your relevant personal information from a database—name, address, policy and group number, and so on. Even the date is filled in automatically. All you have to do is fill in the specifics of your request and click Submit. Now extend that vision to all of the other forms you encounter in business and design—travel reimbursement forms, requisitions, purchase orders, catalog order forms, even print procurement forms—and you begin to see the promise of electronic forms.

THE BEST OF BOTH WORLDS

PDF forms merge the efficiencies of digital technology with the integrity of paper-based form design. Users are comfortable completing electronic PDF forms because they look just like the paper forms they're familiar with. Also, PDF forms are the predominant electronic form format in the state of California and most other governmental agencies. This helps streamline claims processing. Finally, because the electronic forms are tied to our database, form fields are automatically populated, and repetitive data entry is eliminated.

—David DePaolo, president and CEO, Workcompcentral.com

Although you could create electronic forms in HTML and submit them to a database with a CGI script, PDF forms offer numerous benefits over their HTML counterparts.

First and most obviously, they maintain the integrity of the paper-based original, preserving any corporate identity and style built into the design. In addition, PDF forms offer greater flexibility: People can print them and complete them by hand, or (with Acrobat Approval) save them to their hard drives to complete at their leisure. (See Chapter 1, "Which Acrobat Do You Need?" for more on Approval.) Forms completed in Acrobat can be also spell-checked, and they support digital signatures—neither of which is possible with HTML forms. Just think of the hassle that ensues if you enter your social security or policy number incorrectly on a health insurance claim: PDF forms can prevent such miscommunications and errors, save on printing costs and paper-based forms distribution, and reduce inefficiencies in information processing. And finally, PDF form data exchanged between server or database and client is generally more compact than HTML form data.

How Acrobat Handles Forms

Acrobat forms can be as simple and "paperlike" or as interactive as you desire. For the moment, however, let's assume you're leaning toward the latter, complete with online submission and connectivity to a Web server or ODBC database. How does the form data get from Point A, the user's computer, to Point B, the database?

When a user clicks Submit, a chain of data-processing events kicks into action. First, the data is transmitted and saved in one of two formats: either an HTML-compatible, URL-encoded format or Acrobat's own forms data format (FDF), which is also used to store Acrobat annotations and comments (see Chapter 4). Both choices result in smaller, more flexible files than complete PDF files. URL-encoded files are compatible with HTML forms and thus work with any browser-based forms systems you already have in place. FDF, meanwhile, uses PDF-like syntax and constructs to save and reuse data, and it comes in an XFDF flavor that—guess what?—saves XML-encoded, hierarchically structured files that can be tied into XML-based back-end systems.

FDF and XFDF one-up HTML-based forms in that they can also be used to populate form fields. In addition, they bring intelligence to forms, allowing fields to be altered dynamically according to the FDF data received from the server. You can, for example, specify that some fields be hidden or read-only and that others be required. In addition, context-sensitive choices can appear in combo boxes. FDF can even create new PDF documents, drawing on stored, templated forms and populating many of the "spawned" fields automatically. Finally, FDF formatting allows you to control the visual look of buttons, and it lets client and server exchange graphical information such as digital signatures—a feature HTML forms don't support. They reside in your directory with their corresponding PDF files.

Not surprisingly, FDF doesn't make all of these things happen in a vacuum. Other technologies also come into play, including CGI scripts for parsing the information sent to the server, and JavaScripts for interactivity within the form fields. And any serious electronic forms implementation requires the involvement of company IT experts, Webmasters, and database administrators, which goes beyond the scope of this book. However, with a basic understanding of what happens after your forms have been designed and brought online, you should be able to start an intelligent discussion with these folks or your service providers.

Designing Forms

When bringing paper-based forms online, you can take one of two paths: You can scan existing forms into PDF, or you can create the electronic forms from scratch in a page-layout or forms-design application. Both approaches take time and planning: Even scanned paper forms require some clean-up, and you'll have to add fields in Acrobat if you want them to be interactive. You may want to scan old forms simply as a starting point for new forms or to make a template for creating forms from scratch in layout or design software.

Forms design is an art unto itself, as anyone who's filled out a 1040 knows. Pages become crowded mighty quickly. Thus, usability becomes a prime concern in forms design: Forms are no place for what an editor friend of mine dismissively refers to as "art things." A couple rules of thumb: Don't skimp on white space, and leave plenty of room in your fields for users to enter text.

If you're creating your form from scratch, design it completely in your page-layout application: Draw all checkboxes, blank lines for text entry, and buttons with the graphical style you desire. Although you'll add functionality to these elements in Acrobat (and be able to control their appearance), Acrobat is not really a design tool.

Once you've completed the basic design, distill the form to PDF—and keep in mind that when producing electronic forms, it's imperative that you embed your fonts. Nothing can corrupt a form like unreadable or crashing fonts. In addition, don't assume your forms will only be viewed online; save your PDF files at a high enough resolution to allow them to be printed from an office laser printer. Then in Acrobat you can use the Form tool to draw form fields that can be completed interactively.

Creating Form Fields

You can use the Form tool to create text boxes, list boxes, radio buttons, checkboxes, signature fields, and more (Figure 7-25). Click and drag a field on a form, and when you release the mouse button, the Field Properties dialog box will appear. This is where you can define not only the type of field you wish to create but also its appearance, any actions you want triggered when the mouse cursor interacts with it, and more.

Figure 7-25
The Form tool.

Let's start in the Appearance tab (Figure 7-26). The first thing you need to do is enter a name for your field, provide a short description of it, and enter its type. Despite what you might think, choosing a name can be tricky: For starters, if you want the same field on different forms to be automatically populated, those fields must have identical names (this includes the spacing and letter case). In addition, fields with the same name must also be of the same type (radio button, list box, whatever).

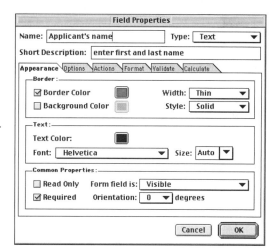

Figure 7-26 The Appearance tab of the Text Field Properties dialog box.

Acrobat recognizes two types of names: flat and hierarchical. Flat names are descriptive and straightforward—for example, "First Name" and "Last Name." With flat names, the fields have no association or relationship. However, by using a parent-child naming convention such as "name.first" and "name.last," you can give your fields a hierarchical structure. This makes them easier to manipulate with JavaScripts and can improve forms-processing performance.

If flat names suit your needs, be specific: For example, don't use "Name" when that could mean either the applicant's name or a dependent's name. In addition, write a brief description of the field to guide users in completing the form: This description will then pop up when the Hand tool is selected and passed over the form field.

Now choose one of the following types from the pop-up list: Button, Check Box, Combo Box, List Box, Radio Button, Text, or Signature. Use Text when you want a user to enter text such as a name, address, or phone number. Use Radio Button when users have only one option and Check Box when they can choose more than one. Combo Box and List Box present the same type of choices in two ways: Combo boxes list choices in a pop-up menu, while list boxes display entire lists (and thus take up more space).

For each field type, you can specify the appearance of borders and entered text, as well as any common properties, such as whether the field is required and whether it is visible onscreen and in print. Acrobat makes some default suggestions about colors and properties based on the type you selected; however, you can customize these to suit your purposes. Before you get carried away, though, remember that consistency improves usability: You probably don't want a lot of bright red form-field outlines and clashing yellow field backgrounds splattering your form like a Jackson Pollock painting. And remember that if you've designed the form in a layout application, you may not want to add to or obscure the graphics you've already created for your form elements.

Depending on what field type you select, the choices in the other tabbed menus will change accordingly. Sticking with a Text field for a hypothetical employment application, let's look at the Options tab (Figure 7-27). The Default field lets you specify default text for the field: Leave this blank if you plan to use the field for user contact information, such as the applicant's name. When you do want default text to appear (say, a department name on a purchase-order form), you might want to make the field read only in the Appearance menu.

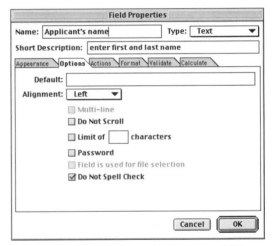

Figure 7-27 The Options tab of the text Field Properties dialog box.

Another option is to specify a limit to the number of characters in the box. Acrobat allows up to 32,000 characters per text field, which is pretty generous, but be careful about cutting fields too short. Checking Password makes typed text appear as asterisks (appropriate for password fields). And you may want to check Do Not Spell Check for fields that contain proper names. By checking "Field is used for file selection," you enable a text field's contents to be a path to a specific file (which would be submitted along with the form). You can also apply a JavaScript to a file-selection field to make a browsable Select File dialog box pop up (more on that when we get to the Actions tab).

Options that appear for buttons and checkboxes let you specify how these form elements are displayed (for example, what happens when they're clicked or checked). There is no Options tab for signature fields; their properties are specified in the Appearance, Actions, and Signed tabs. (For more on digital signatures, see Chapter 4, "Digital Sign Off.") Checkboxes, combo boxes, list boxes, and radio buttons all have an Export Value parameter in the Options tab: CGI applications use this to identify user-selected field contents. You need to enter export values only when you're sending form data to a database over an intranet or the Web *and* when the selection is different from the item designed by the form field, or the form field is a radio button. Enter Yes for checkboxes, list boxes, and radio buttons; enter a specific value for list or combo boxes if you want the exported value to be different from what the user actually specifies.

The Format tab provides further appearance guidelines for text and combo boxes (Figure 7-28). Pick a category such as Number and decide how many decimal places to define, what type of numbers to use, how to format negative values, and so on. The Special category formats Zip codes, phone numbers, and social security numbers.

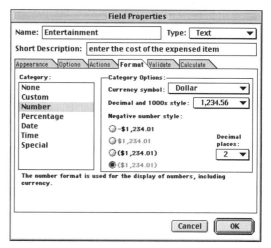

Figure 7-28 The Format tab of the Field Properties dialog box.

Adding Interactivity and Intelligence

The Actions tab of the Field Properties dialog box is where you can add interactivity to your electronic form (Figure 7-29). Since one of the most common actions you'll create is a Submit button, I'll walk you through that process here.

First, determine at what point, or *state*, you want the action to occur. You have six choices: Mouse Up, Mouse Down, Mouse Enter, Mouse Exit, On Focus, and On Blur. For a Submit button, choose Mouse Up: This means the action will occur when the mouse button is released (let up) at the end of a click. Mouse Down means when the mouse button is depressed; Mouse Enter and Mouse Exit refer to when the mouse cursor moves over (enters) and away from (exit) the field. On Focus and On Blur are similar to Mouse Enter and Mouse Exit, respectively, except that they apply to when the mouse enters or leaves the field as a result of a mouse action or by the Tab key being pressed.

After defining the state that triggers the action, click the Add button. In the Add an Action dialog box, select the action you want to occur from the Type pop-up menu (Figure 7-30). All of the possible actions—including Open File, Reset Form, Submit Form, and Execute Menu Item—are invoked by JavaScripts. If you choose JavaScript as your action type, you can apply a custom JavaScript—for example to automatically enter the current date or to hide a field until

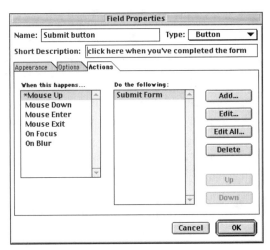

Figure 7-29 The Actions tab of the Field Properties dialog box.

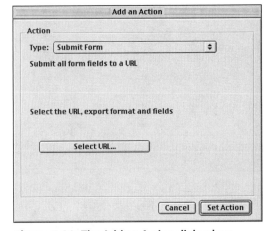

Figure 7-30 The Add an Action dialog box.

a condition is met. (The Acrobat manual includes instructions for writing these and other JavaScript actions.) After selecting Submit Form, click the Select URL button to specify the Web address to which the form should be submitted.

In the Submit Form Selections dialog box, enter the complete URL to which the form should be submitted (Figure 7-31). This is where you decide how you want form data to be saved: By default, Acrobat checks FDF because it offers the most functionality and the smallest file sizes. Note that you can also submit the entire PDF file, which might be a good choice if your forms contain digital signatures.

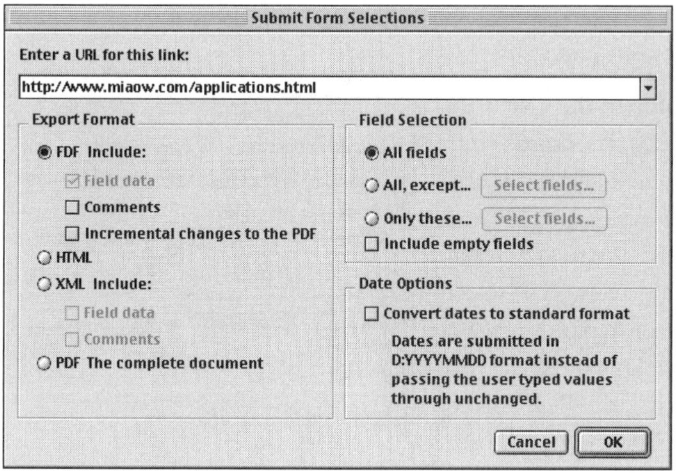

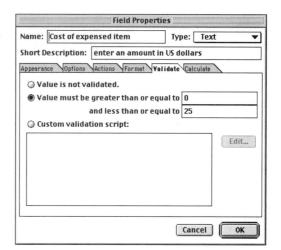

Figure 7-31
The Submit Form
Selections dialog box.

When you've made your selections, click OK and then click Set Action in the Add an Action dialog box. Back in the Field Properties dialog box, you should now see the name of the action in the "Do the following" scrolling list, and an asterisk next to Mouse Up in the "When this happens" list. Once again, for the submission process to work, you need a CGI application on your Web server to collect the data and route it to your database.

There are two additional ways to add intelligence and interactivity to your forms: using the Validate and Calculate tabs of the Field Properties dialog box. When either a text or combo box contains a number or a percentage, as categorized in the Format palette, you can instruct Acrobat to validate the contents of the field. In the Validate tab, check the "Value must be…" radio button and define a range of possible values in the "greater than or equal to" and "less than or equal to" text boxes (Figure 7-32). If a user enters

Figure 7-32 The Validate tab of the Field Properties dialog box.

invalid data, Acrobat will display a "Warning: Invalid Value" message. If you want to validate text (nonnumeric) contents of fields (for example, to screen unacceptable department or product names), check the "Custom validation script" radio button and enter a custom JavaScript.

Finally, we come to the Calculate tab (Figure 7-33). As long as your text or combo box has a numeric value, as defined in the Format palette, you can instruct Acrobat to add, multiply, average, or select the minimum or maximum value of whatever fields you select. To select fields, click the Pick button and highlight and choose two or more fields in the Select a Field dialog box. Click Done when you've chosen all of the fields you want to calculate.

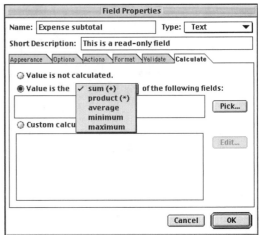

Figure 7-33 The Calculate tab of the Field Properties dialog box.

Many forms require multiple calculations (for example, to generate subtotals and a final total), which means the calculations must occur in a certain order. To set this order, define the calculations in the Field Properties dialog box, then choose Tools > Forms > Set Field Calculation Order. A list of your defined calculations appears in the Calculated Fields dialog box; click to select them and move them up and down in the order list. The one at the top of the list is executed first; the one at the bottom of the list is last.

Editing Form Fields

Now that you know how to create basic form fields, I doubt you'll want to do so manually for every field in every form that you want to bring online. To save time, you can duplicate fields: Simply select a field with the Form tool and then Ctrl/Option-drag it to position a duplicate elsewhere on the page. Alternatively, you could press Alt/Command-C to copy the field and Alt/Command-P to paste it in the center of a different page view. Users will appreciate duplicated fields because any information they enter in one field will be automatically entered in the duplicate field.

To edit fields, select them with the Form tool and double-click or choose Edit > Properties to access Field Properties again. You'll often have dozens, if not hundreds, of form fields to navigate during your editing—which is why the Fields palette is convenient. Choose Window > Fields to display a floating palette that lists all of your form's fields by name, along with icons to indicate field types (Figure 7-34). With the Form tool selected, you can double-click any field listed in the palette, and Acrobat will make it active. Also from the Fields palette, right- or Control-click a field entry to choose from a context menu: Go to Field, Rename Field, Delete Field, Lock Field (to prevent modifications), and Properties (to access the Field Properties dialog box).

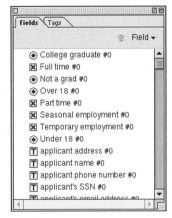

Figure 7-34 The Fields palette.

Acrobat also offers some tools for finessing form fields' placement on the page. Shift-click to select two or more fields whose position you want to alter, then choose Tools > Forms > Fields. Now choose from the four submenus—Align, Center, Distribute, and Size—to adjust their positions. Choose View > Grid and View > Snap to Grid to aid in precision placement. (You can define the grid in the Preferences dialog box, Layout Grid panel.)

With the advent of HTML e-commerce forms, users have grown accustomed to tabbing through form fields. So before you're finished, it's also a good idea to set up a tabbed order for your form fields. After you've set up all of your fields, make sure you've selected the Form tool, then choose Tools > Forms > Fields > Set Tab Order. Acrobat will display a numeric sequence of the fields in the document window (Figure 7-35). To change them, simply click in the new order or sequence that you desire. When you're finished, click outside of any form field or switch tools.

Finally, be aware that there is a Forms panel in Preferences with options that can help both form creators and form users. Choose Edit > Preferences > General, then click Forms from the list on the left. There are three checkboxes in Forms Preferences (Figure 7-36): The first, Auto Calculate Field Values, is great for users; however, it may interfere when you're designing forms. The second and third fields are helpful when individuals fill out forms. Show Focus Rectangle shows when fields are in focus. "In focus" means selected, but a field can come into focus when someone tabs their way into it, instead of just clicking in it. Highlight Form Fields highlights fields when users click on them, in a thin blue (or other color) outline. This is especially useful for text fields.

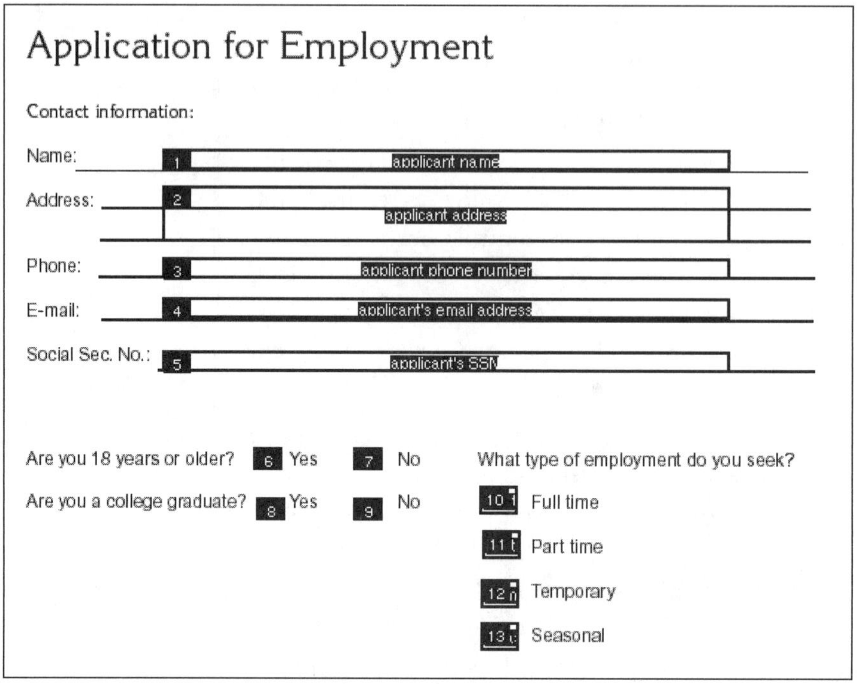

Application for Employment

Contact information:

Name: ___[1]___ applicant name

Address: ___[2]___ applicant address

Phone: ___[3]___ applicant phone number

E-mail: ___[4]___ applicant's email address

Social Sec. No.: ___[5]___ applicant's SSN

Are you 18 years or older? [6] Yes [7] No   What type of employment do you seek?

Are you a college graduate? [8] Yes [9] No   [10] Full time

[11] Part time

[12] Temporary

[13] Seasonal

Figure 7-35 Setting a tabbing order for form fields.

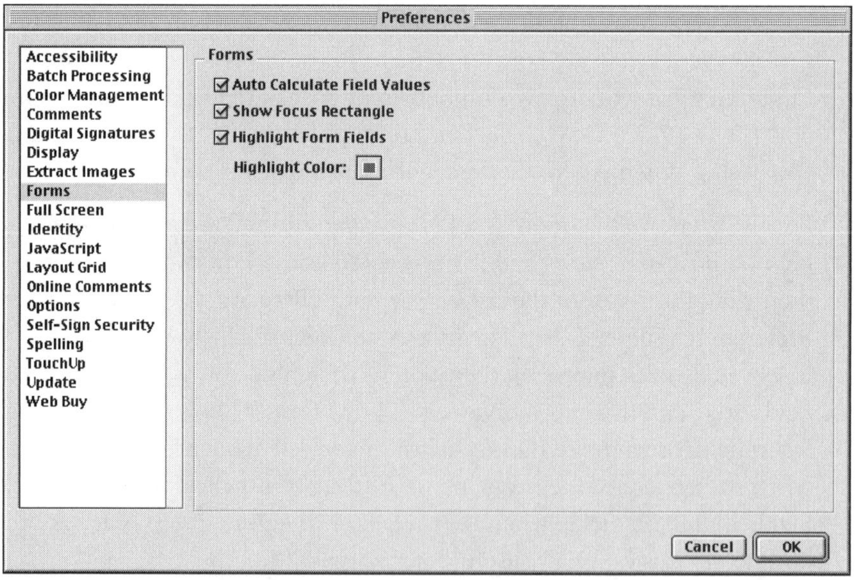

Preferences

Accessibility
Batch Processing
Color Management
Comments
Digital Signatures
Display
Extract Images
Forms
Full Screen
Identity
JavaScript
Layout Grid
Online Comments
Options
Self-Sign Security
Spelling
TouchUp
Update
Web Buy

Forms

☑ Auto Calculate Field Values
☑ Show Focus Rectangle
☑ Highlight Form Fields

Highlight Color: ▣

[Cancel] [OK]

Figure 7-36 The Forms panel of the Preferences dialog box.

Checking Spelling

One other convenient forms feature is the ability to spell-check field contents (as well as comments). To spell-check a completed form, choose Tools > Spelling > Check Form Fields and Comments, then click Start in the Check Spelling dialog box. Misspelled words appear in the Not in Dictionary section of the dialog box, where you can edit them directly, choose a suggested alternative, or ignore the unrecognized word.

The Spelling feature uses whatever dictionary or dictionaries you specify in Preferences (Edit > Preferences > General, and choose the Spelling panel, Figure 7-37). Although spell-checking is the user's responsibility, you can create a button that invokes a spell-check action before a form is submitted. You just need to make sure that your users have the correct dictionary on their systems.

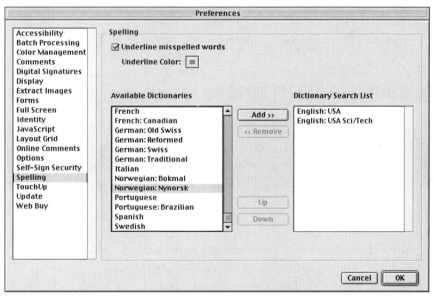

Figure 7-37 The Spelling panel of the Preferences dialog box.

For Form Fanatics

There's still more you can do with forms in Acrobat, such as creating an action that imports data and automatically populates certain fields. However, this requires first setting up a reference form—one that includes the completed fields Acrobat will be searching for to be used as a reference. Acrobat comes with a Personal Field Names (PFN) Specification file, which lets users create profiles of their personal information. This way, when they receive forms that adhere to the PFN specification (including sharing its naming conventions), their personal information is automatically entered into the correct fields. You can also define pages of your forms as templates, which basically generate new pages or forms for users to complete based on the information they've supplied. And of course forms don't have to be tied to a Web server and submitted electronically through a browser; users can simply export form data to an FDF file. But I'll let someone else write the book that explains how to be a complete Acrobat forms whiz. For now, just remember that users must have either the full version of Acrobat or Acrobat Approval to complete electronic forms; Acrobat Reader doesn't offer this capability.

CATALOGING PDF FILES

I've talked a lot about PDF files being "digital masters," and whether you use these masters for print or electronic publishing (or both), one of the most important things you can do with them is save them in a collection, or library. To make any collection of documents manageable, you need a system to organize its content. For PDF files, that system can take the form of Acrobat's Catalog feature: Use it to create a searchable index of your library of PDF files.

Keep in mind, however, that Acrobat's ability to search indexes and collections only extends to local hard drives and networks, not to the Web. Not surprisingly, then, you can only view these collections in Acrobat (not a browser). Nor can typical Web search engines search PDF file contents in the same way they search HTML files. If you want your PDF content to be searchable on your intranet, you need to use a third-party search engine, such as Verity, that supports PDF. Alternatively, Adobe offers the IFilter plug-in, which lets you index PDF files in a site in Microsoft Index Server, allowing site visitors to search for text within the PDF files (in addition to HTML and .doc files, which Index Server supports by default). If you plan to implement either of these technologies, however, you'll need to get your IT department involved.

NO TIME WASTED HERE

We've saved the most money in our graphics repository because it's incredibly organized. We catalog all of the Document Summary metadata, including keywords and authors, on all of our files and artwork. Now everything is in the same format, and we're able to find and pull files up at any time. As a result, we don't have to send out as many jobs to illustrators, because we can locate and reuse art instead of re-creating it, and we can go in and make corrections and do reprints from the PDF files, and we don't have to touch the original application files.

—*Keli Davis, director of production, Evan-Moor Educational Publishers*

Building an Index

Before you create your index, you need to take a couple of steps to ensure that searches will be effective. First, get your files in order: Make sure that all of the documents have their metadata entered in the Document Summary dialog box (choose File > Document Properties > Summary), and that electronic files have all of their links, bookmarks, and form fields set up. Remember, these are "masters." If possible, use an eight-dot-three file-naming convention to minimize cross-platform incompatibilities, and avoid using extended characters because Catalog doesn't recognize ANSI character codes for accented and non-English characters in file and folder names. Break large files into smaller components—give every chapter in a book its own file, for example—to optimize search performance. Finally, disable security. Acrobat cannot catalog password-protected documents. Once the files are in order, store all of a collection's files in one folder on one hard drive or network server volume. This is also where your index will reside, so make sure there's plenty of room.

When you've done all that, you're ready to roll. You don't need to have a PDF file open in Acrobat to begin the cataloging process: Simply choose Tools > Catalog to bring up the Adobe Catalog dialog box, where you'll create your index. The first thing to do here is click Preferences and make sure they meet your needs.

- **General.** There are several settings here that relate to how final indexes are handled at the system level (Figure 7-38). The "Document section size" setting determines the maximum size of a document; if a document exceeds that size, Catalog splits its index into two or more indexes. The range for this setting is 200,000 to 800,000 words: The more memory you have the safer it is to have a higher section size, and the faster the update. In addition, the larger the setting for "Minimum memory for building indexes," the faster the search.

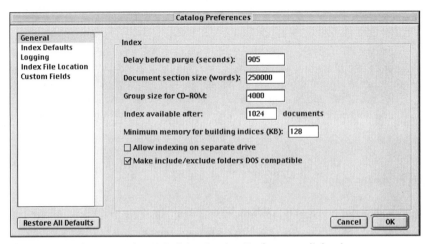

Figure 7-38 The General panel of the Catalog Preferences dialog box.

Do not set "Group size for CD-ROM" higher than 4,000; "Index available after" can range from 16 to 4,000 documents. Catalog will process that many PDF files before making a partial index available, or before updating a current index. Once again, the higher the number, the faster the search.

As for the "Delay before purge" setting, you can set it anywhere between 30 and 905 seconds (15 minutes). Adobe recommends you leave it at the default 905. Indexes that are updated and rebuilt need to be purged periodically to remove old versions of files that are no longer valid to the index. Leaving the delay at a high setting gives users enough time to quit their searches before the purge begins.

On the Mac, checking the "Make include/exclude folders DOS compatible" box allows you to forgo converting all of your PDF files to eight-dot-three names, but you must still store them in a folder that uses the MS-DOS convention.

- **Index Defaults.** In this panel of the preferences dialog box (Figure 7-39), select whether you want to include numbers in indexes (Windows includes them by default), which increases index size; whether you want to optimize index files for CD-ROMs by arranging them for fast access; and whether you want to add unique document identifiers to Acrobat 1.0 files (which resolves file-naming ambiguities that can occur when those files are created on a Mac and translated to MS-DOS conventions). Your selections here will appear in the Options dialog box when you define a new index (we'll get there in a minute); however, you can undo them at that time.

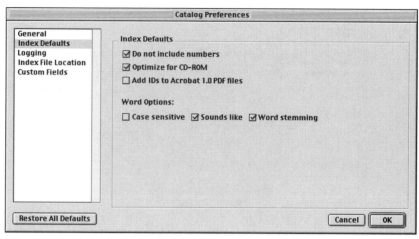

Figure 7-39 The Index Defaults Catalog Preferences dialog box.

Finally, check which types of word-search options you want to allow: Case sensitive, which enables the Match Case option in the Acrobat Search dialog box; Sounds like, which enables the option of the same name in the Acrobat Search dialog box; and Word stemming, which enables the Word Assistant preview in Acrobat Search. The first option restricts searchability; the second improves searchability of proper names; and the last returns words that share a stem (but not necessarily the entire word) with the search term.

- **Logging.** In the Logging panel (Figure 7-40), you can decide whether you want Catalog to produce a log of problems it encounters when it builds the index, and if so, what types of problems you want it to log: search-engine messages or compatibility warnings. You can also specify a maximum log file size, a name, and where you want the log saved. On the Mac, check "Log compatibility warnings" when you're publishing the collection on an ISO 9660 CD and you want to be warned of file names that don't comply with that standard.

- **Index File Locations.** Catalog creates an index definition file (a PDX file) that goes inside the folder that contains the collection of indexed files. This is where you can customize the default index file name or save it outside of the collection folder (Figure 7-41). If you change the index's file name, however, make sure you retain the .pdx extension. In addition, you should probably leave the default Save location as is: If you remove the index from

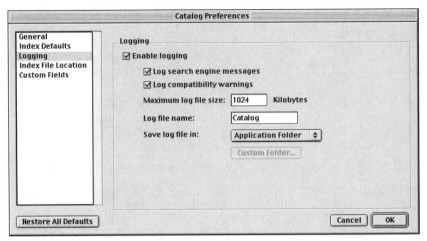

Figure 7-40 The Logging panel of the Catalog Preferences dialog box.

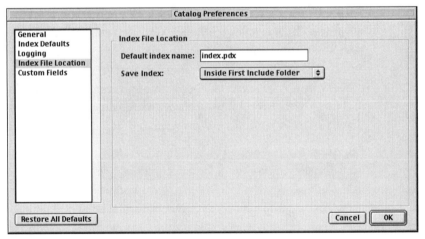

Figure 7-41 The Index File Locations panel of the Catalog Preferences dialog box.

the collection folder, it's easy to lose it. Be aware, also, that Catalog generates a folder of supporting index documents and places it inside the collection folder. That folder shares the index file name and is also something you don't want to move or lose.

- **Custom Fields.** This last preferences panel allows you to add custom fields to your index (Figure 7-42). However, you must also make sure that the indexed documents contain that data field, or a search won't return any results.

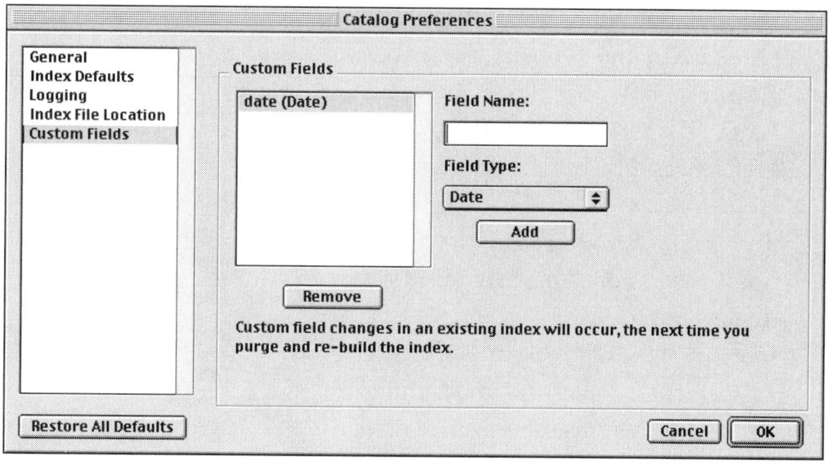

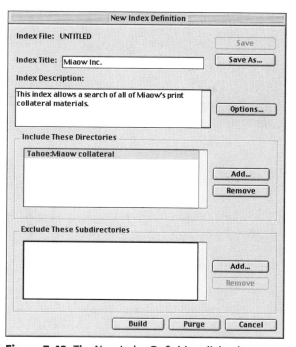

Figure 7-42 The Custom Fields panel of the Catalog Preferences dialog box.

Once your preferences are in order, click OK to return to the Catalog dialog box. *Now* you can create the actual index: Click the New Index button to access the New Index Definition dialog box (Figure 7-43). Give your index a title and a description (the user will see this, though it's not the name of the index file itself, which you specified in Preferences), then click the Add button to select which directories you want to include. You can select individual files or a combination of files and folders. However, if you've set up your collection properly, you should see just a single folder (this also makes it easier to update). If necessary or appropriate, you can exclude subdirectories or subfolders from the collection.

Figure 7-43 The New Index Definition dialog box.

Before you build the index, click Options. In the Options dialog box (Figure 7-44) you can change the Index Defaults you established in Preferences (if you desire) and also create a list of up to 500 words you *don't* want indexed—prepositions, pronouns, and so on. These are called *stop words.* Eliminating *a, the,* and the like from an index can make it as much as 15 percent smaller—a good thing, although it prevents users from searching on text strings that include those words. So add stop words with caution and let everyone who uses the catalog know that they're there.

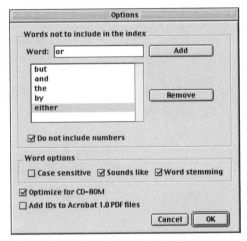

Figure 7-44 The Options dialog box.

Click OK to exit the Options dialog box, then check your choices in the New Index Definition dialog box. When you're ready to go, click the Build button.

Acrobat will prompt you with a Save Index File dialog box, which should contain the index name you defined in the Index File Locations preference panel, as well as the location (inside the collection's folder by default). Change the name and location if desired, then click Save. Catalog will now begin to do its thing, displaying its progress and the status of events as it builds the index (Figure 7-45). When the index is done, the Adobe Catalog dialog box will let you build another.

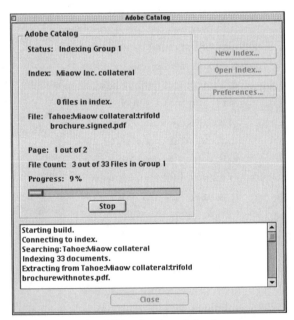

Figure 7-45 The Adobe Catalog dialog box.

To view the results of your catalog, go to the collections folder or directory and take a look: You should find the index file (miaowindex.pdx in my example), a log file (miaowindex.log), and a folder of supporting index files (miaowindex again). If everything is there, you're ready to let people use it (Figure 7-46).

Searching a Catalog

Once collections have been cataloged (indexed), you can search them from within Acrobat. To do so, choose Edit > Search > Select Indexes to locate the list of available indexes. In the Index Selection dialog box (Figure 7-47), you can add and remove indexes from the list, which includes the titles you specified in the New Index Definition dialog box. Click the Info button to see the index's description and path, the number of files in the collection, and the status (available or unavailable).

After you've selected one or more indexes, you can define a query by choosing Edit > Search > Query. In the Adobe Acrobat Search dialog box (Figure 7-48), enter the text you want to search for in the Find Results Containing Text field. The status bar at the bottom of the box indicates which index or indexes will be searched; you can change them by clicking the Indexes button. Then check any options you want, such as Thesaurus (which finds words similar to your search terms) or Proximity (which limits results

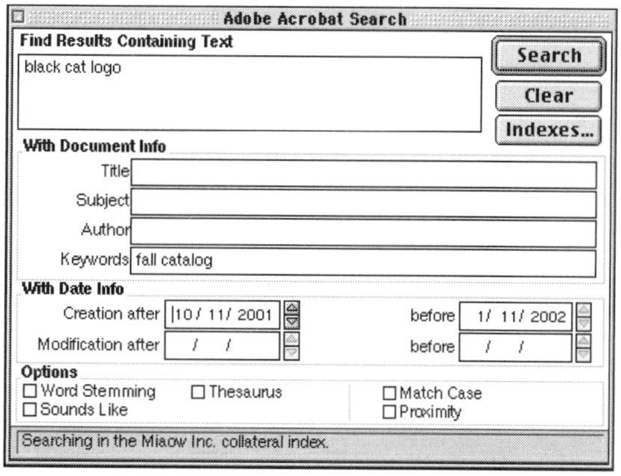

Figure 7-46 The files produced by a Catalog operation.

Figure 7-47 The Index Selection dialog box.

Figure 7-48 The Adobe Acrobat Search (query) dialog box.

of Boolean AND searches to one matched pair per document). Word Stemming and Sounds Like will only work if the index creator built those options into the index.

Acrobat supports all kinds of Boolean, wildcard, and complex searches on both individual words and phrases. You can even search a set of returned documents to find a narrower subset of hits (the command for this is Edit > Search > Results). If you can't decide which options to use in your search, you can use the Word Assistant feature to generate a list of potentially useful search terms.

To use the Word Assistant, choose Edit > Search > Word Assistant while your query window is open. In the Word Assistant dialog box (Figure 7-49), enter a word and choose Word Stemming, Sounds Like, or Thesaurus from the Assist pop-up menu. Then click Look Up. Acrobat returns a list of related words that it found in the selected index, and you can cut and paste any that are helpful into your query box. If nothing turns up, speed your search by skipping those options.

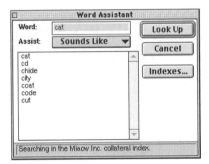

Figure 7-49 The Word Assistant dialog box.

Remember, Word Assistant, Word Stemming, and Sounds Like all have to be built into the index by the creator to be available for the searcher.

You can also narrow your searches by specifying Document and Date Info in the query dialog box: These fields are based on document properties, which is why you should make sure all PDF files contain this metadata. If, by the way, you don't see the Document Info, Date Info, or Options in the search dialog box, go into Edit > Preferences > Search and check all three boxes in the Include in Query section (Figure 7-50).

In addition, you can associate PDF files with a particular index, and that index can be searched without going through the selection process. To associate a file with an index, open it in Acrobat and choose File > Document Properties > Associated Index. In the Document Associated Index dialog box (Figure 7-51), click the Choose Index radio button, then click the Choose button and browse to select the PDX index file. When you find it, click Open and then click OK in the Document Associated Index dialog box. Now when you go to Edit > Search > Query, that index will automatically be selected.

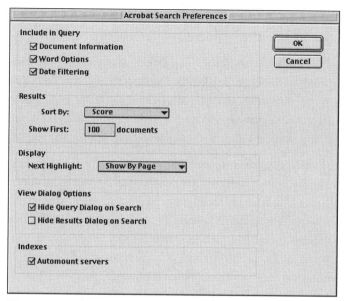

Figure 7-50 The Acrobat Search Preferences dialog box.

One last comment: You probably noticed the Find command right there in the Edit menu above the Search command. Use Find when you're looking for a word or phrase in a specific PDF file; use Search to search multiple files in a collection. Both commands are also available from the toolbar: The Find and Search buttons (Figure 7-52) have a binocular icon, and a binocular icon with a book behind it, respectively.

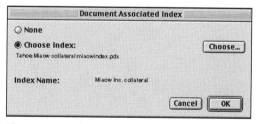

Figure 7-51 The Document Associated Index dialog box.

Figure 7-52 The Find (left) and Search (right) buttons.

Staying Up to Date

You'll need to periodically update your index if files are removed from or added to the collection or if you've moved the collection, causing a change in the relative paths between the index file and the folders containing the indexed documents.

You can open an index anytime from the Catalog dialog and click Build to rebuild it based on the current contents of the collection's folder at their current location.

When you rebuild an index, files that have been deleted or updated remain in the index but are marked invalid so that they're not searched. As you might imagine, this bloats the index, so you should occasionally purge them before rebuilding (click the Purge button). To keep searches optimized and effective, you should also purge and rebuild indexes if you change the optional search criteria or stop words.

Don't hesitate to turn to your IT department for help managing your PDF document collections. They can help you organize, store, and back up your content, as well as help keep users' preferences and systems in sync with the search capabilities you want to allow. Maintaining a collection of PDF documents is a big task, but the more you move toward using PDF to collaborate on document creation, to prepare and send off final files for prepress, and to produce electronic files, the more important it will be to keep your archives in working order. After all, PDF is all about producing and using our digital content more effectively, and helping us all work a little more efficiently in the process.

APPENDIX ONE

Acrobat Assistants

Like any wise performer, Acrobat has a number of helpers and spotters on the ground and in the wings to make sure it lives up to expectations. Trying to develop a comprehensive list of the products that enhance Adobe Acrobat's functionality, however, is rather like trying to catch a nebula: Like interstellar dust and gasses, they come, they go, they collide with other products and form new ones. But to give you an idea of the breadth of products that bring flexibility and functionality to PDF prepress and publishing workflows, this appendix lists more than 80 plug-ins and other applications that do everything from edit transparency to compile form data. Version numbers and list prices are included when available; all prices are in U.S. dollars unless otherwise noted.

ACROBAT PLUG-INS

File Conversion/Compatibility

Company	Product	Description
Adobe Systems 800-833-6687 www.adobe.com	**Make Accessible** Windows Free	Creates tagged versions of untagged PDF files, allowing text reflow for small screens and saving PDF files in Rich Text Format (RTF) for use with word processors.
Adobe Systems 800-833-6687 www.adobe.com	**Save As XML** Windows Macintosh Free	Saves tagged PDF files in XML or HTML formats, including XML 1.00 without styling, HTML 4.01 with CSS 1.00, HTML 3.20, Accessible, HTML 3.20 without CSS, and text-only.

File Conversion/Compatibility *continued*

Company	Product	Description
BCL Computers 408-557-5277 www.bclcomputers.com	**Drake** Windows $199	Converts PDF files into RTF documents using Microsoft Word's text-box features, making them accessible for editing in a word processor.
BCL Computers 408-557-5277 www.bclcomputers.com	**Freebird** Windows $199	Converts PDF files into compressed graphics files for archiving. Formats supported include TIFF, JPEG, and Windows BMP.
BCL Computers 408-557-5277 www.bclcomputers.com	**Magellan** Windows $199	With a click of the mouse, converts PDF pages into HTML pages that are ready to be posted on the Web.
Coptech West 800-932-6783 www.coptech.com	**SmartPDF** Windows Macintosh Free	Makes PDF files into self-updating documents that automatically check an embedded URL to see if a newer version of the file is available.
CreoScitex 604-451-2700 www.creoscitex.com	**PDF Seps2 Comp 1.6** Windows Macintosh $399	Transforms PDF files that have already been color-separated into composite documents that can be viewed and printed in their entirety.

Preflighting

Company	Product	Description
Apago 779-619-1884 www.apago.com	**PDF/X-1 Checkup** Windows Macintosh $149	Preflighting software that checks all elements within a PDF file to ensure that it complies with the ANSI PDF/X-1 standard. Also replaces and corrects missing or damaged ICC profiles.
Enfocus Software 650-358-1210 www.enfocus.com	**Certify PDF 1.01** Windows Macintosh $249	Controls PDF file integrity by allowing preflighting at any step during the document-creation process, storing both the preflight profile and the preflight results within the PDF file, identifying and tracking all edit sessions, and allowing roll-back and comparisons between sessions.

Company	Product	Description
A Round Table Solution (61) 396 865522 www.aroundtablesolution.com	**Duplex** Windows Free	Allows odd and even pages to be printed independently on a non-duplexing printer.
Callas Software (49) 30 4439 0310 www.callas.de	**pdfOutput Pro** Windows Macintosh $299	Adds custom crop and registration marks and color-separates PDF files for output on color printers, imagesetters, and other PostScript devices.
Lantana Research Software 510-744-0282 www.lantanarips.com	**Crackerjack 4.0** Windows Macintosh $495	All-purpose tool for professional color output from PDF files to digital printers, imagesetters, or offset print, including separations, spot-to-process conversion, and screening controls.
Lantana Research Software 510-744-0282 www.lantanarips.com	**Variform PDF** Windows and Macintosh $199	Allows variable-data printing by merging information from any delimited text file into Acrobat forms; can also save results to a file (PostScript or PDF, using Acrobat Distiller).
Quite Software (44) 1631 574089 www.quite.com	**Quite Imposing** Windows Macintosh £199	Graphical page imposition tools for creating a computer-to-plate or computer-to-press workflow.
Quite Software (44) 1631 574089 www.quite.com	**Quite Imposing Plus** Windows Macintosh £389	Expands the standard features of Quite Imposing with features for experienced prepress professionals.

Content Manipulation

Company	Product	Description
Appligent 610-284-4006 www.appligent.com	**DateD** Windows $2,499	Automatically adds time and date stamps and ISO compliance data to PDF documents.
Appligent 610-284-4006 www.appligent.com	**StampPDF** Windows Macintosh $179	Stamps pages in a PDF document with any kind of text: watermarks, page numbers, headers, footers, and so on.

Content Manipulation *continued*

Company	Product	Description
BCL Computers 408-557-5277 www.bclcomputers.com	Jade Windows $199	Extracts text, tables, and graphics from PDF files for use in other applications or PDF documents.
CreoScitex 604-451-2700 www.creoscitex.com	PDF Embedder 1.0 Macintosh $129	Embeds any digital file inside a PDF document; useful for archiving, digital asset-management, prepress file submission, and content delivery.
CreoScitex 604-451-2700 www.creoscitex.com	Pagelet 1.0 Windows Macintosh $249	A page-placement tool that assembles sub-pages or "pagelets" from various PDF documents; an easy method of placing PDF files onto a page.
CreoScitex 604-451-2700 www.creoscitex.com	ShadowFX Macintosh N/A	Adds shadows to any object inside a PDF file, including text.
Datawatch 800-445-3311 www.datawatch.com	Redwing Windows $349	Extracts text and tables from within PDF files and converts them to popular PC data formats.
Enfocus Software 650-358-1210 www.enfocus.com	PitStop Pro 4.6 Windows Macintosh $399	Interactive and automated editing of PDF document contents, including text, graphics, colors, sizes, positions, and page numbering.
Enfocus Software 650-358-1210 www.enfocus.com	PowerUp PDF 1.1 Windows Macintosh $99	Junior version of PitStop allows file features to be edited, including text and graphics, colors, and objects.
Enfocus Software 650-358-1210 www.enfocus.com	EyeDropper 4.0 Windows, Macintosh $29.95	Accurately measures the colors at any location in a PDF document, allowing accurate color editing and matching.
Iceni Technology (44) 1603 628 289 www.iceni.com	Gemini Windows Macintosh $159	Converts text, table, and image elements within PDF documents into formats that can be reused in other applications.
Lantana Research Software 510-744-0282 www.lantanarips.com	PDF ImageWorks Windows Macintosh $295	Edits images directly within PDF files. Tools include cut, copy, paste, resize, rotate, extract, replace, convert color space color, downsample/subsample, adjust brightness/contrast, adjust color, and despeckle.

Content Manipulation *continued*

Company	Product	Description
Lantana Research Software 510-744-0282 www.lantanarips.com	Stratify PDF Windows Macintosh $249	Creates and manages layers in PDF documents, like those used in photo-editing or illustration programs. Layers can be hidden, shuffled, or used to create multiple versions of a single document.
Mapsoft Computer Services (44) 1548 50047 www.mapsoft.com	Maskit Windows $99	Allows you to mask areas of a PDF page to make them invisible. The tool can define the masked area as either inside or outside of a selected area.
Mapsoft Computer Services (44) 1548 50047 www.mapsoft.com	Impress Windows $99	Adds stamps, including watermarks, page numbers, and date/time signatures, to PDF documents.
Mapsoft Computer Services (44) 1548 50047 www.mapsoft.com	Impress Pro Windows $199	A batch version of Impress that lets you treat multiple PDF files with various combinations of watermarks, page numbers, and date/time stamps.
Quite Software (44) 1631 574089 www.quite.com	Quite a Box of Tricks Windows Macintosh £125	Adds commonly needed production functions to Acrobat, including extra file compression; grayscale-to-black-and-white or RGB-to-CMYK conversion; and mirroring, scaling and rotating.

Security

Company	Product	Description
Appligent 610-284-4006 www.appligent.com	Redax Windows Macintosh $349	Protects sensitive or private information in widely distributed PDF documents by allowing you to remove selected text and images.
FileOpen Systems 212-942-2291 www.fileopen.com	Personal Publisher Windows $199	Encrypts and bundles PDF files into secure, copy-protected self-executing files.
VeriSign 650-961-7500 www.verisign.com	Document Signer Windows Free	Adds digital signatures to PDF files using a permanent VeriSign Digital ID.

Utilities

Company	Product	Description
CreoScitex 604-451-2700 www.creoscitex.com	**Synapse Prepare Pro** Macintosh $1,295	Provides printers and trade shops with enhanced control over the creation of PDF files, creating "directives" that can be shipped to remote locations and used to control the actions of Acrobat and EnfocusPitStop.
Dionis 617-730-5557 www.dionis.com	**Ari's Ruler** Windows Macintosh Free	Precisely measures anything on a PDF page: trim size, margins, column widths, distances between objects.
Dionis 617-730-5557 www.dionis.com	**Ari's Link Check** Windows Macintosh $99	Automatically looks for dead-end links and other missing "external dependencies" in PDF files.
Dionis 617-730-5557 www.dionis.com	**Ari's Link Tool** Windows Macintosh $295	Copies and pastes links using standard Edit menu commands, including Paste Multiple, which can be used to paste links onto multiple pages or across multiple documents.
Dionis 617-730-5557 www.dionis.com	**Ari's Bookmark Tool** Windows Macintosh $195	Can copy bookmarks from one PDF file into every PDF file in a given folder. It can also draw book marks from a database, making it easier to create bookmarks that point to other files.
Enfocus Software 650-358-1210 www.enfocus.com	**WebPerfect PDF 1.1** Windows Macintosh $99	Simple prompt-driven tool for optimizing print-based PDF files for use on the Web, minimizing file sizes.
Infodata 800-336-4939 www.infodata.com	**Compose 4.0** Windows $895	A suite of 20 tools for easily adding extra features to PDF files, such as hyperlinked indexes, tables of contents, bookmarks, overlays.
Infodata 800-336-4939 www.infodata.com	**Re:mark** Windows Macintosh $129	Provides an enhanced set of markup, annotation, and commenting tools for easier electronic collaboration when sharing PDF files in workgroups.
Infodata 800-336-4939 www.infodata.com	**Aerial** Windows $149	A suite of tools, including the abilities to use a document's internal page numbers (not those assigned by Acrobat), search an enhanced index, tag frequently used pages, extract text as RTF, and extract tables to the Clipboard.

Utilities *continued*

Company	Product	Description
Mapsoft Computer Services (44) 1548 50047 www.mapsoft.com	**MediaSizer** Windows $39	Changes the media size in PDF files, for example from a letter-size page to A4.
Mapsoft Computer Services (44) 1548 50047 www.mapsoft.com	**AutoSave** Windows $35	Automatically saves your PDF files at regular intervals as you work within Acrobat.
Mapsoft Computer Services (44) 1548 50047 www.mapsoft.com	**PDF Explorer** Windows $39	Allows you to see the contents and components of a PDF file using a Windows Explorer–like interface.
Xman Software 415-945-0910 www.xman.com	**xToolsOne** Windows Macintosh Free	A suite of 10 tools that allows you to see an entire document's annotations in a single window; dog-ear pages for future reference; add footnotes, bookmarks, and links; jump to designated "home" PDF files; reveal the borders of link areas; select page areas for printing; and select text with more flexibility than Acrobat allows.

Telecommunications

Company	Product	Description
A Round Table Solution (61) 396 865522 www.aroundtablesolution.com	**PDF Mail Manager** Windows $99	Sends PDF files—either single pages or whole documents—by email from within Acrobat, while also allowing you to build custom mailing lists.

STAND-ALONE PROGRAMS

Company	Product	Description
A Round Table Solution (61) 396 865522 www.aroundtablesolution.com	**Split & Merge Wizard** Windows $149	Automates splitting and merging PDF files either interactively or in batch mode.

STAND-ALONE PROGRAMS *continued*

Company	Product	Description
A Round Table Solution (61) 396 865522 www.aroundtablesolution.com	**PDF Workshop** Windows $249	Collates PDF document information (title, subject, keywords, etc.) into an Excel spreadsheet for easier file management. From within Excel you can manage (in batch mode) such processes as printing, merging, copying, and updating document information.
A Round Table Solution (61) 396 865522 www.aroundtablesolution.com	**Import** Windows $259	Automates the high-volume conversion of image files (including BMP, GIF, DCX, PCX, PNG, JPEG, TG4, and TIFF) into PDF.
A Round Table Solution (61) 396 865522 www.aroundtablesolution.com	**Security** Windows $350	An ActiveX/COM component that lets you use OLE and Acrobat to open secured PDF files, modify the security on PDF documents, and check for existing security settings.
A Round Table Solution (61) 396 865522 www.aroundtablesolution.com	**ThumbOpt** Windows $125	Creates thumbnails and optimizes PDF files from the command line, either individually or in batches.
ActivePDF 866-468-6733 www.activepdf.com	**PDF Server** Windows $499	Can redirect output from any server-based application to PDF. Professional version also supports encryption.
ActivePDF 866-468-6733users www.activepdf.com	**PDF Printer** Windows $129	An add-on for PDF Server that allows to "print" directly to PDF.
ActivePDF 866-468-6733 www.activepdf.com	**PDF Toolkit** Windows $249	For use with PDF Server, a collection of tools for forms creation, text extraction, watermarking, file merging, database support, and so on.
ActivePDF 866-468-6733 www.activepdf.com	**PDF WebGrabber** Windows $229	Add-on to PDF Server that converts HTML-based Web pages into PDF.
ActivePDF 866-468-6733 www.activepdf.com	**Spooler** Windows $129	Directs PDF files to any printer, either directly or through a spooled queue.
ActivePDF 866-468-6733 www.activepdf.com	**PDF DocConverter** Windows $299	An add-on for PDF Server that converts files in more than 280 document types directly into PDF.
Ansyr Technology 425-688-1600 www.ansyr.com	**Primer 3.1** Pocket PC, Win CE $79.95	PDF file reader for handheld devices.

STAND-ALONE PROGRAMS *continued*

Company	Product	Description
Appligent 610-284-4006 www.appligent.com	**AppendPDF** Windows Macintosh $2,495	Creates a single PDF document from multiple PDF files, individual PDF pages, or ranges of PDF pages.
Appligent 610-284-4006 www.appligent.com	**AppendPDF Pro** Windows Macintosh $3,995	Creates a single PDF document from multiple PDF files, individual PDF pages, or ranges of pages, plus adds custom covers, tables of contents, and text and image stamps.
Appligent 610-284-4006 www.appligent.com	**FDFMerge** Windows Macintosh $2,995	Merges form data into PDF forms.
Appligent 610-284-4006 www.appligent.com	**PDFText** Windows Macintosh N/A	Extracts text from PDF documents and saves it as ASCII text.
Appligent 610-284-4006 www.appligent.com	**SecurSign** Windows Macintosh $2,495	Server-based application for automatically encrypting PDF files.
Appligent 610-284-4006 www.appligent.com	**StampPDF Batch** Windows Macintosh $2,995	Stamps text and JPEG files inside single or multiple PDF files.
BCL Computers 408-557-5277 www.bclcomputers.com	**easyPDF** Windows $49	A printer driver that creates PDF disk files from any application without a lot of complicated options (for example, letter is the only available page size).
Callas Software (49) 30 4439 0310 www.callas.de	**pdfPreviewMaker** Windows NT $1,999	Running in batch mode with pdfBatchProcess Pro (included), it converts PDF files (including multipage documents) into BMP, JPEG, TIFF, or thumbnail files.
Callas Software (49) 30 4439 0310 www.callas.de	**pdfToolbox** Windows Macintosh $369	Includes pdfBatchProcess Pro (distill, preflight, and convert to EPS), pdfBatchMeister (controls settings for batch distilling), pdfInspektor (automatic pre-flighting), pdfCropMarks (adds crop and registration marks), pdfOutput (conversion to multipage EPS format), and PDF CropMeasure (verify page crop sizes).

STAND-ALONE PROGRAMS *continued*

Company	Product	Description
Callas Software (49) 30 4439 0310 www.callas.de	**pdfInspektor2** Windows Macintosh $149	Preflighting software that analyzes PDF files and reports on their condition and standards compliance.
Callas Software (49) 30 4439 0310 www.callas.de	**AutoPilot** Windows Macintosh $1,999	A server-based PDF workflow program for processing and routing PDF files, AutoPilot can automatically activate other Acrobat plug-ins for flighting and making color separations.
Dionis 617-730-5557 www.dionis.com	**Ari's PDF Splitter** Windows Macintosh $349	Can break up large PDF files into smaller ones while maintaining links and bookmarks.
E-Lock Technologies 800-453-9345 www.elock.com	**E-Lock Reader** Windows freeFree	Verifies digital signatures on a range of electronic documents, including PDF files.
FileOpen Systems 212-942-2291 www.fileopen.com	**FileOpen Publisher** Windows $2,500	High-volume batch version of FileOpen Personal Publisher that adds such capabilities as time limitation for file viewing and printing; restriction of file use to particular device; and watermarking.
Krause-Biagosch (49) 521 45 99 127 www.krause.de	**KIM PDF** Windows	Imposition software that creates complete composed sheets as PDF files that can be viewed from within Acrobat.
OneVision 201-938-0500 www.onevision.com	**Asura 3.5** Win NT Mac OS X N/A	Fully automated PDF preflighting program, with automatic file correction or routing to OneVision Solvero for manual repairs.
OneVision 201-938-0500 www.onevision.com	**Secare 4.0** Win NT Mac OS X N/A	Imposition software for assembling forms using PDF files.
OneVision 201-938-0500 www.onevision.com	**Solvero 4.5** Win NT Mac OS X N/A	Complete suite of tools for editing all aspects of PDF files in full WYSIWYG mode.
Shira 781-376-4181 www.shira.com	**Tattoo** Windows N/A	Creates personalized PDF files by superimposing image files in PDF, PJTF, TIFF, JPEG, EPS, or ScitexCT formats during output.

ACROBAT DISTILLER CLONES

Company	Product	Description
Artifex Software 415-492-9862 www.aladdin.com	**GhostScript** Windows Free	A set of PostScript-compatible tools that include a PostScript interpreter plus facilities for creating PDF files.
Global Graphics 781-392-1600 www.globalgraphics.com	**Jaws PDF Creator** Windows Macintosh $120	Creates PDF files by acting either as a print driver that you select in your application, or as a Distiller-like application onto which you can drag PostScript or EPS files.

BROWSER PLUG-INS

Company	Product	Description
ActivePDF 866-468-6733 www.activepdf.com	**PDFPrint** Windows $299	A plug-in to Microsoft Internet Explorer or Netscape Navigator that allows direct printing from within the browser to the printer of your choosing.

QuarkXPress EXTENSIONS

Company	Product	Description
Callas Software (49) 30 4439 0310 www.callas.de	**MadeToPrint** Windows Macintosh $349	Creates PDF files directly from within QuarkXPress, translating page and bounding box sizes with extreme accuracy for output on high-resolution imagesetters.

APPENDIX TWO

Online Resources

A wealth of information about using PDF in publishing and graphic arts work-flows is available online. The following is a compendium of resources.

INFORMATION SOURCES

Site	URL	Description
Planet PDF	www.planetpdf.com	The world of PDF in one stop: news, conference transcripts, training tips, consultant and developer listings, forums, tools, and more.
PDF Zone	www.pdfzone.com	Like Planet PDF but smaller, offering news, tools, tips, user forums, and a range of online newsletters.
Adobe ePaper	www.adobe.com/epaper	Adobe's homepage for PDF Online resources, including products, plug-ins, and tutorials.
Adobe PDF	www.adobe.com/support	Online user forums and information exchanges for all of Adobe's products, including Acrobat and PDF.
Adobe Technical	www.adobe.com	Provides access to Adobe's library of support data-base, html, technical notes, and white papers on all Adobe products, including Acrobat and PDF.
Adobe Access	access.adobe.com	PDF-related services for people with visual impair-ment, including PDF-to-HTML and PDF-to-ASCII conversion and free Acrobat Make Accessible plug-in.

ONLINE SERVICES

Service	URL	Description
Preflight Online	www.extensis.com	Subscription-based service for preflighting PDF, EPS, and QuarkXPress files. Entails a $6,000 setup fee plus $.10 to $.95 per transaction.
TextCafe	www.textcafe.com	Texterity's online service for converting PDF, QuarkXPress, and Microsoft Word files into XML, plus a range of popular eBook formats and HTML. Online price quotes available.
Create PDF Online	createpdf.adobe.com	Let Adobe create your PDF files. Costs $9.99 per month or $99.99 per year for an unlimited number of files. Available in United States and Canada only.
Power XChange	www.powerxchange.com	Buy a wide variety of Acrobat plug-ins and add-ons online.

INDEX

1-2-3 Touchup Order tool, 153
4-bit compression, 88–89
8-bit compression, 88–89

A

Acrobat
   assistants, 289–299
   described, 1
   helper programs, 295–298
   history of, 1–3
   plug-ins. *See* plug-ins
   resources. *See* resources
   versions of, 3–9
Acrobat 1.0, 1–4
Acrobat 2.0, 2–3, 4
Acrobat 3.0, 3–5, 85, 86
Acrobat 4.0, 3–6, 85, 86
Acrobat 5.0, 3–4, 6–9, 85
Acrobat Approval Business tools, 9, 278
Acrobat Capture, 9
Acrobat Distiller. *See* Distiller; distilling
Acrobat Distiller Printing Preferences dialog
      box, 34
Acrobat Distiller Server, 9
Acrobat eBook Reader, 7, 9, 264
Acrobat Messenger, 9
Acrobat Reader, 2, 7, 9
Acrobat Self-Sign Security handler, 139–146
Acrobat Standard Security, 265
Actions palette, 147
Actions tab, 271
Add an Action dialog box, 272, 273
Adobe Access site, 301
Adobe Acrobat. *See* Acrobat
Adobe Acrobat Search dialog box, 285
Adobe Catalog dialog box, 279, 284
Adobe Content Server, 9, 265
Adobe Document Server, 9
Adobe ePaper site, 301
Adobe FrameMaker. *See* FrameMaker
Adobe Illustrator. *See* Illustrator

Adobe InDesign. *See* InDesign
Adobe PageMaker. *See* PageMaker
Adobe Photoshop. *See* Photoshop
Adobe Technical site, 301
Adobe Type Manager (ATM), 94, 97, 98
Adobe XAP properties, 246
Advanced panel, 104–106
Advanced Print Settings dialog box, 167–168
Aerial plug-in, 294
Agfa Apogee system, 218, 221–222, 234
Allow PostScript File to Override Job
      Options setting, 105
AM (amplitude-modulated) screening, 209
American National Standards Institute. *See*
      ANSI
amplitude-modulated (AM) screening, 209
Analyze command, 170–171
annotations. *See also* comments
   Acrobat version and, 3
   described, 119
   managing, 128–138
   sequence numbers, 128
   uses for, 119
ANSI (American National Standards
      Institute), 234–235
ANSI text, 158
Anti-Alias to Gray option, 89
Apogee system, 218, 221–222, 234
Appearance palette, 147
Appearance tab, 269–270
AppendPDF Pro program, 297
AppendPDF program, 297
Apple Web site, 99
application files, 19, 20
application-based trapping, 190–191
applications. *See also specific applications*
   exporting from, 29–30, 32–34
   moving text/graphics into, 157–159
   printing from, 26–28, 32–34
   stand-alone, 295–298
archiving PDF files, 21
Ari's Bookmark Tool plug-in, 294

Ari's Link Check plug-in, 294
Ari's PDF Splitter program, 298
Ari's Ruler plug-in, 294
Article Properties dialog box, 261
article threads, 260–262
Article tool, 260–261
Articles palette, 261–262
ASCII Format option, 105
Ask for PDF File Destination option, 109
Ask to Replace Existing PDF File option, 109
Asura program, 188–189, 298
ATM (Adobe Type Manager), 94, 97, 98
Attachment Properties dialog box, 123, 124
attachments, 122–124, 171
Automatic option, 89
AutoPilot plug-in, 184, 298
Auto-Rotate Pages option, 86
AutoSave plug-in, 295

B
Base 14 Fonts, 93
batch processing, 172–176
batch sequence files, 172, 174
bicubic downsampling, 91
Binding option, 86
binocular icon, 287
bit depth, 88
bitmap images, 89
black ink generation, 103, 168
black points, 165, 166
black-point compensation, 165, 166
blends, 157
blind exchange, 235
bluelines, 214
bookmarks, 258–260
    analyzing, 170–171
    creating, 251, 258–260
    deleting, 260
    described, 258, 259
    eBooks, 251, 256–260
    editing, 259
    linking, 260
    nesting, 259–260
    preflight tools and, 183
    removing, 171
Brisque system, 228–229, 234
browsers. See Web browsers
buttons, 269–270, 271
byte serving, 85–86

C
Calculate tab, 274
Calculated fields dialog box, 274
Callas AutoPilot plug-in, 184, 298
Callas PDF Toolbox, 184
Callas pdfInspecktor plug-in, 184
Callas pdfOutputPro tool, 213
Capture Suspects, 153
Catalog plug-in, 9
cataloging PDF files, 278–288. See also indexes
    building indexes, 279–285
    searching catalogs, 278, 285–287
    security, 279
    updating indexes, 287–288
CCIT (Consultive Committee on International Telephony and Telegraphy), 89
CelebraNT system, 225–226, 234
Certify PDF plug-in, 290
CGATS (Committee for Graphic Arts Technologies Standards), 234–235
channels, 17
checkboxes, 270, 271
chokes, 194
CIE color space, 99
CIP3 PPF standard, 230, 231–234
CIP4 JDF standard, 230, 231–234
Circle tool, 124–127
Clipboard, 158
CMYK color, 99, 105, 209
CMYK press profiles, 164
collaborative tools, 117–149
    comments. See comments
    digital signatures, 138–147
    document comparison, 147–149
    page markups, 124–127
    purpose of, 117
color. See also color management
    Acrobat version and, 3
    black-point compensation, 165, 166
    calibration, 100
    CIE color space, 99
    CMYK, 99, 105, 209
    comments, 127
    compression and, 88–89
    continuous-tone, 209
    DeviceN color space, 214
    Distiller, 98–104
    eBooks, 250
    halftone information, 103

HSB color, 194
ICC color management, 21
images, 87, 88, 89, 156
Mac OS–based systems, 99, 101–102
markup tools, 127
objects, 156
overprinting and, 103, 193
PostScript version and, 12
precautions, 101
prepress and, 100, 101, 102–104
printing managed color, 166–168
process colors, 194
proofing conditions, 165–166
rendering intent algorithm, 99
RGB, 89, 99, 209
separations. *See* separations
soft proofing, 166
spot colors, 209, 214
sRGB color space, 100, 250
transfer function settings, 103
undercolors, 194
unmanaged, 100, 101, 102
color engine, 99, 165–166
color management, 98–104
    host-based, 166–168
    ICC, 21, 98, 99, 102
    overview, 99
    PostScript files, 99–102
    preferences, 163–165
    printing managed color, 166–168
    resources, 99
    turning off, 102
Color Management Off option, 102
Color Management panel, 164
Color panel, 98–104
Color Picker, 194
color profiles, 99, 156, 165, 167
color rendering dictionary, 166
Color Settings file, 99–102
color space array, 166
ColorCentral program, 198
color-separating files, 208–211
ColorSync, 99, 101–102
ColorSync settings file, 101–102
ColorSync workflow, 164
Column Select tool, 158
combo boxes, 270, 271, 273, 274
comments, 118–124. *See also* annotations
    DSC comments, 105
    exporting, 133

File Attachment tool, 122–124
filtering, 131–133
finding, 130–131
Free Text tool, 120
importing, 133, 135
logging, 105
managing, 128–138
markup tools, 124–127
methods for, 118
Note tool, 118–120
OPI comments, 105–106, 199
preferences, 128–129, 134–136
printing, 128–129
problematic, 105
removing, 170–171
sequence numbers, 128
sharing online, 134–138
Sound Attachment tool, 122, 123
spell checking, 277
Stamp tool, 120–122
summaries, 130, 131
Comments palette, 129–130, 148
Committee for Graphic Arts Technologies
    Standards (CGATS), 234–235
Common Ground, 2
Compare Document Revisions dialog box,
    147–149
Compatibility pop-up menu, 85
Compose plug-in, 294
composite files, 17, 20, 207, 208
composite workflows, 17
Compress Text and Line Art option, 87–88
compression
    4-bit compression, 88–89
    8-bit compression, 88–89
    Automatic option, 89
    CCITT and, 89
    described, 87
    Distiller, 87–91
    downsampling, 89–91
    graphics, 88
    images, 86, 87–91
    JPEG, 84, 88, 89, 90
    lossless, 87–89
    lossy, 88
    number of colors and, 88–89
    Optimize For Fast Web View option,
        85–86
    photographs, 88
    Run-Length Encoding, 89

compression, *continued*
  text, 87–88
  ZIP, 87–89
Compression panel, 87–91
Configure Signature Appearance dialog box,
  142, 143
Consultive Committee on International
  Telephony and Telegraphy (CCIT), 89
content
  Adobe Content Server, 9, 265
  editing, 149–157
  embedded, 7
  extracting, 157–163
Content Server, 9, 265
content-manipulation plug-ins, 291–293
contents, table of (eBooks), 256
Convert Gradients To Smooth Shades option,
  105
Copy command, 158
CorelDraw, 68–75
Crackerjack plug-in, 213, 214, 291
Create Adobe PDF Online service, 77–79,
  302
Create New User profile dialog box, 141
CreoScitex Brisque system, 228–229, 234
CreoScitex Prinergy system, 218, 222–225,
  234
Crop Pages command, 161–162
Crop Pages dialog box, 162
Crop tool, 161–162
cropping pages, 161–162
CTLW format, 220, 228–229

D
Dalim Litho system, 238
Dalim Swing system, 238
Dalim Twist system, 238
dashes, 154, 254
databases, 267
DateD plug-in, 291
DCS 2.0 files, 17, 20
DCS (desktop color separations), 17, 111
DCS files, 17, 18
Default field, 270
Default Page Size option, 86
Delete Clip command, 155
Delete Pages command, 161
deleting items
  bookmarks, 171, 260

  comments, 170–171
  digital signatures, 144
  indexes, 285
  links, 171
  metadata, 171
  pages, 161
  unwanted data, 170–171
Delta RIP, 220
desktop color separations. *See* DCS
destination links, 171
Detect and Remove command, 170–171, 175
Detect and Remove dialog box, 170–171
DeviceN color space, 214
devices
  output, 89–91, 210, 211
  parameters specific to, 168, 183
Digital Signature tool, 142–143
digital signatures, 138–147
  deleting, 144
  invisible, 144
  legality of, 139
  passwords, 140–141, 144
  preferences, 140
display list, 13
Distiller
  Advanced panel, 104–106
  clones, 299
  Color panel, 98–104
  Compression panel, 87–91
  described, 9, 83
  Fonts panel, 92–98
  General panel, 85–87
  job options, 84–106
  Normalizer, 218, 230
  passwords, 107
  PostScript files and, 16
  preferences, 108–109
  version 4 enhancements, 6
distilling, 83–116
  page ranges, 86
  PostScript files into PDF files, 110–115
  PostScript files manually, 30–32
  security settings, 106–108
DK&A INposition program, 204
DK&A Trapper program, 204
.doc files, 278
Document Associated Index dialog box, 287
Document Fonts dialog box, 151
Document Metadata dialog box, 244–245

Document Open Options dialog box, 263
Document Properties command, 95
Document Security command, 107, 172
Document Security dialog box, 107
Document Server, 9
Document Structuring Convention. *See* DSC
Document Structuring Conventions option, 105
Document Summary dialog box, 105, 279
document type definitions (DTDs), 242–243
documents. *See also* files; pages
    comparing, 147–149
    eBooks. *See* eBooks
    electronic. *See* electronic documents
    oversized, 168
dot gain, 212
double-byte fonts, 94–95
downsampling, 89–91
Drake plug-in, 290
drivers. *See* printer drivers
DSC comments, 105
DSC (Document Structuring Convention), 14, 105
DTDs (document type definitions), 242–243
Dublin Core Properties, 246
duotones, 214
Duplex plug-in, 291
Dynagram DynaStrip software, 205
DynaStrip software, 205

E
easyPDF program, 297
eBook job option, 84, 90, 150, 248
eBook Reader, 7, 9, 264
eBooks, 246–265. *See also* tagged PDF files
    article threads, 260–262
    bookmarks, 251, 256–260
    colors, 250
    columns and, 249
    covers for, 264
    creating with InDesign, 251–252
    creating with PageMaker, 247, 248–251
    default page view, 263
    editing tags, 255–256
    editing text, 254
    finishing touches, 263–265
    fonts, 249, 254
    graphics, 250
    indexes, 256

links, 256–258, 260
    monitors and, 248, 250
    multiple chapters, 256
    page numbering, 264–265
    reflowing text, 252–254
    resolution, 249
    security, 265
    size of, 248
    structure, 247
    tables of contents, 256
    thumbnails, 264
    viewing in browsers, 264
eBookstores, 264
e-commerce transactions, 139
Edit Batch Sequences command, 174
Edit Sequence dialog box, 174, 175
editing items
    bookmarks, 259
    content, 149–157
    eBooks, 254
    e-form fields, 274–276
    fonts, 150
    graphics, 154–157
    links, 258
    objects, 154–157
    text, 149–154, 254
editing tags, 255–256
editing tools, 149–157
e-forms, 266–278
    Acrobat handling of, 267–268
    adding actions, 271–273, 278
    appearance of, 269–270, 271
    described, 266
    designing, 268
    fields in. *See* fields, e-form
    imposition and, 201
    intelligent forms, 271–274
    interactivity, 271–274
    names and, 269
    performing calculations in, 274
    preferences, 275–276
    spell checking, 277
    tips for, 278
    validation features, 273–274
    vs. HTML forms, 266–267
electronic documents, 241–288
    eBooks. *See* eBooks
    e-forms. *See* e-forms
    PDF *vs.* XML, 242–246
    XMP, 244–246

electronic forms. *See* forms
E-Lock Reader program, 298
em dashes, 154, 254
Embed All Fonts option, 92, 93
Embed Thumbnails option, 86
embedded items
    content, 7
    fonts, 92–97, 151–153
    PDF Embedder plug-in, 292
    sound, 183
    thumbnails, 86
Encapsulated PostScript. *See* EPS
encryption, 107, 108, 139, 172
Enfocus PitStop Professional plug-in,
        162–163, 185–186, 292
ENU folder, 120, 121
EPS (Encapsulated PostScript), 14, 203
.eps extension, 115
EPS files, 105, 111, 202–203
EPS images, 105
errors
    batch-processing, 173
    fatal, 109
    PostScript workflows and, 13, 14
    preflight software and, 183
E-Sign Act, 139
Export command
    CorelDraw, 72–75
    FreeHand, 61–62
    InDesign, 45–52
    PageMaker, 53–56
    QuarkXPress, 66–68
Export Comments command, 134
exporting comments, 133
exporting PDF files
    from applications, 29–30, 32–34
    CorelDraw, 72–75
    FrameMaker, 58–59, 247
    FreeHand, 61–62
    Illustrator, 36–38
    InDesign, 45–52, 247
    PageMaker, 53–56, 247
    Photoshop, 41–42
    QuarkXPress, 66–68
Extensible Authoring and Publishing (XAP),
        246
Extensible Markup Language. *See* XML
Extensible Metadata Platform (XMP),
        244–246
Extensis Preflight Online service, 186

Extensis Preflight Pro package, 186
Extensis Suitcase, 97, 98
Extract Images command, 158
Extract Images panel, 158
Extract Pages command, 159–160
Extract Pages dialog box, 158–159
Extreme workflows, 217–238
    Apogee system, 218, 221–222, 234
    benefits of, 219
    Brisque system, 228–229, 234
    CelebraNT system, 225–226, 234
    CIP3/CIP4, 231–234
    described, 217–218
    in-RIP trapping, 191
    JDF format, 229–231
    PDF/X format, 234–237
    PJTF format, 229–231
    PPML/VDX standard, 237–238
    Prinergy system, 218, 222–225, 234
    process management, 219
    process players, 218–219
    products for, 219–229
    RIPs and, 219–221, 238–239
    TIFF/IT format, 234–237
    Trueflow system, 226–228, 234
    vs. PDF workflows, 220–221
EyeDropper plug-in, 292

F

Facing Page-Continuous view, 86
fatal errors, 109
FDF data, 267–268
FDF (Form Data Format) documents, 133,
        134, 267, 268
FDFMerge program, 297
Field Properties dialog box, 146–147, 269–274
fields, e-form
    creating, 269–271
    duplicating, 274
    editing, 274–276
    password fields, 270
    tabbed order for, 275, 276
    text fields, 270
fields, index, 282–285
File Attachment tool, 122–124
file compatibility plug-ins, 289–290
file conversion plug-ins, 289–290
file formats. *See also specific formats*
    options for, 17–20

preflighting and, 182
FileOpen Publisher program, 298
files. *See also* documents
    application files, 19, 20
    attaching to PDFs, 122–124
    batch sequence files, 172, 174
    color-separating, 208–211
    comparing, 147–149
    composite files, 17, 20, 207, 208
    compression. *See* compression
    DCS files, 17, 18
    .doc files, 278
    EPS files, 105, 111, 202–203
    FDF documents, 133, 134
    flattening, 14, 29, 79
    PDF files. *See* PDF files
    PostScript files. *See* PostScript files
    PPD files, 28
    unsecuring, 172
Filter Comments dialog box, 132
filtering comments, 131–133
Find button, 287
Find command, 130–131, 287
Find Comment dialog box, 131
finding items
    catalogs, 285–287
    comments, 130–131
Fit Text to Selection command, 153
flat names, 269
flattening files, 14, 29, 79
FlightCheck program, 186–188
FM (frequency-modulated) screening,
    211–212
folders
    ENU folder, 120, 121
    Sequences folder, 120, 172
    Stamps folder, 120
    watched, 109, 115–116
Font Locations dialog box, 94
Font Properties Extension (Windows), 97
fonts
    Acrobat version and, 4
    Adobe fonts, 96
    Adobe Type Manager, 94, 97, 98
    Agfa/Monotype fonts, 96
    Base 14 Fonts, 93
    changing, 153
    checking, 95–96
    determining foundry, 97, 98
    displaying, 150

Distiller, 92–98
double-byte, 94–95
eBooks, 249, 254
editing and, 150
embedded, 92–97, 151–153
Emigre fonts, 96–97
licensing, 96–97
locating, 93
Mac OS–based systems, 97
managing, 97–98
Multiple Master, 152
non-English, 94–95
OpenType fonts, 94
PDF files and, 19
PostScript fonts, 94
PostScript version and, 12
previewing, 95–96
problems with, 93, 182
selecting, 93
subsets, 92, 93
substitutions, 92–96, 152–153
Suitcase utility, 97, 98
TrueType fonts, 94, 95–96, 97
Type 1 fonts, 93, 94, 95–96
Type 3 fonts, 94
unembedding, 151
Windows-based systems, 97
Fonts panel, 92–98
for position only (FPO) images, 197
Form Data Format (FDF) documents, 133,
    134, 267, 268
Form tool, 268, 269, 274
Format tab, 271
formats. *See* file formats
forms
    e-forms. *See* e-forms
    HTML, 266–267
foundry, font, 97, 98
FPO (for position only) images, 197
FrameMaker
    exporting from, 58–59, 247
    printing from, 56–58
Free Text tool, 120
Freebird plug-in, 290
FreeHand
    exporting from, 61–62
    printing from, 59–61
frequency-modulated (FM) screening,
    211–212
Fuji film CelebraNT system, 225–226, 234

G

Gemini plug-in, 292
General panel, 85–87
Geschke, Chuck, 11
Get Info command (Mac), 97
GhostScript program, 230, 299
Ghostview program, 230
gradients, 105, 157
Graphic Select tool, 158
graphics. *See also* images; objects
    color, 156
    compression, 86, 87–91
    eBooks, 250
    editing, 154–157
    extracting from PDF files, 158
    markup tools, 124–127
    moving into applications, 157–159
    saving to Clipboard, 158
    signatures as, 142, 143
grayscale images, 87, 88, 89
grids, 155

H

halftone information, 103
halftone screening, 209–210, 211
halftones, 168, 209–210
Hand tool, 127
handlers, 139–146
Heidelberg MetaDimension, 234, 238, 239
Heidelberg Supertrap plug-in, 196–197
Heidelberg Supertrap Plus plug-in, 197
Helios PDF Handshake program, 199
hierarchical names, 269
HSB color, 194
HTML forms, 266–267
hyphens, 154, 254

I

ICC color management, 21, 98, 99, 102
ICC (International Color Consortium), 99
Ifilter plug-in, 278
Illustrator
    exporting from, 36–38
    overprinting and, 105
    printing from, 34–36
images. *See also* graphics
    bitmap, 89

    color, 87, 88, 89, 156
    compression, 86, 87–91
    continuous-tone, 90
    eBooks, 250
    editing, 154–157
    EPS, 105
    extracting from PDF files, 158
    FPO, 197
    grayscale, 87, 88, 89
    JPEG format, 83
    moving into applications, 157–159
    photographs, 88
    problems with, 182
    processing technology, 10–13
    quality of, 90
    resolution, 89, 91, 197
    size of, 86, 90
imagesetters, 10–11
imaging
    Acrobat version and, 4
    PostScript version and, 12
Import Comments command, 135
Import program, 296
Import Scan command, 31
importing comments, 133, 135
imposition, 200–207
    described, 201
    EPS files, 202–203
    overview, 201–202
    PDF files, 202–203, 208
    PostScript files, 202–203
    terminology, 201–202
    tools for, 204–207
Impostrip program, 207
ImpozeIt product, 205
Impress plug-in, 207, 293
Impress Pro plug-in, 293
InDesign
    creating eBooks with, 251–252
    exporting from, 45–52, 247, 251–252
    generating tagged PDF from, 251–252
    printing from, 43–45
Index Selection dialog box, 285
indexes, 279–285. *See also* cataloging PDF files
    adding to list, 285
    associating PDF files with, 286
    creating, 283–284
    custom fields, 282–285
    defaults, 280–281
    file locations, 281–282

logging problems, 281
metadata in, 279
numbers in, 280
preferences, 279–283
rebuilding, 288
removing from list, 285
updating, 279, 287–288
word-search options, 281
ink, overprinted, 194
in-RIP separations, 212
in-RIP trapping, 191
Insert Pages command, 160
Insert Pages dialog box, 160
interactivity
    forms, 271–274
    links, 257
International Color Consortium. *See* ICC
Internet Explorer, 5
Internet publishing strategies, 15
invisible signatures, 144
IPTech ImpozeIt product, 205

J

Jade plug-in, 292
JavaScript actions, 172
Jaws PDF Creator program, 230, 299
JDF (job definition format), 229–231
JDF schema, 243
JDF specification, 232–233
job definition format (JDF), 229–231
job ticket workflows, 105
job tickets
    described, 219
    JDF tickets, 229–231
    PJTF tickets, 229–231
    portable, 218, 219, 229–231
    processors, 218
    vs. XMP metadata, 246
JPEG 2000 format, 200
JPEG compression, 84, 88, 89, 90
JPEG format, 83, 88

K

KIM PDF program, 204, 298

L

Lantana Crackerjack plug-in, 213, 214, 291
late binding, 191
licensing fonts, 96–97
line breaks, 154, 254
line screen, 210–211
Line tool, 124–127
Link Properties dialog box, 257–258
Link tool, 257, 258
links
    adding interactivity to, 257
    analyzing, 170–171
    to application files, 19, 20
    bookmarks to pages, 260
    creating, 257–258
    destination, 171
    eBooks, 256–258, 260
    editing, 258
    to PostScript files, 14
    preflight tools and, 183
    removing, 171
List All Fonts command, 150
list boxes, 270, 271
Litho system, 238
logging
    batch-processing messages, 173
    index problems, 281
    preferences, 281, 282
    problematic comments, 105
lossless compression, 38, 87–89
lossy compression, 88
low-resolution proxy, 197
luminance, 194

M

Mac OS–based systems
    color, 99, 101–102
    fonts, 97
    OS X, 32
    PostScript commands, 113
    printer drivers, 26, 33
    printing from applications, 26–27, 28
MacGSView program, 230
Macromedia FreeHand. *See* FreeHand
MadeToPrint extension, 299
magazine advertising production, 19
Magellan plug-in, 290
Make Accessible plug-in, 248, 289
margins, 161–162

marking up pages, 124–127
markup tools, 124–127
Markzware FlightCheck program, 186–188
Markzware MarkzNet service, 186–188
Maskit plug-in, 293
MediaSizer plug-in, 295
metadata
    analyzing, 170–171
    building indexes and, 279
    removing, 170–171
    XMP, 244–246
MetaDimension, 234, 238, 239
Microsoft Index Server, 278
Microsoft Internet Explorer, 5
Microsoft Office applications
    distilling documents from, 6
    generating tagged PDF from, 247–248
    printing from, 75–77
Millennium Digital Commerce Act, 139
misregistration, 189–190, 194
moiré patterns, 209, 211
monitors
    eBooks and, 248, 250
    soft proofing and, 166
mouse actions, 271–272
multimedia, 2–3
Multiple Master fonts, 151–152

N

Netscape Navigator, 5
neutral density, 194
New Index Definition dialog box, 283
NikNak program. *See* Jaws PDF Creator pro-
    gram
No Hands Software, 2
nonbreaking spaces, 154, 254
Normalizer, 218, 230
Note tool, 118–120
Number Pages feature, 169–170

O

objects. *See also* graphics
    clipping and, 155
    color, 156
    editing, 154–157
    moving, 154–155
    pasting, 155, 158
    repositioning, 154–155
    selecting, 154, 158
    snapping to grid, 155
ODBC database, 267
OEB (Open E-Book), 243
OEB schema, 243
OneVision Asura program, 188–189
OneVision Secare package, 205
OneVision Solvero program, 188, 298
Open as Adobe PDF command, 31
Open E-Book (OEB), 243
Open Prepress Interface. *See* OPI
Open Web Page command, 31
OpenType fonts, 94
OPI comments, 105–106, 199
OPI (Open Prepress Interface), 178, 197–200
OPI workflows, 105–106, 198–199
Optimize For Fast Web View option, 85–86
Optimize Space dialog box, 171
Options dialog box, 284
Options tab, 270–271
Output Options dialog box, 175, 176
overprinting, 103, 192, 193–195

P

Page Numbering dialog box, 169–170
page pairing, 203
Page Templates dialog box, 121, 122
Pagelet plug-in, 292
PageMaker
    exporting from, 53–56, 247, 248–251
    generating eBooks with, 247, 248–251
    generating tagged PDF from, 247, 248–251
    printing from, 52–53
pages. *See also* documents
    adjusting margins, 161–162
    cropping, 161–162
    deleting in PDF files, 161
    displaying in Facing Page-Continuous
        view, 86
    distilling. *See* Distiller; distilling
    eBooks, 264–265
    extracting content from, 157–163
    extracting from PDF files, 159–160
    inserting into PDF files, 160
    managing, 159–162
    marking up, 124–127
    numbering, 169–170, 264–265
    oversized, 168
    preparing final pages, 169–172

renumbering, 169–170
replacing in PDF files, 160–161
rotating(in PDF files), 86, 161
size of, 86
Palm OS Reader, 7, 9
Paper Capture online service, 31
Paper Capture plug-in, 9
Paper White option, 165, 166
password fields, 270
passwords
    digital signatures, 140–141, 144
    PDF files, 106–108, 116
    watched folders, 116
Paste command, 158
pasting objects, 155, 158
pasting text, 158
PDF 1.2, 85, 235, 236
PDF 1.3, 85, 235, 236
PDF 1.4, 85, 235, 236
PDF Consultant feature, 170–171
PDF DocConverter program, 296
PDF Embedder plug-in, 292
PDF Explorer plug-in, 295
PDF files
    archiving and, 21
    assessing problems with, 181, 182–183
    associating with indexes, 286
    attachments to, 122–124
    batch processing, 172–176
    capturing, 31
    cataloging. See cataloging PDF files
    comments in. See comments
    comparing, 147–149
    Create Adobe PDF Online service, 77–79, 302
    creating automatically, 115–116
    creating for prepress. See prepress
    deleting pages in, 161
    described, 2
    digital content in, 7
    displaying fonts in, 150
    distilling PostScript files into, 110–115
    editability of, 17, 20
    embedded content, 7
    encrypting, 107
    exported vs. distilled, 29, 30
    exporting. See exporting
    extracting content from, 157–163
    extracting pages from, 159–160
    features, 20

fonts and, 19
imposition, 202–203, 208
inserting pages into, 160
managing pages in, 159–162
marking up pages, 124–127
optimizing for Web viewing, 85–86
poorly designed, 21
poorly prepared, 83
preparation checklist, 81
previewing, 86
printing. See printing
redistilling, 149
removing unwanted data from, 170–171
replacing pages in, 160–161
resolution and, 86
rotating pages in, 86, 161
security settings, 106–108
separations and, 208
size of, 15, 16, 20, 29, 123
structured, 6, 247
tagged. See tagged PDF files
thumbnails of. See thumbnails
transparency in, 29, 79–81, 168
viewing, 2
vs. PostScript files, 15–17
XML-tagged, 6
PDF forms. See e-forms
PDF Handshake program, 199
PDF ImageWorks plug-in, 292
PDF Mail Manager plug-in, 295
PDF Merchant, 9
PDF (Portable Document Format)
    resources, 301–302
    versions, 3, 8, 85
    vs. EPS, 203
    vs. XML, 242–246
PDF Printer program, 296
PDF Sept2 plug-in, 290
PDF Server program, 296
PDF Toolkit program, 296
PDF Viewer, 32
PDF WebGrabber program, 296
PDF workflows
    advantages, 20–21
    collaborative tools, 117–149
    disadvantages, 21
    examples, 16, 178–180
    OPI technology and, 198, 200
    separations and, 213–214
    transitioning to, 22–23

PDF workflows, *continued*
  transparency in, 79–81, 168
  trapping and, 192–193
  typical tasks, 178–180
  vs. Extreme workflows, 220–221
  vs. ROOM workflows, 220–221
  XML and, 200
PDF Workshop program, 296
PDF Writer printer driver, 2
PDF Zone site, 301
PDFFormat plug-in, 156
pdfInspecktor plug-in, 184
pdfInspektor2 program, 298
PDFMaker plug-in, 247–248
pdfmark operators, 248
pdfOutputPro plug-in, 213, 291
pdfPreviewMaker program, 297
PDFPrint plug-in, 299
PDFText program, 297
pdfToolbox program, 297
PDFWriter utility, 32
PDF/X format, 19, 207, 218, 234–237
PDF/X-1 Checkup plug-in, 290
.pdx extension, 281
Pencil tool, 124–127
permissions, 106–108, 116
Personal Field Names (PFN) file, 278
photographs, 88
Photoshop
  exporting from, 41–42
  image editing and, 155
  printing from, 39–40
PitStop Professional plug-in, 162–163,
    185–186, 292
pixels, 88, 91, 155, 156
PJTF (Portable Job Ticket Format), 219,
    229–232, 234
PKCS#7 syntax, 145
Planet PDF site, 301
plug-ins. *See also specific plug-ins*
  browser plug-ins, 299
  collaboration tools, 162–163
  content-manipulation plug-ins, 291–293
  editing tools, 162–163
  file compatibility plug-ins, 289–290
  file conversion plug-ins, 289–290
  listed, 289–295
  output plug-ins, 291
  preflighting plug-ins, 290
  resources, 289–295, 302

  security plug-ins, 293
  telecommunications plug-ins, 295
  third-party plug-ins, 162–163, 290–295
  utilities, 294–295
Pocket PC Reader, 7, 9
Portable Document Format. *See* PDF
Portable Job Ticket Format (PJTF), 219,
    229–232, 234
portable job tickets, 218, 219, 229–231
PostScript
  Acrobat version and, 4
  Default Page Size option and, 86
  described, 10, 11
  encapsulated, 14
  history of, 10–13
  preprocessing and, 14
  printer drivers, 110
  Resolution option and, 86
  transparency and, 29
  versions of, 12
PostScript drivers, 26, 28, 110
PostScript files
  color management, 99–102
  disregarding job settings, 105
  Distiller and, 16
  distilling into PDF files, 110–115
  distilling manually, 30–32
  features, 20
  imposition, 202–203
  links to, 14
  rasterizing, 13
  resolution and, 86, 105
  separations and, 208
  size of, 15, 20, 111
  trapping and, 105, 192
  vs. PDF files, 15–17
PostScript fonts, 94
PostScript Level 1, 12
PostScript Level 2, 12, 211
PostScript Level 3, 12, 191, 211, 218
PostScript Printer Descriptions (PPDs), 28,
    110
PostScript printers, 13, 166
PostScript Settings panel (Mac), 33
PostScript workflows, 13, 14, 16, 79
Power XChange site, 302
PowerUp PDF plug-in, 292
PPDs (PostScript Printer Descriptions), 28,
    110
PPF (print production format), 231

PPML schema, 243
PPML/VDX standard, 237–238
preferences
    batch processing, 173
    color management, 163–165
    comments, 128–129, 134–136
    digital signatures, 140
    Distiller, 108–109
    formatted text, 158–159
    forms, 275–276
    indexes, 279–283
    logging, 281, 282
    search, 286, 287
    spelling, 277
    tables, 158–159
    touchups, 155, 156
Preflight Online service, 186, 302
Preflight Pro package, 186
preflighting, 180–189
    Asura program, 188–189
    bookmarks, 183
    error reporting, 183
    file formats and, 182
    FlightCheck program, 186–188
    links, 183
    MarkzNet service, 186–188
    need for, 180–181
    PDF preflight tools, 184–189
    pdfInspecktor plug-in, 184
    PitStop Professional plug-in, 185–186
    plug-ins for, 290
    Preflight Online service, 186
    Preflight Pro package, 186
    QuarkXPress files, 186
    repairing problems, 183
    resources, 290, 302
    security settings, 183
    separations, 214
    software requirements, 181–183
    sound, 183
    thumbnails and, 45
    video, 183
prepress, 177–215
    Acrobat versions and, 4, 85
    advanced options, 104–106
    color and, 100, 101–104
    creating PDF files for, 25–81
    exported vs. distilled files, 29, 30
    imposition, 200–206
    job option parameters, 102–104

OPI, 197–200
PDF role in, 10–23, 177–178
PostScript versions and, 12
precautions, 31–32
preflighting. See preflighting
RIPs and, 215
separations, 207–214
trapping, 189–197
workflows, 178–180
prepress partners
    communications with, 25
    PDF guidelines, 86
    security and, 106–108
    watched folders and, 115
Preserve Halftone Information option, 103
Preserve OPI Comments option, 105–106
Preserve Overprint settings option, 103
Press job option, 84, 90
Primer program, 296
Prinergy system, 218, 222–225, 234
Print command
    CorelDraw, 68–72
    FrameMaker, 56–58
    FreeHand, 59–61
    Illustrator, 34–36
    InDesign, 43–45
    Microsoft Office, 75–77
    PageMaker, 52–53
    Photoshop, 39–40
    QuarkXPress, 62–66
Print dialog boxes, 26, 27, 33
Print job option, 84
print production format (PPF), 231
printer drivers
    described, 28
    Mac OS–based systems, 26, 33
    PDF files and, 28
    PDF Writer driver, 2
    PostScript drivers, 26, 28, 110
    role of, 28
    setting up, 33–34
    Windows-based systems, 26, 33, 34
printers
    drivers for. See printer drivers
    PostScript printers, 13, 166
    PPDs, 28, 110
    setting up Distiller as, 27–28
    virtual printers, 28
Printers Control Panel (Windows), 34

printing
   advanced options, 167, 168
   from applications, 26–28, 32–34
   comments, 128–129
   from CorelDraw, 68–75
   from FrameMaker, 56–58
   from FreeHand, 59–61
   from Illustrator, 34–36
   from InDesign, 43–45
   MadeToPrint extension, 299
   from Microsoft Office, 75–77
   overprinting, 193–195
   from PageMaker, 52–53
   PDFPrint plug-in, 299
   from Photoshop, 39–40
   from QuarkXPress, 62–66
   trapping. See trapping
private key, 138
process colors, 194
process players, 218–219
processing technology, 10–13
profiles, color, 99, 156, 165, 167
programs. See applications
Proof Colors command, 165, 166
Proof Setup command, 165–166
proofing tools, 163–168
.ps extension, 112, 115
public key, 139
publishing strategies, 15

Q
QuarkXPress
   exporting from, 66–68
   extensions, 299
   imposition and, 203
   preflighting and, 186
   printing from, 62–66
   trapping and, 190, 192
Quite a Box of Tricks plug-in, 293
Quite Imposing plug-in, 204, 205, 291
Quite Imposing Plus plug-in, 291

R
radio buttons, 269–270, 271
raster image processors. See RIPs
rasterization process, 13–14, 168, 219–221
readers
   Acrobat Reader, 2, 7, 9

eBook Reader, 7, 9, 264
E-Lock Reader, 298
free readers, 9
Palm OS Reader, 7, 9
Pocket PC Reader, 7, 9
Redwing plug-in, 292
Re:mark plug-in, 294
Remove command, 171
rendering intent algorithm, 99, 165
Replace Pages command, 160–161
Replace Pages dialog box, 161
reports, 171
resampling, 89–91
resolution
   controlling, 108
   defaults, 86
   eBooks, 249
   images, 89, 91, 197
   output devices and, 89–91, 210, 211
   PDF files and, 86
   PostScript files and, 86, 105
   resampling and, 89–91
Resolution option, 86
resources
   Acrobat plug-ins, 289–295, 302
   browser plug-ins, 299
   color management, 99
   Distiller clones, 299
   information sources, 301–302
   online, 289–302
   preflighting, 290, 302
   QuarkXPress extensions, 299
   stand-alone programs, 295–298
   Web sites, 289–302
RGB color, 89, 99, 209
RGB profiles, 165
RIP once, output many (ROOM) workflows,
   219, 220
RIP process, 13–15
RIPs (raster image processors)
   Delta RIP, 220
   described, 11
   downsampling and, 89
   Extreme systems and, 219–221, 238–239
   in-RIP separations, 212
   in-RIP trapping, 191
   non-Extreme, 238–239
   prepress decisions and, 215
   ROOM workflows, 219, 220, 221
   separations and, 207

RLE (Run-Length Encoding), 89
ROOM (RIP once, output many) workflows, 219, 220, 221
Rotate Pages command, 161
Rotate Pages dialog box, 161
rotating pages, 86, 161
RTF text, 158
rulers, 155
Run Sequence Confirmation dialog box, 172–173
RunDirEx.txt file, 110, 114
RunFilEx.ps program (Mac), 110, 112
Runfilex.ps program (Windows), 110
Run-Length Encoding (RLE), 89

S

Save As command
    copying text/graphics, 157–158
    digital signatures, 144
    extracting PDF pages and, 158
    FrameMaker, 58–59
    Illustrator, 36–38
    Photoshop, 41–42
    touched-up images, 157
    transparency and, 80
Save As XML plug-in, 289
Save command, 144
Save Portable Job Ticket Inside PDF File option, 105
Save Warnings and Errors in Log File option, 173
Scan command, 31
ScenicSoft ColorCentral program, 198
ScenicSoft Preps program, 205–206
ScenicSoft TrapWise program, 195, 196
schemas, 242–246
screen angle, 209
screen frequency, 210
Screen job option, 84, 90, 150
Screen Trueflow system, 226–228, 234
screening, 208–212
Search button, 287
search engines, 278, 281
searching for items
    catalogs, 278, 285–287
    comments, 130–131
Secare program, 205, 298
security
    Acrobat Standard Security, 265

cataloging and, 279
    digital signatures, 138–147, 172
    eBooks, 265
    encryption, 107, 108, 172
    passwords, 106–108, 116
    PDF files, 106–108
    permissions, 106–108, 116
    plug-ins for, 293
    preflight tools and, 183
    prepress partners and, 106–108
    unsecuring files, 172
    watched folders, 115–116
Security Handler pop-up menu, 173
Security program, 296
SecurSign program, 297
Select All command, 154–155, 158
Self-Sign certificates, 145
Self-Sign Security dialog box, 140–147
separations, 207–214
    color separating software, 212–214
    composite files, 207, 208
    considerations, 213–214
    creating, 17–18, 208
    in-RIP separations, 212
    PDF files and, 208
    PostScript files, 208
    preflighting, 214
    RIPs and, 207
    screening, 208–212
    tools for, 213, 214
.sequ extension, 172
Sequences folder, 120, 172
servers
    Acrobat Distiller Server, 9
    Adobe Content Server, 9, 265
    Adobe Document Server, 9
    Microsoft Index Server, 278
    PDF Server program, 296
    Web servers, 134–138, 267
ShadowFX plug-in, 292
Shira PDF Organizer package, 207
signature certificates, 144–145
signatures, digital, 138–147
signatures, press sheet, 201
Signatures palette, 140, 144–146
Signed palette, 147
Simulate Black Ink option, 165, 166
SmartPDF plug-in, 290
Snap to Grid commands, 154
soft hyphens, 154, 254

soft proofing, 166
Solvero program, 188, 298
sound
    comments, 122, 123
    embedded, 183
    preflight tools and, 183
Sound Attachment tool, 122, 123
Sound Properties dialog box, 122, 123
Sound Recorder dialog box, 122
Space Audit dialog box, 171
spaces, nonbreaking, 154, 254
Special category, 271
Specifications for Web Offset Publications
        (SWOP) standard, 101
spell checking, 277
Split & Merge Wizard program, 295
Spooler program, 296
spot colors, 209, 214
spreads, 194
Square tool, 124–127
sRGB color space, 100, 250
Stamp tool, 120–122
StampPDF Batch program, 297
StampPDF plug-in, 291
Stamps folder, 120
startup volume, 108–109
stochastic screening, 211–212
Stratify PDF plug-in, 163, 293
Strikeout tool, 127
strikethrough text, 127
subject moiré, 209
Submit Form Selections dialog box, 272–273
subsampling, 89–91
Subset Embedded Fonts option, 92
Suitcase utility, 97, 98
Summarize Comments dialog box, 130
Supertrap plug-in, 196–197
Supertrap Plus plug-in, 197
SVG schema, 243
Swing system, 238
SWOP (Specifications for Web Offset
        Publications) standard, 101
Synapse Prepare Pro plug-in, 294

T

Table/Formatted Text Select tool, 158
tables, 158–159
tables of contents, eBooks, 256
tagged image file format. *See* TIFF

tagged PDF files. *See also* eBooks
    bookmarks, 251, 256–260
    creating, 247–252
    editing, 255–256
    links, 256–258, 260
    overview, 6–7, 8, 247
    reflowing, 154, 252–254
    XML and, 6
tags
    XML, 6, 200, 242, 256
    XMP, 246
Tags palette, 8
Tattoo program, 298
telecommunications plug-ins, 295
text
    ANSI, 158
    compression, 87–88
    eBooks, 249
    editing, 149–154, 254
    extracting from PDF files, 158–159
    fitting to selection, 153
    formatted, 158–159
    markup tools, 124–127
    moving into applications, 157–159
    pasting, 158
    reflowing, 154, 252–254
    removing unwanted, 170–171
    saving to Clipboard, 158
    selecting, 158
    strikethrough text, 127
    unembedding, 151
Text Attributes palette, 151–154
text boxes, 269, 273, 274
text breaks, 154
text fields, 270
Text Select tool, 158
TextCafe site, 302
threads, article, 260–262
thumbnails
    Binding option, 86
    copying, 160
    eBooks, 264
    moving, 160
    page previews, 86
    preflighting and, 45
    uses for, 45
Thumbnails palette, 86, 160
ThumbOpt program, 296
TIFF (tagged image file format), 19, 88
TIFF/IT format, 19, 234–237

Tiling feature, 167, 168
tools. *See also specific tools*
    Acrobat Approval Business tools, 9, 278
    collaborative. *See* collaborative tools
    editing tools, 149–157
    Extreme workflows, 219–229
    imposition tools, 204–207
    markup tools, 124–127
    preflight tools, 184–189
    proofing tools, 163–168
    for separations, 213, 214
    trapping tools, 195–197
Touchup Object tool, 154–157
Touchup Order tool, 255, 256
touchup preferences, 155, 156
Touchup Text tool, 149, 150–154, 254
transfer functions, 103, 168
transparency
    controlling in printed pieces, 168
    editing graphics and, 156–157
    PostScript and, 29
    using in PDF workflows, 79–81
Trapeze Artist program, 195
Trapper program, 204
trapping, 189–197
    application-based, 190–191
    chokes, 194
    considerations, 192–193
    creating good traps, 193–195
    dedicated, 191–192
    in-RIP, 191
    late binding, 191
    luminance, 194
    misregistration, 189–190, 194
    neutral density, 194
    overprinting, 103, 192, 193–195
    PDF workflows and, 192–193
    PostScript files and, 105, 192
    QuarkXPress and, 190, 192
    spreads, 194
    Supertrap plug-in, 196–197
    tools for, 195–197
    trap size, 194–195
    Trapeze Artist program, 195
    TrapWise program, 195, 196
Trapping Key dialog box, 193
TrapWise program, 195, 196
troubleshooting. *See also* errors
    assessing PDF problems, 181, 182–183
    font problems, 93, 182

image problems, 182
index problems, 281–282
PDF files, 181, 182–183
preflight tools and, 181, 182–183
Trueflow system, 226–228, 234
TrueType fonts, 94, 95–96, 97
Twist system, 238
Type 1 fonts, 93, 94, 95–96
Type 3 fonts, 94

U

UCR (Under Color Removal), 103, 168
Ultimate Technographics Impostrip program, 207
Ultimate Technographics Impress program, 207
Ultimate Technographics Trapeze Artist program, 195
Under Color Removal (UCR), 103, 168
undercolors, 194
underline marks, 127
Undo feature, 149–150
Unicode standard, 94
Unix-based systems, 113
U.S. Prepress Default setting, 101
Use Local Fonts command, 95, 150
Use Prologue.ps and Epilogue.ps option, 105
User Information panel, 141
User Settings dialog box, 141–142
utilities. *See* applications; plug-ins

V

Validate tab, 273–274
Variform PDF plug-in, 291
vectors, 155
video preflight tools, 183
View PDF When Using Distiller option, 109
Virtual Printer plug-in, 28
virtual printers, 28

W

Warnock, John, 11
watched folders, 109, 115–116
Web browsers, 4–5
    digital signatures, 138, 144
    Internet Explorer, 5

Web browsers, *continued*
  Netscape Navigator, 5
  optimizing PDF files for, 85–86
  plug-ins, 299
  viewing comments in, 134–138
  viewing eBooks in, 264
Web Capture feature, 6, 9, 247, 248
Web servers, 267
  sharing comments via, 134–138
Web sites
  Acrobat plug-ins, 289–295, 302
  Adobe Access, 301
  pardAdobe ePaper, 301
  Adobe Technical, 301
  browser plug-ins, 299
  color management, 99
  ColorSync, 99
  Create Adobe PDF Online service, 77–79, 302
  Distiller clones, 299
  information sources, 301–302
  PDF Zone, 301
  Planet PDF, 301
  plug-ins, 289–295, 299, 302
  Power XChange, 302
  Preflight Online, 186, 302
  QuarkXPress extensions, 299
  resources, 289–302
  stand-alone programs, 295–298
  TextCafe, 302
WebPerfect PDF plug-in, 294
white points, 165, 166
Windows-based systems
  fonts, 97
  PostScript commands, 113
  printer drivers, 26, 33, 34
  printing from applications, 26, 27–28
Word Assistant, 281, 286
workflows
  ColorSync workflow, 164
  composite workflows, 17
  Extreme workflows. *See* Extreme workflows
  homegrown PDF workflows, 178–180
  job ticket workflows, 105
  OPI workflows, 105–106, 198–199
  PDF workflows. *See* PDF workflows
  PostScript workflows, 13, 14, 16, 79
  prepress workflows, 178–180
  ROOM workflows, 220, 221

X
XAP (Extensible Authoring and Publishing), 246
XFDF data, 267
XHTML schema, 243
XML (Extensible Markup Language)
  CIP4 standard, 232
  JDF job tickets, 229–231
  PDF workflows and, 200
  PPML standard, 237
  vs. PDF, 242–246
XML schemas, 242–244
XML tags, 200, 242, 256
XML-tagged PDF files, 6
XMP (Extensible Metadata Platform), 244–246
XMP metadata, 244–246
XMP schemas, 244–246
XMP tags, 246
xToolsOne plug-in, 295

Z
ZIP compression, 87–88

COLOPHON

Real World PDF with Adobe Acrobat 5 was written in Microsoft Word on an Apple Macintosh G3 running OS 9.1, and all creating and testing of PDF files was done on the same system, as well as on a Pentium 3 PC running Windows 2000 Professional.

Chapters were laid out in QuarkXPress 4.04 on a Power Computing Power Tower Pro 225 running OS 8.6. They were then distilled to Acrobat PDF 1.3 files (using Distiller 4.0) and e-mailed to the author, developmental editor, and tech reviewers, who marked up the copy using Acrobat's annotation and comments tools.

Final pages were sent as application files to VonHoffmann Graphics, Inc. in Owensville, Missouri, where they were prepared for CTP printing using a Prinergy prepress workflow. Separations were imaged on a Creo 3344 thermal platesetter and printed on a 6-unit Heidelberg 40-inch UV press.

The paper is 50-pound Weyerhauser Lynx Opaque. Body text is Bitstream Aldine401 and Adobe Myriad Multiple Master.

PEACHPIT PRESS

Quality How-to Computer Books

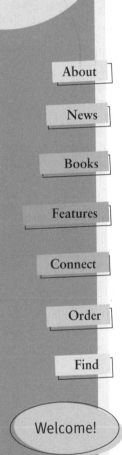

About

News

Books

Features

Connect

Order

Find

Welcome!

Visit Peachpit Press on the Web at www.peachpit.com

- Check out new feature articles each Monday: excerpts, interviews, tips, and plenty of how-tos

- Find any Peachpit book by title, series, author, or topic in Books

- See what our authors are up to on the News page: signings, chats, appearances, and more

- Meet the Peachpit staff and authors in the About section: bios, profiles, and candid shots

- Use Connect to reach our academic, sales, customer service, and tech support areas

Peachpit.com is also the place to:

- Chat with our authors online
- Take advantage of special Web-only offers
- Get the latest info on new books